Thomas Becket

HIS LAST DAYS

William Urry

Edited with an Introduction
by Peter A. Rowe

SUTTON PUBLISHING

First published in 1999 by
Sutton Publishing Limited · Phoenix Mill
Thrupp · Stroud · Gloucestershire · GL5 2BU

Reprinted in 2001

British Library Cataloguing in Publication Data
A catalogue record for this book is available from the British Library

ISBN 0-7509-2179-X

Typeset in 11/14pt Garamond.
Typesetting and origination by
Sutton Publishing Limited.
Printed in Great Britain by
J.H. Haynes & Co. Ltd, Sparkford.

Contents

FOREWORD BY DR HENRY MAYR-HARTING   vii

INTRODUCTION   xiii

Prologue
THE KING AND BECKET   1

Chapter One
THE RETURN FROM EXILE   31

Chapter Two
THE PLOT   65

Chapter Three
CHRISTMAS AT CANTERBURY, 1170   74

Chapter Four
THE INTERVIEW AT THE PALACE   100

Chapter Five
THE MURDER   127

Chapter Six
THE AFTERMATH   150

Epilogue
THE HOLY BLISFUL MARTIR   169

NOTES   182

FURTHER READING   186

INDEX   187

Foreword

*Address given at the Memorial Service for William
Urry on 1 May 1981 in the Church of St Mary the
Virgin, Oxford, by Dr Henry Mayr-Harting*

In commemorating the life and work of William Urry, we celebrate
one of the most life-enhancing men whom any of us could possibly
have met, generous and stimulating to his fellow scholars, a
delight to his friends, and deeply happy in and with his wife Katie
and his family. My own first encounter with William came in 1958
when as a research student I went to work in the Canterbury
Cathedral Library and Archives of which he was then in charge. It
was a not uncharacteristic encounter. He began by questioning me
in the most friendly way about where I was staying, explained to
me – not too briefly – who had lived there in the twelfth century,
and then fetched the documents I wanted to see and gave me
interesting and totally unpatronizing advice about them. It was
not long before a group of people came in by appointment to see
the library. I could not quite hear what was said from my position,
but the effect was rather like a bassoon concerto, the orchestral
part being largely composed of gales of laughter in response to a
decidedly *allegro vivace* soloist. In the course of the week one of the
documents which I wished to see eluded him, namely the
profession of obedience by Bishop Godfrey of Chichester, who was
bishop for less than a year in 1088, to the Archbishop of
Canterbury. As we parted he suddenly said to me, 'Don't go telling
Katie Major (here he referred to my excellent but at the time
slightly awe-inspiring supervisor, the then Principal of St Hilda's)
– 'don't go telling Katie Major that I can't lay my hands on vital
documents'. Amid all his love of ritual and formality, there lurked

something of the naughty schoolboy, which helped to make him the completely unstuffy person he was. Bishop Godfrey of Chichester, it will be apparent, was not one of the leading figures of the Anglo-Norman Church. Whether William referred to his profession as a 'vital' document ironically, therefore, or because he considered any document that reinforced a Canterbury right to be vital, I shall never know.

I make no excuse for coming to the subject of Canterbury so soon. William was born in Canterbury; he was always proud to have served in the Buffs, the Kentish regiment par excellence, during the war; and Canterbury was central to his whole life's work as an historian. Besides his published *magnum opus*, *Canterbury under the Angevin Kings*, he has left two completed books in manuscript, *The Marlowes of Canterbury* and a book on Thomas Becket. Much love and an unrivalled local knowledge have been poured into both books on subjects where local knowledge is greatly needed. In the case of Thomas Becket, many have wondered at the zest with which William could write and lecture about a historical figure whom he heartily disliked. The dislike is *not* easy to explain. Perhaps it was occasioned by the sensitivity which anyone who has worked for a great church must feel about the high-handed exercise of ecclesiastical authority, no matter what his actual relations with the church in question. About the zest there is less difficulty. William was the one man who had, so to speak, the complete file on every minor actor in the drama, who knew all the Kentishmen who had made hay while the sun shone and the Archbishop had been in exile, impeded from looking after his own, who understood every little grievance which the locals had against Becket, who had even spotted which houses the Archbishop's enemies conveniently (for their activities of 29 December 1170) had in the town. Where others have done fine work on the broad setting of the Becket conflict, he seized the opportunity to tell a story for which the local element is fundamental.

William would not have disdained to apply to himself a word now not much in vogue, the word 'antiquary'. When Marion Stowell of the History Faculty Office and I attended his funeral service in Canterbury Cathedral, we heard someone behind us say, 'Wonderful man, Dr Urry; I once took a train journey with him out of Canterbury and he lit up every field on the way with History'. Listen, again, to the words of one of his graduate pupils:

I am certain that I gained more from his lectures than from any other series I have ever attended; not broad knowledge as such, but an even more valuable quality, his overwhelming and irrepressible enthusiasm for the human details of History: the price of bread in the twelfth-century market, the age of the speaking-tube in the Canterbury cloisters, the hour of Vespers, the paths across an Elizabethan pea-field, or whether Boots or Lloyds Bank now occupied the site of a monastic outhouse.

And he added, 'it was really quite a moving experience to see the crowds of undergraduates queuing up in the Schools for an hour before William Urry's lectures on Becket'.

It would be a great mistake, however, to suppose that antiquarianism was a soft form of intellectual and historical endeavour in his case. He had a very solid linguistic discipline behind his studies, for it happened that he had read a general degree in Latin, French and Anglo-Saxon at Birkbeck College, London, before the war, and maintained that it was quite as hard as the History Honours degree which he subsequently took. Moreover, the antiquarianism of his masterly *Canterbury under the Angevin Kings* is controlled and channelled into true History by his thematic treatment of crucial topics in medieval urban history, while the brilliant introduction on the manuscript sources and their dating give an insight into the kind of instruction he could offer as Reader in Western Palaeography in this university.

When William became Reader in Palaeography he was elected to a fellowship at St Edmund Hall. He loved his college and would stand in the lodge lost in rapt and admiring contemplation of it. How different from those who stalk through their lodges, under the impression that it is they who grace their colleges! Here, although a professorial fellow, he was well known to, and knew, the undergraduates; he attended the college chapel regularly; and his eminently courteous personality formed one of the principal recollections which many a guest carried away from its common room. Apart from the fact that William found the college a friendly and historic one, with its Canterbury connections, he was glad to think himself following in the tradition of its antiquary of earlier times, Thomas Hearne. He had indeed Hearne's accurate and meticulous scholarship, Hearne's way of seizing on morsels of antiquity with a voracious appetite, Hearne's love of miscellaneous appendices, and some of Hearne's caustic wit. He would cite Hearne unexpectedly at disconcerting turns, as when the college kitchen failed to produce pancakes on Shrove Tuesday. What he lacked was Hearne's malice. He had far too much inner peace and assurance for that. He was not averse to an attacking move, in print or *viva voce*, but one may say of him, as Adam Smith wrote of Hume, that it was never the meaning of his raillery to mortify.

The picture of William standing in admiration of his college and his good fortune to be a fellow of it not only tells us something about St Edmund Hall and about himself generally, but I believe it also holds the clue to his extraordinary power as a teacher, which is testified on all sides. Partly, of course, this power was due to his incomparable flow of words. The members of the History Faculty Office remember the veritable fusillade of words which he fired into the room when the bullet holes made by Cromwell's soldiers in two medieval painted panels at Canterbury were filled in, which offended his notions of what ought to be preserved as historic. But partly this power was due to the fact that he never lost his sense of wonder. One of the most moving sermons preached at St Edmund Hall in the past decade was his on the smallness of human time, or time scales, in which he recounted how he had been gazing at the records under his care at Canterbury, reflecting on how a mere two yards of shelf space covered so many centuries. Surely this sense of wonder, this streak of naïvety without which no one can be truly human, lay behind his gift to convey enthusiasm for the human details of History. This same sense of wonder is captured by a friend who once saw him staring with rapt attention at a highly polished traction engine at the St Giles Fair.

During his last twenty years William suffered with admirable courage a succession of crises in his health. Mr Lowe of the History Faculty Building recalls his saying of himself that he was a man with one foot in the grave and the other on a banana skin. But despite often desperate illness, the banana skin was always much more in evidence than the grave. He once told me a delightful story against himself which illustrates the point. He owned a small house in Canterbury in which he had installed an old lady of ninety as a tenant. He was naturally the soul of kindness towards her, but it pleased him to represent himself as a Rachman-type landlord, eagerly waiting for the demise of this lady so that he could retake possession of his house. On one occasion, when he had been given only months or even weeks to live but was recovering, he went down to Canterbury and called on his tenant, who, in his version, said to him, 'I know why you've come to see me, Dr Urry, but you don't look none too good yourself, you know.' Not five years ago, with his irrepressible interest in the fabric of Canterbury Cathedral, he appeared on the roof having mounted the scaffolding, and when the wicked deed was exposed by his son and daughter, he said, 'Don't go telling your mother that I've been up on the roof of the cathedral.' He never brooded on his illnesses and was indeed always planning his future work during them. On the very last Sunday before he finally lost consciousness he felt that he was going to get better and he avowed emphatically that the keys of his typewriter would become red hot as he made up for lost time.

The Book of Proverbs sees Wisdom engaged as if in play, with the children of men for his playfellows. Never was there a more obvious instance than William Urry of a playfellow of Wisdom passing from this life to the next with, it may be added, the confident faith of a believing and practising Christian. His bodily remains lie now in the cloister of Canterbury Cathedral, close to the staircase leading up to the library. Many scholars and visitors will have passed that place during the twenty-three years when he was Cathedral Librarian and Archivist, quite unaware of the unusual gusts of wit and learning, warmth and generosity, which were to blow on them a few moments later.

William Urry, *c*. 1962, when he was Keeper of the Manuscripts and Librarian, Canterbury Cathedral, and City Archivist of Canterbury.

Acknowledgement

The editor and publishers gratefully acknowledge the kindness of Sir Paul Getty KBE (The Wormsley Library) in allowing the reproduction of numerous illustrations from the Becket Leaves.

Introduction

Writing an obituary in *Archaeologia Cantiana* for 1981, Dr Frank Jenkins said that William Urry had 'left two completed books in manuscript, one on the family of Christopher Marlowe for whom he had great respect, and the other on Thomas Becket whom for some reason he heartily detested'. In due course *Christopher Marlowe and Canterbury* was published, but the ensuing years brought no news of the book on Becket. Then in 1995 I learned from John Butler's book, *The Quest for Becket's Bones*, that he had been allowed to consult Dr Urry's manuscript. Reviewing the book in the *Journal of Kent History* I expressed regret that William Urry's book remained unpublished.

Following up this remark I got in touch with Dr Urry's widow, Mrs Kate Urry, who kindly lent me a copy of the work and told me something of its history. I found that the author's intention had been to present the Becket story with the same vividness that had drawn crowds to his Oxford lectures, but in a way that would appeal to a far wider audience than merely students of history. When I saw the manuscript I quickly realised that this work, the product of William Urry's own 'last days', which he finished just before his death, was not one book but at least one and a half books. Although voluminous and discursive, there was within its pages a truly gripping story, told with the verve and command of detail which brought Dr Urry renown first in Canterbury and then at Oxford. Unfortunately I never met or heard Dr Urry in the flesh, but I have listened to the tapes of his Oxford lectures and they are riveting!

Reluctant as I was to tamper with the work of an author whose consent could not be given to any proposed changes, I soon realized that an attempt must be made to prune the digressions (fascinating though many of these were, and some of which are perhaps publishable on their own account) and to reduce the excessive length. This has been achieved mainly by condensing the four original opening chapters into one, now entitled 'Prologue'. To a large extent Dr Urry's own wording has been retained in this part of the book. This proved even more feasible in the later chapters, which are as he wrote them apart from cuts and some minor sub-editorial changes. Although I have corrected obvious errors, I have throughout tried to make only such alterations and abridgements as would have been made by the author in collaboration with a publisher's editor. In this I have been enormously helped by Kenneth Pinnock, who knew William Urry well and has many years' experience of publishing.

For the benefit of scholars and others who want to know precisely what authorities Dr Urry was relying on at various points of the narrative, a copy of the original typescript, together with the many pages of notes, has been deposited at the Cathedral Library in Canterbury. Anyone who consults this will find that, although his last book was designed for a general rather than a specialist audience, Dr Urry never forsook the scholarly habits of a lifetime.

In the course of the work William Urry makes several references to the 1970 biography by Dom David Knowles, which many consider the most sympathetic account of St Thomas in recent times. He could not, of course, refer to Frank Barlow's more recent biography, since it appeared five years after his death. Professor Barlow's work has rapidly established itself as the standard Life. Far more frequent than any references to modern works, however, are those to the contemporary chroniclers, about whom a word needs to be said here. They include William of Canterbury and Benedict of Peterborough, both monks of the cathedral monastery at Canterbury; Edward Grim, who happened to be at Canterbury at the time of the murder during which he was seriously injured; Guernes de Pont Ste-Maxence (also known as Garnier), a Frenchman who was not involved in the story himself but who wrote it up shortly afterwards, and who seems to have been William Urry's 'favourite'; William FitzStephen, who was with Thomas at the end, and whose biography is considered by many to be the most attractive; John of Salisbury, who stuck by the Archbishop in spite of all, until the last moment when he fled; and Herbert of Bosham, whose flowery style is not to modern taste but for whom Dr Urry had a sneaking regard. There are other accounts too, of which the most important is the Icelandic saga *Thómas Saga Erkibyskups*.

As he sifted and welded together these various accounts, what conclusions about Becket did Dr Urry reach? Working myself on his text I have concluded that he neither loved Becket, as Canon Derek Ingram Hill suggested at his funeral in Canterbury Cathedral, nor heartily disliked or detested him as Frank Jenkins and Professor Mayr-Harting thought. The truth seems to be rather that he was intrigued by this endlessly fascinating man. Although we know more about Becket than about almost anyone else in medieval history, we can never quite fathom him. William Urry brings out with unique clarity the intense pain that Becket suffered in his last years. Was he, towards, the end, weary of life and deliberately inviting death? Such are the endless questions and uncertainties that Becket poses. Every conclusion becomes merely the prelude to further questions. Perhaps T.S. Eliot gets nearest to firm ground. In conversation with Kate Urry, she reminded me of the lines from *Murder in the Cathedral*:

> When king is dead, there's another king,
> And one more king is another reign.
> King is forgotten, when another shall come:
> Saint and Martyr rule from the tomb.

We wondered whether the subtle idea of being a saint and martyr ruling from the tomb might have weighed with St Thomas.

I am grateful to Mrs Urry for entrusting the manuscript to me, and to Kenneth Pinnock for much help on this book. Kenneth was also responsible for the selection of the illustrations, in which Anne Oakley has also given valuable assistance. I am also grateful to the Revd John Cowdrey of St Edmund Hall, Oxford, for his encouragement and suggestions, and to the staff of the Canterbury Cathedral Archives. On a personal note, I wish to express my thanks to all those medieval scholars – including Dr Emma Mason at Birkbeck (William Urry's own college), Dr Margaret Aston and Dr Phyllis Roberts of New York – who have so generously given help to me, an amateur historian. Nor must I fail to put on record my gratitude to my former secretaries, Tina Ades and Karen Wood, who did the preliminary work of making a fair copy of the original manuscript, which ran to well over one hundred thousand words!

Above all I thank my wife Liz and our children Barnaby, Sophie and Gregory, who have wondered sometimes when I was going to stop tapping away at the word processor and take a proper part in the life of our family. Thank you, my dears, for your love, patience and support.

Peter A. Rowe
Hamstreet, Ashford, Kent
7 July 1999
Feast of the Translation of St Thomas

The King and Becket

A t ten o'clock on the day of his enthronement as Archbishop of Canterbury, Sunday 3 June 1162, Thomas Becket emerged from the vestry of Canterbury Cathedral, modestly clad in a simple surplice with a cloak of black above it. He made his way to the high altar and prostrated himself in prayer for a while. Then he turned and went down into the choir where all the bishops and clergy sat (the barons being accommodated in the nave). Assurance was demanded afresh on the part of the Church that Becket was free of worldly obligations. 'If this person', said the monks, 'is handed over to us thus free, then we are prepared to receive him and pass him over to the bishops for ordination.'

The young Prince Henry, who was there deputizing for his father King Henry II, and Robert de Beaumont, Earl of Leicester, together with all the officials and barons, repeated the guarantee given at the time when Becket's election as archbishop was confirmed at Westminster. Thomas was consecrated by Bishop Henry of Winchester, the powerful and wealthy brother of King Stephen. No doubt there was held at the end of the day the usual splendid banquet without which no medieval event would be complete. Next day came a crowd of jesters importuning the new archbishop for rewards. Probably they had performed at the banquet. They received an unexpected response. 'I am not the man I was when chancellor,' he told them. 'Church funds are for the Church and the poor. I have nothing to give you.'

Thomas Becket was born in the family home on the site of the present Mercers' Hall off Cheapside on 21 December 1120, St Thomas the Apostle's day. He seems to have been the youngest in a family that consisted of three girls and him. The family most likely took its origin from a hamlet called Becquet on the Le Havre peninsula. His father Gilbert was a member of the merchant class at Rouen, whence he gravitated to London in a second wave of migration following the Norman Conquest. Thomas' mother Matilda, a pious woman, came from Caen.

As a boy Thomas was sent to the equivalent of a preparatory school conducted at Merton Priory, south west of London. He later moved back to London to attend one of the great schools in the metropolis. After a break in his studies he went to Paris, then Europe's leading university. Thomas was not a dedicated scholar and had to force himself to work, aided by pressure from his mother.

Tragedy came when he was about twenty-one. His mother Matilda died. Having lost the most influential person in his life, Thomas abandoned his studies and drifted back to the bereaved household in London where his father, now at an unprosperous point in his own career (possibly through losses by fire), was not glad to see him without career prospects. Gilbert Becket did not long survive his wife and when he died the young man had to find a job. A kinsman, Osbert 'Huitdeniers' or 'Eightpence', gave him an opening, either as his own assistant or as clerk to the sheriffs in London governmental service.[1] Pen-pushing in a city office could hardly have fulfilled Becket's vision of a satisfying career. He endured it for around three years before escape came.

Thomas was invited to join the staff of Archbishop Theobald of Canterbury, where he found himself among a remarkable group of rising young men, the *eruditi*, some of the best brains in the country and certainly more learned than Thomas. Conspicuous among them was the sinister figure of Roger of Pont l'Evêque, a murderer and sexual pervert who was destined to be Becket's great enemy until the end of his life. Roger hated Thomas from the word go, and twice engineered his ejection from the archbishop's ménage; but twice Becket returned. The household was dominated by church discipline, for Theobald was an ex-monk of Bec. But not all was hard administrative work and liturgy, for Becket enjoyed following hawks and hunting and when himself archbishop kept a pack of hounds.

In the twelfth-century Church senior clergy had no shame in amassing several prosperous benefices, putting in ill-paid curates to do the work while pocketing the balance themselves. There was a borderland between 'clerk' and 'cleric' and the identification of literacy with ecclesiastical status blurred the issue. For the Crown, of course, which needed a civil service made up of literate clerks, ecclesiastical preferment was an admirable way of paying for the administrative machinery which served it. Becket, who was ordained a deacon, acquired several benefices. In 1154, when Archbishop Theobald wished Roger of Pont l'Evêque on to the chapter of York as their archbishop, Becket took over his office of Archdeacon of Canterbury.

Theobald realised that although Thomas had dropped out of his studies at Paris, he had ability and so sent him on special study courses in law at Bologna and Auxerre. He was later involved in negotiations at Rome and it was largely due to his advocacy there that Henry, son of Geoffrey of Anjou, was confirmed as heir to the throne of England in place of Eustace, son of King Stephen, who then conveniently predeceased his father. Stephen's disorderly reign ended with his death on 15 October 1154. Henry II became king and was crowned on 19 December at the age of twenty-one.

Becket's great opportunity had arrived. Through Theobald's influence, he became secretary or chancellor to the new young king. He was thirteen years older than his monarch and by now well-versed in administration and the ways of the world. King Henry was an astonishing mixture. He could use his charm to overcome opposition but when this failed his self-control could give way to savage bursts of rage and fiendish cruelty. He could also be unbelievably generous. His restlessness made him almost impossible to live with, and hunting and hawking came before important business.

Henry was constantly preoccupied with the military aspects of maintaining his enormous domains. These stretched from the Scottish border far into modern France, and had been vastly increased when in May 1152 he had married Eleanor of Aquitaine, the very recently divorced wife of King Louis, thus securing all her wide, sunny and prosperous lands and extending his territories as far as the Pyrenees. The new chancellor devoted his administrative skills to support of Henry and set about reducing England to order; illegal castles were flattened all across the realm, and ruinous royal fortresses brought back into commission. Becket was also a gifted army commander, not merely as a headquarters organiser but also as an actual general in the field, participating personally in combat. Becket's military activities are not attractive to the modern mind. His biographer Edward Grim paints a frightening picture of the slaughter and damage that he caused.

A close friendship grew up between the young king and his chancellor. Outwardly at least the friendship was secure although it is impossible to know whether there was any real affection between the two men. Thomas was not a man of great personal loves, and the only emotional tie we can be sure of was that with his mother. It may be, however, that their eventual estrangement was a manifestation of that perennial phenomenon, a great love turning into a great hate.

The chancellor, a born and competent bureaucrat, built up a headquarters staff to collect money on his master's behalf, as when vacant bishoprics and abbacies fell to the Crown. The Chancery was a profitable investment and it is quite certain that Becket bought it. Whatever he might have paid for the post, however, he would easily recoup himself from the fees charged.

More than one description is available of Thomas Becket's appearance at this period. He was tall and dark with an aquiline nose and pale complexion which tended to flush over at moments of excitement. He had a tendency to stammer but outgrew this in time. Perhaps he already wore the black beard shown in some representations. His senses were acute, particularly his capacity for hearing and his ability to detect any smell.

Henry's eldest surviving son, Prince Henry, was destined by his father to become King of England and was to be crowned in the elder Henry's lifetime to secure his succession. The king determined to marry the child to Margaret, daughter of King Louis and his second wife, Constance of Castille. Though the proposed marriage would appear on any count to be incestuous, since the boy's mother Queen Eleanor had been married to the girl's father, Becket overcame his scruples about promoting the betrothal and set off for Paris in 1158 in one of the most extraordinary expeditions ever to leave England. The mission was a complete success and the children were declared duly affianced.

Becket made many enemies. The barons, from old-established families, were irritated by the rise of the London burgess's son. All and sundry had been forced to pay the 'aid to marry the king's daughter' and even before all the contributions had been collected the truce, supposedly effected by the betrothal of the young people, was broken by expensive war the very next year.

We know of one family group which was full of envy and spite where Becket was concerned. These were the Brocs. The head of the clan was Rannulph de Broc. In the absence of a son to Rannulph, the position of second-in-command devolved upon a nephew, Robert de Broc, who had been a Cistercian monk and clerk, but had then gone back into the world. Among his retainers Robert de Broc had a clerk named Hugh of Horsea, or Mauclerk, and it was he who administered the last dreadful blow upon Becket's body when the archbishop was murdered.

In 1159 King Henry laid claim to Toulouse as a fief of his wife, Eleanor of Aquitaine. It was now in the hands of Count Raymond whose wife, Constance, was sister to King Louis. Vast military preparations were made and in the campaign which followed Becket proved himself to be a talented general, leading into the field a force of no fewer than seven hundred picked warriors, himself clad in helmet and coat of mail. He took supposedly impregnable castles, seized Cahors and crossed the Garonne, and would have taken Toulouse, where King Louis had joined the garrison, but for King Henry's feudal scruples which forbade the move. Becket fell back on Quercy and conducted a savage and cruel dragonnade, slaughtering and burning, as recorded by shocked biographers. Becket is next heard of five hundred miles to the north on the borderland between Norman and French territory at Trie where he conducted a fresh bloody *chevauchée*. He even engaged in single combat, unhorsing and disarming the French knight Engelram de Trie.

This warrior Thomas Becket, as men noted, was actually a clerk in holy orders, Archdeacon of Canterbury, Provost of Beverley, rector or prebend here and there, Dean of Hastings and so forth. Archbishop Theobald's misgivings increased as age began to tell on him. A full-blooded enjoyment of secular and military life, and a way of dealing with the Church which often displeased his fellow clerics, was not what he had foreseen for Thomas in 1154. By 1161 Theobald knew he was dying and sent a pathetic series of requests to Thomas to return to the fold and comfort him in his departing moments. Thomas did not come and the archbishop died without ever seeing him again.

Henry very soon told Becket that he intended him to become the new Archbishop of Canterbury. Becket's protests were silenced by friends. A royal deputation journeyed to Canterbury ostensibly to consult with Prior Wibert and his monks about a successor to Theobald. The astute prior went through the motions of consulting his brethren and came back to announce that choice had fallen *nemine contradicente* on the chancellor, Thomas Becket.

Confirmation of election and other formalities were completed at Westminster, though there was one significant dissident, Gilbert Foliot, Bishop of Hereford and soon to be Bishop of London. It was formally declared that Becket stood completely free from any secular

on enim eſt deus noſter ut diſ

Becket's consecration as archbishop, from Queen Mary's Psalter, early fourteenth century. (By permission of The British Library; Ms Royal 2B vii f.29)

obligations. The enthronement was to take place at Canterbury on 3 June 1162. The archbishop-elect was not yet even in priest's orders, a defect remedied on the eve of his enthronement. As the great day dawned, vast crowds of barons and retainers rode to Canterbury. How they were accommodated is hard to say, for the whole place had been devastated by fire in the previous year. The city may be imagined as surrounded by a forest of knightly pavilions, like some scene from King Arthur. Fifteen diocesan bishops with attendant staff added to the congestion.

The twelfth century was one of the great ages of the Church. After long centuries of simony and corruption, a series of reforming popes emerged, conspicuous among whom was Gregory VII, known as Hildebrand (1073–85). The ambition of men like Gregory was to reform the Church and to win its liberty from subjection to lay authority.

A great contest unrolled between secular and religious power, *regnum* and *sacerdotium*. The German Emperor Henry IV came up against the iron will of Pope Gregory VII. At Roman synods Gregory twice sentenced him to be excommunicated and deposed; in 1076, after the first sentence, the German opposition compelled him to receive absolution. In despair, at midwinter Henry crossed the Mount Cenis pass to Canossa, there to wait barefoot in the snow at the castle gate, until after three days the Pope condescended to absolve him. To Canterbury nearly a century later, another Henry was to come on a similar penitential journey.

It was into this context of a revivified Church, growing steadily more powerful, that Thomas Becket had entered at as high a level as he could have wished – short of the papacy itself. The Archbishop of Canterbury was one of the outstanding pontiffs of Christendom. There must have been a heady realization, once he had accepted office and acclimatized himself to the idea despite initial misgivings, that the archbishopric offered an opportunity for greatness at least equal to the chancellorship which he was soon to relinquish.

On the day after his enthronement Becket had said that 'I am not the man I was when chancellor.' Much has been written of the conversion undergone by Thomas Becket on his accession to the archbishopric. It is true that some moves towards austerity were made, such as the adoption of a hairshirt (kept secret from all but intimate members of his household such as his chaplain, Robert of Merton, and his manservant, the faithful Osbert or Osbern). He rigorously followed a *horarium* which included midnight prayers and, at dawn, the 'Maundy' or ceremonial washing of the feet of poor men, together with the distribution of alms and food to the so-called 'poor prebendaries' and other hungry folk. But was this conversion as complete as imagined?

It was some time before he broke himself of the habit of wearing fine secular dress, which irritated his monks, although in time he went down to Merton and invested himself with the habit of an Augustinian canon of that place. The previously faithful supporter of the Crown turned his ardour towards service (as he saw it) of the Church. Well-organized penitential floggings were carried out daily, and Robert of Merton was always at hand to beat his master and was often urged to lay on harder.

Perhaps the ruthless commander of 1159 and other years, who rode against Toulouse unnerving even his monarch, had not changed all that much and was not so different in mentality from the archbishop who in later days was to frighten the Pope by his opposition to King Henry. Nor again is the warrior-chancellor who did single combat with the French knight in 1159 much different, surely, from the archbishop who in 1166, about to anathematize his enemies at Vézelay, performed vigils at Soissons at the shrine of St Drausius, where champions about to engage in combat were wont to have recourse.

The monks of Canterbury were for a long time uncertain about the supposed conversion of their *ex officio* abbot, and were never fully convinced that he was one of themselves until his body was stripped after the murder in 1170 and the mortifying, verminous undergarments came to light. There is evidence that Becket himself had some misgivings about his new vocation. More than once he confessed that he had come from a worldly court, all unworthy of his high office.

The new archbishop quickly set to work to recruit a body of *eruditi* as headquarters staff. Principal among these were John of Salisbury, a brilliant classical scholar, and Herbert of Bosham, a learned clerk, biblical scholar and even hebraist (an unusual accomplishment). Some of the *eruditi* later rose to very high office in the Church. Humbert of Milan, recruited by Becket during his later exile, became Pope Urban III in 1185. An entertaining member of the group was Llewelyn, the loquacious Welshman, also called Alexander. Some of these and others, such as William FitzNigel who was to replace William de Capes as Becket's household marshal during the exile, are among the principal actors in the chroniclers' accounts of the day of the murder.

The physical wants of all these *eruditi*, knights and professionals were attended to by a large contingent of domestic servants. There were cookhouse staff, of whom one, the scullion Robert 'Shinbone', is known to history for a minor part in the great drama. Closest to Becket in terms of service was the faithful Osbern, his chamber-servant, who stood by him in circumstances of great bravery three or four times in his career. In addition to staff there were many noble young boys about, undergoing training as pages. As archbishop, Becket had the pick of the barons' second sons, and to these was added Prince Henry, heir to the throne.

The new archbishop must have felt himself sorely confined in his position as diocesan bishop, having to administer a diocese which was tiny in comparison with others. Unable to restrict himself to his own modest field of activity he found excuses to ride far and wide. News of his expeditions and his extravagant mode of life reached the ears of Pope Alexander III, who gave him some firm counsel: 'My brother, you must shut yourself up in the church of Canterbury. Reduce yourself to mere necessities, and *do* stop chasing about all over the country.'

It is significant that in this period Becket's measures usually concern not his own see of Canterbury but intrude into someone else's diocese, as in the case of the matrimonial affairs of Isabella, Countess Warenne, in the diocese of Winchester. This case had echoes in the last seconds of the murder in 1170. In the Toulouse campaign of 1159, a fatal casualty through sickness had been William, husband to the countess. Another William, King Henry's brother, wanted to marry the widow, but Becket claimed that they were within the prohibited degrees (not at all certain) and the Lord William died, as was thought, of sheer grief, to the great resentment of his friends. All this was remembered a decade later.

Although Becket and the king had been fast friends it is difficult not to believe that the archbishop, by his constant interference in matters which did not strictly concern him, was now in some measure trying to take on Henry. A real crisis soon developed in the shape of the question of criminous clerks. Henry was determined that there were to be no exemptions from his own laws and customs, while the Church was equally determined that the clerks should stay outside the frightful penal system of the day. Henry's natural hope had been that with his own chancellor as archbishop some kind of working arrangement could be arrived at. The king held that 'ancestral laws' required that anyone in holy orders caught out in theft, homicide or treason should be spoiled of his orders and handed over for condign punishment. Becket's own position was that *laymen cannot be the judges of clerks*.

The issue came up at the royal council summoned to Westminster in October 1163. The king made it clear that he wanted criminous clerks handed over to the royal courts for proper punishment after degradation. Becket argued that the clergy were a separate estate not subject to temporal power. There was much citation of canon law, as yet in an amorphous state, while the continued use by Becket of the expression *salvo ordine* ('saving our order') drove the king into such a wild state of exasperation that he suddenly rode off from the council, incandescent with rage, not bothering to offer formal farewell to the bishops.

A further ineffectual meeting was held very soon afterwards at Northampton, characterized by insulting exchanges between the two principal opponents in which Henry caught Becket on a very raw nerve, demanding of him if he were not the son of one of his villeins. The inevitable expression *salvo ordine* was brought out again to inflame the king. In the meantime Pope Alexander, with all his own troubles, grew worried at the dispute in England and sent a distinguished deputation to beg Becket to climb down, or at least soft-pedal.

Matters reached boiling point early in 1164 when Henry summoned the court to Clarendon, the hunting lodge on the hilltop near Salisbury. Henry wanted set down in writing a series of working arrangements which had been effective enough in practice between Church and Crown over the years. If Becket had not been so recalcitrant, the king might not have clamoured for definition. To us the king's proposals, which are known to history as the Constitutions of Clarendon, may seem harmless enough but, with sharp tempers on either side and threats against the privileged position occupied by the churchmen, some of the clauses were contentious indeed. For instance, Becket objected to clauses which precluded appeals to Rome, or even departures from the realm on pilgrimage. That clerics should appear when summoned by the king's justices was naturally anathema.

There was an atmosphere of crisis. Henry made furious demands while Becket remained inflexible. The bishops were victims of conflicting loyalties. At length they came round courageously to the archbishop's support. Becket went aside, ostensibly to meditate. To the consternation and wild confusion of his colleagues, he then announced that he was prepared to give way. His great rival, Bishop Gilbert Foliot of London, was later to claim that Becket had secretly intended to feign consent but withdraw it later whenever it suited him. To this charge, which may account for much of the loathing Becket displayed towards Foliot, no plausible denial was ever made.

After the conference, Becket in deep shame suspended himself from priestly duties for forty days, as he informed the Pope, who remitted this self-imposed penance. He returned to Canterbury and soon his mind ran on escape from the realm. During the summer of 1164 he seems to have made at least two unsuccessful attempts to flee, although King Henry had no great desire that Becket should fly.

Henry found a real excuse for dealing with Thomas Becket late in 1164, not on the hazardous grounds of canon law but as a secular feudal tenant. One of the king's senior Exchequer officials was John the Marshal, who happened likewise to be a vassal of the archbishop. John swore that Becket denied him feudal justice and Henry summoned Becket to answer the marshal's charges in court at

Westminster on 16 September 1164. The archbishop failed to turn up on grounds of illness. Henry was enraged and gave orders for a fresh appearance at Northampton on Tuesday 6 October. This time Becket obeyed, although Henry delayed his own appearance by a day. Little was accomplished on Wednesday 7 October, the first working day, because John the Marshal had hung back at Westminster. On the following day, when the marshal's case was formally opened, Becket's defence was soon dismissed and a substantial fine imposed. None of the barons wanted to deliver sentence and at length Bishop Henry of Winchester was induced to act. The bishops (except Gilbert of London) stood surety for Becket.

Full of resentment at Becket's opposition during the last couple of years, Henry now determined to break his old friend. With grossest injustice he embarked upon outrageous demands, without prior notice raking up old business from the days of the chancellorship. Becket agreed to pay the large fine imposed, for the sake of peace, and sureties were nominated to cover £100 each. On Friday 9 October even more extreme demands were made and fines imposed. More sureties were designated. On Saturday 10 October came an absolutely impossible demand showing that Henry had taken leave of all reason: a figure of 30,000 marks was named. To all this Becket could rightly claim that when he was made archbishop he had been exonerated from any worldly obligations in the presence of the king's son and the leading barons.

Becket's entourage was becoming very alarmed and started to slink away. On that Saturday, food was left uneaten in the refectory at St Andrew's (a Cluniac priory where Becket and his immediate circle were housed) and poor people were invited in to finish it. The Bishop of Winchester tried in vain to placate Henry with a free will offering of 2,000 marks. Some other bishops, unfriendly to Becket, tried to induce him to resign. Consultations continued during Sunday but the strain on Becket started to tell. He went off his food and was overtaken with a violent sensation of cold and pain in his side, continuing through the night and into the next day.

Accurate diagnosis from vague symptoms is impossible after eight centuries but it is likely that Becket had an attack of renal colic, that is, the descent of solid particles with excruciating agony through the ureter, although cold and pain in the side are also not inconsistent with intestinal blockage. Whatever the cause, it seems to have been a manifestation of a chronic condition, for this cold and pain in the side were commented upon at the time of his death six years later. As he lay suffering, attendants warmed up pillows and applied them to his abdomen. In the morning, officials came demanding his presence but, in agony from his griping bowels, he gasped that he was unable to move, though he would come on the morrow even if carried on a stretcher. Henry swore by the eyes of God that he certainly would come.

By the morning of Tuesday 13 October he was sufficiently recovered to make a move. He decided to attend at the castle clad in all his pontifical raiment, just like a knight armed for battle. His agitated staff dissuaded him and he set out instead in a cloak above a canon's surplice. Ahead of him rode Alexander Llewelyn carrying the primatial cross. Taking hold of the cross himself, the archbishop entered the castle hall. On the day in question the floor was strewn with the customary greenery and in the middle burned a fire on an open hearth. At the far end of the hall were two chambers, one above the other. To the upper one the king withdrew, in another of his rages, while the bishops and Becket assembled in the lower room. Messengers went to and fro announcing what was happening in either chamber, an arrangement hardly conducive to good debate. In his anger Henry now put forward the grave charge of contempt. 'Traitor!' bawled many of the barons, while the bishops implored Becket to see reason. The king wanted them to pass sentence upon Becket but they asked the king if they might request the Pope to depose the archbishop, and thus be excused from passing sentence themselves. The king agreed and Becket added his own appeal to the Pope.

Finally, Robert de Beaumont, the 'good Earl' of Leicester, was commissioned to deliver sentence. Becket told the earl that he had been faithful to the king after the ways of the world. He had been declared free of all entanglements. He had been summoned only in the case of John the Marshal, and as a spiritual leader he was not going to listen to judgment by laymen. Taking up the cross he then swept out of the chamber into the main hall. Violent jeers arose from all and sundry, who flung hay and twigs from the floor after him, including even the castle serving lads and the court prostitutes who had sidled in to watch.

As he went through the door the official court usher, the hateful Rannulph de Broc, sneered 'Off you go like the traitor you are.' Becket ignored the remark for the moment, and intent on a dramatic withdrawal failed to notice a faggot lying ready to be cast on the central fire. He tripped over it, although he did not actually fall to the floor. As he staggered up Broc's insult came home to Becket and he swung round calling back, 'One of your family got himself hanged for a felony which is more than ever happened in my family,' showing yet again his touchiness about his own background.

By now it was about midday. The archbishop's party sought their horses amid the vast mass of tethered beasts awaiting the barons and their retainers. Becket managed to find his steed, as did his clerk William FitzStephen, but Herbert of Bosham had a parking problem, for his horse was hemmed in. In their frantic haste to be gone, Herbert was accommodated on the crupper behind Becket. They moved across to the castle gate which had been shut all day. Still clutching the cross, Becket sat for a moment paralysed with fear as one of his staff, Peter de Mortorio, spotted the bunch of castle keys hanging on a hook near the gate. The gatekeeper was busy chastising a boy, and they managed to light on the right key and let themselves out into the town. With Herbert behind him and only one hand free as he continued to hold the cross, Becket had difficulty in governing his horse, while importunate crowds of townsfolk, particularly the poor, cried for his blessing which he gave first with one hand and then with the other.

Back at the priory the primatial cross was deposited at the altar of St Mary, beyond the high altar. A word must be said about the cross – a wooden staff surmounted by a bronze cross, probably gilded, with a figure of the Saviour superimposed – which had figured so prominently in the day's events. It was not seen again by Becket until some six years later, when he returned from exile, and it is heard of more than once on the very day of his death when he narrowly escaped being brained by it.

Most of Becket's staff forsook him and flight was certainly in his mind now. Bishops and barons came and went in states of agitation, making suggestions for peace. The archbishop sent a message to Henry asking permission to quit the realm, and answer was returned that proper debate on the matter would have to be made the next day. However, Becket decided to go there and then. Such staff as had not forsaken him were sent to rest. A bed had been made for him within the safety of the church, and the monks of St Andrew's crept in to say their Compline quietly so as not to disturb the sleeper behind the altar. But in fact there was no sleeper there, for it seems that the faithful Osbern had made up the bed with a pillow and a dummy beneath the lambskin cover, the standard schoolboy dormitory practice.

The night was stormy and a great tempest of wind and rain developed. Accompanied by two lay brothers of the Order of

Sempringham, Scailman and Roger de Cave, who had attached themselves to his party, and by the squire Robert de Brai, Becket mounted and finding the north gate of Northampton alone unguarded, they all set off northward in the fearful weather. The idea seems to have been to make for Boston in Lincolnshire from where a ship could take Becket across to Flanders. Cash was clearly a problem after the fearsome fines in the royal court, and Herbert of Bosham was told to slip away quietly to Canterbury, there to pick up what he could in the way of plate or money, after which he was to cross the Channel and find his way to the Abbey of St Bertin at St Omer, where his master hoped, before long, to join him.

The Gilbertine brothers knew the route northwards to their Lincolnshire houses very well, and led the archbishop across the open, dark, rainswept countryside avoiding the roads. The party came into Lincoln as dawn was breaking on Thursday 15 October. Becket was taken to a house just above the bridge over the River Witham, and spent the day concealed there. To avoid identification he adopted the white smock of a lay-brother of Sempringham together with ill-fitting shoes to match, and took on the name 'Christian'. As it became dark he stepped out into a small boat which moved the few yards to the bridge and thence into the gloom down river to where muddy islets rose out of the brackish waters of Wildmore Fen. One of these islets, called the 'Hermitage', was a grange of the Order of Sempringham. Leaving Becket there, the two brethren went off across the fens to the headquarters of their order to make ready horses for further flight.

Back at Northampton messengers came from the castle to hasten the archbishop to court. The unbelievably courageous Osbern sent word that his master must rest a little longer. Repeated summons came from the king and at length there arrived Bishop Henry of Winchester to whom Osbern let out the secret. Bishop Henry sighed in relief. Back at the castle King Henry was told the news, and breathing hard said, 'We haven't finished with *him* yet.' Becket had left his household staff in the lurch and the king's partisans promptly and vengefully set about beating them up. William de Capes went boldly to Henry to complain, and orders were issued to stop it, while Rannulph de Broc (of all people) was told to make sure that the order was obeyed, which he did with very ill grace.

At his chilly lodging at the Hermitage in the fens, Becket fed miserably off a dish of peas. Shortly afterwards he slipped down river to the port of Boston where there were plenty of wool-ships which might supply passage to Flanders. Either there was no such passage to be had or his nerve gave out, for he returned up river. Henry had ordered the ports to be watched and perhaps royal officials were already alert on the quayside. Giving up hope of getting a boat from a northern port, Becket decided to move southwards on the horses made ready at Sempringham.

At length his party found some way of crossing the Thames and entering Kent, and passed through Canterbury in the dark, making for Eastry, one of the cathedral manors where Becket secreted himself. Eastry is very close to Sandwich and one morning a priest produced a boat and Becket and three companions, including Scailman, put out to sea on the hazardous early winter English Channel, on Sunday 1 November. The vessel was rowed the thirty miles to the Franco-Flemish coast. Landfall was made at low tide that evening on the mudflats near Gravelines. As it became light on Monday 2 November 1164, they started off along the coast.

The party came to Gravelines at last, and after an overnight rest in an inn they plodded through the Flanders mud along the banks of the River Aa. After twelve miles they came to the Abbey of Clairmarais, but news had flashed round that the archbishop had entered the land. At once Becket was whisked away to another damp grange, also called the Hermitage, on the island known as 'Eldemenstre' (now St Momelin). In this watery spot Becket stayed a few days. Meanwhile his clerk, Herbert of Bosham, had turned up four or five days earlier at St Bertin. He came over to Becket's refuge on the night of 3 November and heard the story of his master's odyssey. Herbert was unable to give Becket much comfort over money for all he had collected was a hundred marks with some plate from the palace at Canterbury.

Had he realized it, Becket was now embarking on a six-year exile abroad. It is the great wearisome passage in Becket's life, amorphous and resembling some trackless desert, or a stream lost in the marshes, with no consistent story other than the principal actor's total incapacity to agree with anyone on anything. He manipulates the most important people in Europe first one way and then the other. He spurns attempts at reconciliation, insults his own monarch, annoys his patron the French king, makes things awkward for the Pope, who had enough troubles of his own, and quarrels with almost unparalleled viciousness with men like Bishop Gilbert of London who, but for Becket's unbridled attacks, might be considered one of the great and distinguished churchmen of his century. He would

Becket escapes into exile, from Queen Mary's Psalter, early fourteenth century. (By permission of The British Library; Ms Royal 2B vii f.292r)

certainly have made a better archbishop. Becket condemned himself not by the company he kept but by some of the enemies he made, such as Bishop Gilbert and Richard de Lucy, the Justiciar of England and virtuous and faithful minister of the Crown.

Becket was anxious to reach the Abbey of St Bertin where he was welcomed enthusiastically. He was not alone as a refugee, for monks of Canterbury had fled thither headed by Prior Wibert, but that wily individual soon took his party back to make friends with the king and, indeed, for nearly three years until his death in 1167, he managed to maintain an astute balance between his clerical and lay masters. Also at St Bertin was Richard de Lucy, returning from a pilgrimage to Compostella. De Lucy was a vassal of the archbishop in Kent, but he promptly repudiated his homage to Becket. Shortly afterwards Becket went in search of King Louis and at Soissons secured sympathetic audience. Herbert of Bosham was sent off to find the Pope at Sens, where he was in temporary exile from Rome.

In the meantime King Henry determined to get his own version of events heard, and sent powerful deputations to both King Louis and Pope Alexander. They had no great success with King Louis, who took violent exception to a reference to Becket as 'former archbishop'. They then went off to find the Pope at Sens. The Pope was in an unenviable position. His title to the papal throne was under threat because the Emperor of Germany, Frederick Barbarossa, supported the anti-pope Paschal III. Pope Alexander relied on the continued support of Henry of England, the other powerful monarch in Europe, which did not make supporting Becket any easier for him. For all that, the king's party had little success with the Pope and at length made off back to England.

Becket himself, after his interview with Louis, now rode to see the Pope who met him in the papal bedchamber. Becket dramatically produced the text of the Constitutions of Clarendon, and was severely upbraided for consenting to them. Remembering that he had accepted the mitre virtually from King Henry's lay hands, he now drew off his archiepiscopal ring and resigned his office into Alexander's hands, but was very soon reinstated. Any remaining scruples about how he had become Archbishop of Canterbury were now laid to rest by this papal action.

As the archbishop could not return home, where was he to stay? In the no-man's-land between French and Burgundian territories lay the Cistercian Abbey of Pontigny. Thither Becket and his staff were sent, and there they settled in for a couple of years. During his sojourn at Pontigny, Becket resolved to live as far as possible as a monk.

Back in England, Henry was thirsting for revenge. Unable to reach Becket, he expelled in the bitter midwinter his kinsfolk (down to babes in arms) and his clerks. Some managed to reach Pontigny, and on hearing at mealtime from William de Capes that a group of refugees might arrive at any moment, Becket made an unbelievably harsh remark, observing that provided they were spiritually saved he did not care if his servants were cut to pieces and his kinfolk, including his sisters and nephews, flayed. Generous people opened their houses, mothers with babies being taken into French nunneries.

The archbishop had automatically forfeited his great barony by flight. It was seized upon by the king who put in as agent for collection of the income the loyal and ruthless Rannulph de Broc, who accounted for huge sums. Some income due to Becket's clerks went through the diocesan office of Bishop Gilbert Foliot of London, where it was dealt with by a fraudulent agent, a practice in due course interrupted by the Pope. But not all was blind confiscation,

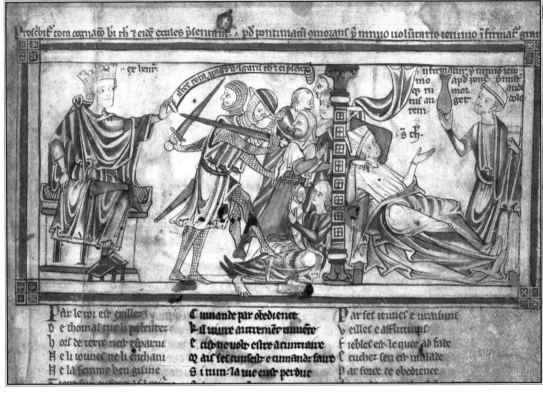

Henry II sends Becket's relatives (including a babe in arms) into exile. On the right, Becket is shown on his sickbed in Pontigny Abbey, ill from excessive fasting, with a doctor examining a specimen flask. (The Becket Leaves)

for some of the cash was spent on demonstrably useful purposes such as repairs to Canterbury's city walls.

Becket's time at Pontigny was not wasted. The party found a store of ancient books and Becket caused transcriptions to be made, some of which appear in later years in the cathedral library at Canterbury. Becket's great problem was to settle quietly into moderated activities after a long, vigorous and busy career. In enforced idleness he found, to his shock, that sexual urges were still upon him, and in panic he flung himself into penances, particularly in immersion in the drains beneath the abbey. Infection entered his system and dangerous abscesses developed on his cheek. Communicating to his jawbone, these resulted in a calamitous attack of osteomyelitis with necrosis of the bone, the whole accompanied, of course, with unendurable pain.[2]

A primitive operation was conducted by one William, undoubtedly the 'W. *medicus*' once in Archbishop Theobald's household, who will appear at the end of Becket's career in 1170. William extracted two

Becket takes leave of Pope Alexander III in 1165. The Pope embraces him and urges him to stand firm. (The Becket Leaves)

splinters of bone, and the sufferings of the patient without anaesthetic can hardly be contemplated. Thereafter, for the remainder of his life, Becket must have suffered recurrent bouts of pain, with high temperature and impaired judgement, which might account for the violence of his language, his unrestrained use of the fearful weapon of excommunication, and his from time to time erratic conduct, all of which is otherwise so difficult to understand.

Early in 1166 some of Becket's clerks set off for the papal court in Italy, whither Alexander had removed in the middle of 1165, to ask that their master be accorded the status of legate for England. He agreed, though not without misgivings, and warned the archbishop to use moderation. Becket lost little time in making use of his new powers. At Vézelay, about thirty miles south of Pontigny, and in the presence of a great crowd of pilgrims, he excommunicated on Whit Sunday 1166 several of his enemies, episcopal and baronial. He had even considered excommunicating King Henry himself, who was ill at the time. In the event, Becket contented himself on this occasion

(Left) Becket excommunicates the bishops and barons, who recoil in horror; (right) he argues before the kings of England and France, while boys shout abuse. (The Becket Leaves)

with stern warnings to Henry as to what might follow if he did not cease from scheming against the Church. The English bishops appealed to the Pope against the excommunications.

The events at Vézelay also provoked a whole spate of letters, and in late 1166 Gilbert Foliot wrote the most celebrated epistle in the whole controversy, called from its opening *Multiplicem*.[3] It is so damning to Becket that some of the saint's admirers have been unwilling to accept it as genuine. It contains, for example, the notorious charge that Becket compromised his integrity at the Council of Clarendon by forswearing himself, with the idea of retracting his promises later. The general feeling now is that the letter is genuine. If Gilbert makes a dreadful accusation then it must be conceded that he was certainly in the know, though his utterance must be read in the light of the fact that it was made at the height of a quarrel. Dom David Knowles calls the letter 'a rhetorical masterpiece', adding that 'its cold and unrelenting hatred . . . comes from the abundance of a heart in which humility and love had long ceased to harbour'.[4] Others might see it as the product of a fine if embittered mind, couched in terms of astounding restraint in the face of a now fanatical opponent.

King Henry decided to take further action against Becket. Pontigny was Cistercian and great numbers of houses of that order lay scattered through Henry's domains. Pressure was accordingly brought to bear and, at the end of 1166, Becket was dislodged from Pontigny, moving to St Colombe, the Benedictine house on the Yonne, close to the walls of Sens, under the aegis of King Louis. There he made his base for the next four years.

Pope Alexander, bewildered at events, appointed legates who in the manner of their kind succeeded in doing very little and that very slowly. They met Becket in November 1167 and asked if he would resign his see if the king renounced the Constitutions of Clarendon. Resignation was quite out of the question, they were told. Later the same month the king in tears besought the cardinals to ask the Pope to rid him altogether of Archbishop Thomas.

The sequence of events during 1168 is difficult to follow. Pope Alexander ordered Henry to receive Becket back and offer a thousand marks' compensation to enable him to set up house again. He must renounce the Constitutions, and interdict was threatened to induce King Henry to come to terms with Thomas.

In January 1169 the king and archbishop were actually brought together in the presence of King Louis at Montmirail, about forty miles south-west of Chartres. Becket was prepared to observe the long-standing customs that governed the relationship between Church and Crown in England, but his agreement was qualified by the perennial saving of his dignity and 'the honour of God', and so nothing was agreed. Even the sympathetic King Louis was exasperated with Becket. At some time in this period, Henry's temper rose so high against Thomas that he actually plotted to slay him. Another papal legation was appointed in February 1169 but its actions were as ineffectual as those of its predecessor.

Archbishop Thomas was again itching to be at the throats of his enemies, principally Bishop Gilbert of London. The last great batch of anathemas had been promulgated against the splendid background of Vézelay, and now a similar site was chosen, St Bernard's own Abbey of Clairvaux, some eighty miles east of Sens. After riding through the lovely countryside bursting with spring blossom to the great Cistercian monastery standing in its green gorge, on Palm Sunday Becket called down damnation on the person of Gilbert Foliot, Bishop of London, and several others.

The hatred nurtured by Becket for Foliot is easy enough to comprehend. The latter came from an aristocratic family, while the

Becket departs from the English and French kings, having failed to reach agreement. The royal guards show their contempt but the common people (*vulgus*, at right) welcome him. (The Becket Leaves)

former was of burgess origin, and ill at ease with him on that count alone. Foliot was a scholar, well-versed in the Scriptures and learning of the day, while Becket had dropped out as a young student and was obliged to fall back on better-equipped staff. Becket was a late starter on the ecclesiastical scene, whereas Foliot was a dyed-in-the-wool churchman. Again, some of the exploitation and misuse of the rights of the see of Canterbury had been carried on in Foliot's office.

Foliot was to be left in no doubt about his humiliation. Two violently worded letters, bordering on the irrational and outstanding for their venom even in the sorry literature of ecclesiastical controversy, were sent off. For one thing, Bishop Gilbert's taunts in the letter *Multiplicem*, particularly the charge of forswearing, were unforgivable even if, because quite unrepudiated by Becket, they sound all too true. Bishop Gilbert furthermore had been engaged in historical research and had long since made the engaging discovery that Pope Gregory the Great had originally planned to make London, not Canterbury, an archbishopric!

The two letters from Becket, addressed to Bishop Gilbert and his Dean of St Paul's, arrived in London on Ascension Day 1169. On the same day, far away (probably at Sens), Becket was busy publishing yet more excommunications. The complete list ran to no fewer than twenty-seven names, though some offenders were unknown to Becket and indeed charges were hardly specified. The old familiar names were in the list. Bishop Gilbert headed it, followed by Bishop Jocelin of Salisbury, Richard de Lucy and two archdeacons, Richard of Ilchester (charged with supporting the anti-pope) and Geoffrey Ridel, Archdeacon of Canterbury and King Henry's acting chancellor. Rannulph de Broc, not unexpectedly, remains unforgiven since he had been exploiting the archiepiscopal estates. Other smaller people were also on the list.

The sheer lack of wisdom of Becket's action is hard to comprehend. His grievances had clearly worked themselves up into an irrational obsession, and perhaps there was some unbearable surge of pain from the osteomyelitis, or one of the other chronic conditions which he suffered, demanding outlet somehow or other. Gilbert took action to release himself and, circumventing Becket, made for the papal court, where he engineered his absolution.

The last-appointed legates were still moving ponderously around and King Henry saw them at Domfront in the summer of 1169. There were also meetings between the king and the archbishop. Becket tried to induce the king to give him the kiss of peace, but without success. King Henry, far from intending to abrogate the Constitutions of Clarendon, set about enhancing them. A whole new set of decrees was brought into force by 9 October 1169. They controlled the movements of clerics through the ports. Passports were to be demanded, and all those over fifteen years of age were to swear an oath of allegiance to the Crown. The decrees were to have consequences for Becket upon his landing at Sandwich on 1 December 1170.

King Henry crossed into French territory in November 1169, with the ostensible purpose of making pilgrimage to St Denis. Occasion was taken for a further meeting between the two foes at Montmartre, but the kiss of peace was still not given. Any schemes for peace were thrown into disarray by the news which now circulated: King Henry proposed to have his son Prince Henry crowned as King of England, to ensure the succession. The project for the coronation of Prince Henry had nearly come to fruition in 1161–2, with papal approval. The Pope, by a letter which can now be dated 17 June 1161, had written to Roger, Archbishop of York, authorizing him to crown Prince Henry. Archbishop Theobald of Canterbury had died in April and the epistle sounds like an answer to an application. Alexander was clearly unaware of the rights of the see of Canterbury.

It is remarkable that Henry decided to go ahead with his plans when peace and reconciliation with Becket were in the air. The coronation of the king's son by the newly returned archbishop would have been the absolute crown of reconciliation. Yet Henry, motivated by we know not what burst of emotion, decided to proceed without Becket and the date in June 1170 was fixed. Becket knew what was going on and felt doubly betrayed when Pope Alexander lifted the excommunication of Gilbert Foliot who had struggled to him across the Alps.

When news of the imminent coronation reached the Pope, he sent off letters to the Archbishop of York and the other bishops forbidding the ceremony unless the king cancelled the Constitutions of Clarendon and the anti-papal oaths which he had exacted from his subjects. He stipulated that the ceremony must at all costs be performed by the Archbishop of Canterbury. The letters were sent to Thomas at Sens for forwarding to England. The archbishop added his own covering letter and entrusted the whole to Bishop Roger of Worcester (who was then in Normandy), for immediate delivery to Roger of York and his colleagues. It is not certain if the letters reached their addressees. King Henry reinforced existing regulations against bringing letters from the Pope or Becket into England. Bishop Roger of Worcester, who had recently been with Becket, was forbidden to cross the Channel from Normandy.

Lavish preparations were made for the coronation, which duly took place on 14 June at Westminster with all the accompanying splendid ceremonial. The actual crowning was performed by the Archbishop of York, Roger of Pont l'Evêque, assisted by Jocelin, Bishop of Salisbury and Gilbert Foliot, Bishop of London. Later they salved their consciences by purporting to rely on the papal letter of 1161. Archbishop Thomas and his circle were stunned by news of the coronation when it reached them. Here was another outrage to take the place of the Constitutions of Clarendon as the major obsession in Becket's mind.

Becket set his clerks to work drafting a whole series of letters of interdict. There were dozens of addressees, including all the bishops of England and Wales. Monastic houses were included and letters

C n pef fe nenr e panence   M   L eperef li fin: roie fi gianr

The coronation of the 'young king' in June 1170, followed by a banquet. Note the minstrel-boy in the foreground. (The Becket Leaves)

were sent to William, Subprior of Canterbury Cathedral and to Clarembald, the evil Abbot of St Augustine's Abbey (with whom Becket was hardly on speaking terms). They were all told to ensure that church doors were closed, bells silenced and religious rites refused to all save baptism to infants and the last rites to the dying. It is quite certain that the documents were never delivered in England. Royal officials would very soon have tracked them down.

Soon after the coronation Henry crossed over to Normandy, leaving England under its youthful new monarch, who was heavily surrounded by tutors and advisers. Henry first journeyed to see King Louis at a rendezvous near Fréteval, a castle about halfway between Chartres and Tours, within French territory but not far from King Henry's own frontiers. Louis wanted to know why his daughter Margaret, the young King Henry's wife, had been left behind at Caen and not taken to England to be crowned with her husband. After discussions, he was pacified for the time being. A distinguished group of French and Norman clerics was present and also hundreds of knights and barons, among whom Becket thought he saw (as he later affirmed) Reginald FitzUrse who was to strike him down half a year later.

A messenger brings news of the coronation to Becket, who claps his hand to his brow and forthwith sends a letter of complaint to the Pope. (The Becket Leaves)

Becket met King Henry at Fréteval on the following day, the feast of St Mary Magdalen, 22 July 1170. The old feeling of friendship between the two antagonists re-asserted itself. Henry had in mind a far-reaching and dramatic proposal, a tremendous climb-down and a drastic change of policy for which Becket was to prove entirely unprepared. He told Becket that nothing had gone right since he lost his good counsel, adding: 'I want to entrust my son Henry to your care. I will make my son and kingdom over to you.' He wanted to take the Cross, he said. Becket was being offered not only a regency but also the tutelage of a crowned king. He had no inkling of what was coming and was clearly overwhelmed and taken aback. 'No,' he responded, 'I will never accept it. I am already overburdened with the work I have.' If Henry wanted to take the Cross, then he advised him to seek another as tutor for the youth and controller of the realm.

Having thrown Henry's magnificent offer back at him, Becket could not keep from recrimination. He complained about the expulsion of his relations, now nearly six years before, and was quite unable to keep off the subject of the coronation. Henry promised amendment and the punishment of evil counsellors and declared himself convinced of the historic rights of the see of Canterbury over the coronation. At the end of the meeting, Henry swallowed the great rebuff over the proffered regency and invited Becket to be his guest in a progress through Normandy so that they might exhibit the restitution of harmony. But the archbishop begged post-ponement, saying he had to take his leave of King Louis and the French Church.

After so many years of absence Becket's clerks were very homesick. Guernes puts into Gunter's mouth an expression of this longing to return, and gives Becket's reply that after six weeks in England he would well wish to pay five hundred marks to be elsewhere. Henry told Becket he might send a clerk over into England to take possession of the land seized from the archbishop and his kindred. To this business Becket appointed his *eruditus* Herbert of Bosham.

Becket's grievances over his archiepiscopal fiefs still festered in his mind. One great bone of contention in the story of the crisis was the castle of Saltwood in Kent. It stands in a prime strategic position some way back from the coast near Hythe. The manor and castle of Saltwood were fiefs of the see of Canterbury but over the years had become annexed to the office of Constable of England, the commander of the kingdom's land forces. Henry of Essex was Constable until 1163 when he was disgraced and his holdings were seized by the Crown. Saltwood Castle should have escheated to its immediate lord, the Archbishop of Canterbury, but did not. At the beginning of Becket's exile at the end of 1164, King Henry empowered Rannulph de Broc, Becket's bitter enemy, to take possession of the castle where he was able to keep watch on the archbishop's Kentish estates and tyrannize over the neighbourhood generally. This minor baron had never been so well off in his life and was very unwilling to vacate his comfortable home on Becket's return in 1170. Becket sent a list of demands, including the return of Saltwood Castle, to King Henry. Henry sent word that he would look into matters when he came back into Normandy and in due course both John of Salisbury and Herbert of Bosham rode over the border to meet him there, but their mission was fruitless.

Early in October some unnamed emissaries of Becket went to England to find out what was happening to the estates. They made contact with the young King Henry and with Robert, sacrist of

Canterbury Cathedral. The emissaries could not report much satisfactory progress to Becket towards the middle of October, when they also gave him the disquieting news that Henry proposed to fill sees at the moment lacking bishops and had summoned Roger of York, Gilbert of London and Jocelin of Salisbury to meet him, together with four or six clerks from each of the dioceses in question. The nominees were then to proceed to the Pope for consecration, to the further detriment of the see of Canterbury.

Becket learned of an interview to be held near Tours between King Henry and Count Theobald of Blois on 12 October. He decided to attend and arrived on the day before the conference. Henry heard that he was coming and sent out members of the court to welcome him, and followed along himself, though the archbishop's staff noted that the king seemed anxious to avoid meeting the other's eyes, both then and later on in the evening. Becket again failed to receive from the king the very much wanted kiss of peace. The next morning Henry set out for the meeting with Count Theobald. Becket followed a little later and caught up with the king, exchanging arguments along the way with him about unfulfilled promises.

A few days later Becket went over to intercept Henry at Chaumont, not to argue with him but just to see him. Henry received him agreeably enough. They had a long conversation together. Help with cash was promised to the extent of 500 marks. Settlement of Becket's debts was undertaken, very necessary given his large staff and expensive tastes, especially in books. The creditors must have become very insistent now that news was circulating of Becket's departure out of their reach.

The king promised to meet Becket at Rouen and bestow the kiss of peace. Then the pair were to travel back in amity to England. Becket asked leave to depart. 'Go in peace,' said the king, 'and I will see you at Rouen or in England as soon as I can.' The archbishop had a moment of prophetic intuition. 'My lord,' he said, 'my spirit tells me that now as I leave you, you will never see me again in this life.' 'What?' said Henry, 'do you think I won't keep my word?' 'Be that far from me,' said the other and soon rode off to Sens to set his affairs in order and to make ready to leave for England.

Becket then moved back into Louis' territory and went round thanking his French hosts one by one. Louis urged him to stay and told Becket that since he had not had the kiss of peace, he must not trust Henry. On 15 October 1170 King Henry sent a writ to his son in England, ordering restitution of the property that the archbishop and all his men who left England for his sake had lost. They were to have restored to them their possessions as they had them three months before the archbishop fled.

John of Salisbury wrote off to the monks of Canterbury telling them the good news that the long exile might at last be coming to an end. He addressed himself particularly to William the subprior (ignoring Odo the prior, irregularly elected in Becket's absence), and to Robert the cathedral sacrist. 'He will soon be casting light on Canterbury, the city of saints,' he told them, 'and will be leaving Sens on All Saints' Day [1 November].' He also asked for help for the archbishop. Whatever practical help was given, someone had a brilliant idea for morale-building. There was returned to Becket his revered primatial cross, last seen at Northampton in late 1164. When Robert the sacrist set out for Sens in response to John's appeal, he took it with him. Possibly he took money as well but however much it may have been it was not enough to settle the archbishop's debts.

Although the king had behaved remarkably leniently with the monastic community at Canterbury, they were much troubled by the Broc family, particularly by Robert, nephew of Rannulph, installed only a dozen miles away in Saltwood Castle. Robert was in and out of the archbishop's palace next door to the cathedral monastery and seems to have operated an efficient spy system, finding out what was going on and even reporting to the king the contents of letters from the Pope. The king was unlikely to countenance aid and comfort to the enemy, and the monks of Canterbury did not venture for a long time, closely watched as they were, to send any practical or financial help to their archbishop in exile. They were continuously apprehensive that royal agents would take over their house. Prior Wibert died on 27 September 1167 and was buried amid his great building achievements in the chapter house within the cloister door. The monks elected Odo as the next prior, but Becket never accepted him as Wibert's legitimate successor.

John of Salisbury visited the young king, probably in the Winchester area. He was quite well received although the young man's guardians were in a nervous, hostile and suspicious state, believing that even if peace were openly established there were still plenty of occasions for trouble. John behaved very cautiously. He found that royal officials had made inventories of property of the see and that proclamation had been made at the ports that no one of the archiepiscopal party was to be allowed to leave the realm under pain of their departure being made permanent as exile. They had made it their business to ensure that if the archbishop did come back, nothing would be ready for him but empty buildings, demolished barns and fields stripped of crops, despite the specific agreements reached during the summer and subsequently confirmed by King Henry.

Far away in Italy the Pope remained not over-accurately informed of events in the west. Alexander was not very happy at his own part played in the story, under various pressures as he was, and excused himself for devious diplomacy saying he was anxious for the peace of the Church. On 16 September 1170 he issued two letters, one suspending Roger of York and Hugh of Durham for participation in the coronation, and the other suspending and excommunicating Gilbert of London and Jocelin of Salisbury. Other bishops were suspended from episcopal functions, while other offenders were left to Becket's discretion.

These letters had been requested by Becket, but by the time they arrived Becket had made his uneasy peace with Henry and so could not use them. He was intent on returning to England and publication of the papal sentences would have put that return in jeopardy. After an intervention by King Louis, the archbishop wrote again to Alexander, asking that the Pope should leave the publication of the sentences of suspension or excommunication of Archbishop Roger and the other bishops to his, Becket's, discretion, to use according to his judgment and the circumstances prevailing. The Pope agreed, replying from Tusculum (Frascati) on 24 November 1170. When Becket at Wissant at the end of November decided to suspend the Archbishop of York and to excommunicate the Bishops of Salisbury and London, it was impossible that he could have received the answer given by the Pope at Tusculum only a few days earlier. When taking action against the prelates he must, after all, have relied on the papal letters of 16 September.

CHAPTER ONE

The Return from Exile

It was on 3 November 1170, six years to the day after his arrival in exile at Gravelines, that Thomas Becket left Sens. His immediate objective was Rouen, where according to promise he expected to meet King Henry and pick up 500 marks. At that moment Becket was deeply in debt, but whatever his laments about poverty, he was accompanied by a cavalcade of a hundred horsemen, although some were evidently not of his household. Trailing along with him went a crowd of creditors in hope of collecting what was owed them from King Henry. When Thomas arrived at Rouen, there was no king and no money, only a curt letter explaining that Henry had been obliged to go off to deal with a French foray across the frontiers in Auvergne. To Rotrou, Archbishop of Rouen, Becket cried out bitterly, 'What price now the agreement between the king and me? Why hasn't the king come along himself? What about the kiss of peace? And what about the money? I have brought my creditors along with me. The king doesn't stick to his word!' To help him with his immediate money problems, Archbishop Rotrou there and then gave him £300, a very considerable sum, even if in money of Rouen.

Unwilling to forgo French cheer when back in England, Becket had taken steps to lay in a good stock of wine before his departure, thereby adding to his burden of debt. The king gave permission for the consignment to pass through his territories, and we know that the shipload came in not far from Pevensey, where it was seized by the archbishop's enemies. The most valuable and prized part of the luggage was unquestionably Becket's private library. It seems that about half a ton of parchment came trundling out of Sens late in 1170 with the rest of the archiepiscopal baggage. It is not surprising that (as he was to say) the archbishop desired sepulture at Canterbury, close to the cathedral library designated as a home for his collection.

A page from an illuminated Gospels belonging to his own library which Becket brought back from France to Canterbury. In the middle is the figure of Christ, and below that a mitred archbishop – probably Becket himself. (Cambridge, Trinity College; Ms B.5.5. f.130v)

By late November Becket was among his old friends at St Bertin. The Count of Flanders, Philip of Alsace, personally conducted the archbishop out of St Omer towards Ardres and Guisnes where the local Count Baldwin took over. At the castle of Guisnes Becket stayed at least one night, taking spiritual counsel with the chaplain before setting off for the coast in the morning. Then the way lay straight on for some ten miles to the port of Wissant, the usual crossing place for Archbishops of Canterbury through the Middle Ages. Here the party found themselves lodgings and looked for transport for the crowd of clerks and attendants with their horses, and for Becket's loads of books and other luggage.

Several ships were commissioned. One vessel was reserved for Thomas himself and some of the clerks, while others were loaded and set sail almost at once. The clerks impatiently besought him to go aboard, anxious to see their native land again after so long a time. 'Are we going to be like Moses,' they demanded, 'who saw the promised land and could not enter?' Becket replied, addressing himself particularly to Gunter the clerk who had voiced the question before, 'What is the hurry? Before forty days are up you will wish yourself anywhere but in England.'

Thomas and his companions took a walk along the beach, speculating on the weather prospects as travellers will. The air was clear and they could see the white cliffs of Dover thirty miles away, rising out of the Channel. While they were thus walking they were accosted by the Dean of Boulogne, an Englishman called Milo, who had sailed up the coast. Becket at first suggested with a smile that he had come to ask for a lift, to go over into his native land to see his kinsfolk. But Milo explained that he had come with a warning from the Count of Boulogne, to the effect that Becket had numerous enemies and that they were on watch on the other side (news no doubt picked up from one of the numerous cross-Channel ships), adding that 'if you land, you will be seized and flung into bonds in some mighty castle'.

Becket answered that nothing would stop him from the journey. His flock had now waited for him for seven years, he said, using a biblical number. He was determined to reach his church of Canterbury, even if unable to get there alive, 'should I depart suddenly from this world'. He asked for everyone's prayers for his last wish, which was that he should be buried at Canterbury. His collection of books was very much in his mind, for he went out of his way to say that they were to go likewise to Canterbury with his body.

On the beach at Wissant Becket meets Milo, who warns him against sailing to England. But his boat is already close to land and he embarks on 30 November 1170. (The Becket Leaves)

Twilight came on as they walked on the shore, and so they made their way back to their lodgings.

Meanwhile across the water events were moving fast. The old enemies Roger of York, Gilbert of London and Jocelin of Salisbury had come down to Dover intending to cross over into Normandy to see the king. No doubt they had learned of the provisional papal suspension of Archbishop Roger (which Becket had up his sleeve), and of the reserved excommunication of the other two for participation in the coronation of the young king, an act quite beyond forgiveness in Becket's eyes. Then, as will be related, they were aggravating their offence by being involved in the forthcoming election of bishops to vacant sees which Henry, with complete lack of excuse, had set in motion without reference to the archbishop. The urge to implement the suspension and excommunications suddenly became irresistible.

On any rational view, launching the sentences at this stage seems almost inexplicable. A Christian father-in-God would surely have waited for an interview with the delinquents, to see if there were any signs of submission and repentance, while even a more worldly politician would have curbed his feelings until entry into England allowed him to sense the atmosphere. Possibly, knowing that the three prelates were on the move and would reach court to tell their tale into King Henry's ears before he could do so, he decided to paralyse their activities. Yet there were ways other than excommunication, with all its frightful implications.

How can such irrational and self-defeating actions be explained? The archbishop had long been in a bad psychological state and was now smarting from the disappointment of his let-down by the king at Rouen. Importunate creditors were still hovering around him, demanding cash. The explanation may lie in something physical and perhaps Becket acted impulsively in response to bouts of pain. He had just ridden three hundred miles from Sens to Rouen over poor mid-winter roads, and so up into the notoriously inhospitable climate of Flanders, with its rain and mud. Jolted by his steed and exposed to the cold winds, no doubt the ragged and inflamed nerve-endings in his diseased jawbone were giving trouble. Perhaps there was one of the inevitable flare-ups of osteomyelitis, incurable before the days of modern surgery and drugs. Perhaps he was in pain from his chronic abdominal condition, very likely after long shaking in the saddle.

The archbishop now gave orders to his faithful and courageous servant Osbern. To him were entrusted the damning documents with sentence of suspension or excommunication for delivery to the three prelates. He found a cross-Channel boat bound for Dover and slipped aboard. He managed to step ashore unidentified and found that his quarries were quite close at hand. The day was Advent Sunday, 29 November. Roger of Pont l'Evêque, Archbishop of York, was chanting his office in the Church of St Peter (long since disappeared) on the north side of Dover market-place, a hundred yards from the harbour front. It is quite likely that Becket was using his humble chamber-servant not merely as an unlikely and unsuspected messenger, but as a studied insult to his bitter rival. He had certainly placed him in a position of grave personal danger.

Osbern had learned well the professional language of his masters, or had been well briefed. 'The Pope', he told Archbishop Roger, 'sends you by me such greeting as you deserve. Here, read this letter which he has sent you. . . . You are cut off from all appeal and from your sacred calling.' Quickly upon this dangerous *démarche* Osbern located the other two offenders, just as they had finished performing their offices in one or other of the local churches. He served the notice of excommunication on each of them with the words, 'Take this, my lord. . . . It expels you from the community of the Church!' At this the two bishops turned white with grief, shock and anger.

After all this the town of Dover was far too hot to hold Osbern. The townsfolk themselves were all ready, as Gervase says, to turn out in defence of their archbishop, and Osbern found it easy to obtain shelter. But Rannulph de Broc was there. He drew his sword and went about raging for the messenger's blood. Well-wishers hid Osbern, and at length Broc and his knights went back up the steep hill to Dover Castle, while the stricken prelates returned to their lodgings. Becket, across the water, soon had news of his 'revenge', and gloated on it, 'rejoicing with exceeding great joy'.

The three men in charge at Dover were in league with the bishops and were certainly well known to Becket. Rannulph de Broc 'of the horny conscience', as William of Canterbury describes him, was an old enemy with whom the archbishop had had a violent brush at Northampton six years before. Reginald of Warenne was brother of William, Earl of Surrey, and a leading member of the court. Gervase of Cornhill served as Justiciar of London and Becket, born in Cheapside only yards from Cornhill, could have known him since boyhood. Their families were millionaires by the standards of the day, and had acquired their wealth in city finance. William says that Gervase, who had moved into the county class and became Sheriff of Kent, was much keener on getting his percentages than on promoting rectitude and justice.

Robert, the Sacrist of Canterbury Cathedral, had travelled over to France, probably meeting Becket before his departure from Sens, and had handed over to him the archbishop's much-prized cross. He could be useful as a harbinger for the return and accordingly was sent back to make things ready at Canterbury. However, as soon as he stepped ashore at Dover he was seized and demand was made upon him for his entry-permit, as required by the enlarged Constitutions of Clarendon enacted in the previous year. He was unable to produce authorization to land and was forthwith put under oath to go back across the water as soon as tide and wind allowed.

Robert the Sacrist's captors demanded to know whether Becket was coming and were told, 'He certainly is coming, if the weather is all right; and then you will see him for yourselves.' The day after Osbern had performed his mission, while they were still awaiting

Four kings of England, from the *Historia Anglorum*, written and illustrated by Matthew Paris in the latter half of the thirteenth century. The panel shows (clockwise from top left) Henry II, Richard I, Henry III and John. (By permission of The British Library; Ms Royal 14C vii f.9)

passage, the archbishop with a crowd of companions went down to have a look at the ships in which they were to travel. They saw a vessel from England coming into port and as soon as it tied up they asked the sailors what their prospects were like on the other side. Herbert of Bosham got hold of the helmsman. 'What do you think you're up to? You're out of luck,' said the sailor. 'There are a lot of knights in port ready to set about you and the archbishop when you

Hplhonr le ch mangha.   o ecun ſruit opatore leenuref. ǝ oli regales annuanuit

egnles ꝼ broͤenſei

Ꝟ e douſ malf doir boͤte mediꝛ·   Ꝟanir eu engleterre aruue·   Ꝟ iiir que uuſ i paruenuſtes
e ſlur meuꝛ uuc uaur atenſ   ꝙ uꝛ larendenr a la riue   Ꝟ eſ euefquef lu roi meiſtet
Ꝑ e deſtre haſtuſs e engieꝛ   Ꝑ ourei la beneiꝙin   e n ſentence eſcuuuacuun
Ꝑ ar quei repentrum apres   Ꝟ emandenc par deuoeuun   Ꝟ unt ſurfe efe ia contentum
L arceues qi lur reſpunt   ꝙ aiſ reauſ demadec ppr quei·   ꝉ i li unr dir a grant manace

The arrival at Sandwich. The poor and lame struggle out in a little boat to be blessed by the Archbishop. On shore are 'Regales et Brokenses' – henchmen of the king and of Rannulph de Broc. (The Becket Leaves)

land. You have made everyone furious, especially the king's faithful men, what with your excommunication and suspension of these bishops. The clergymen and clever people are saying that this is Advent-time, a good time for the world, and things ought to be all peaceful. But you have upset everything.' Herbert took Becket aside and told him what the sailor had said. Gunter, the simple soul, became very worried and tried to dissuade Becket from crossing the water. 'If the country is upset like this,' he said, 'what is it going to be like when the king finds out?' 'Gunter,' said Becket, 'I can see land, and with God's help I mean to cross. And I well know that the time of my suffering is very close.'

Becket and his party went on board ship either on the night of 30 November or 1 December. Dover lies some thirty miles from Wissant, and a quite moderate breeze would have carried the vessel across the Channel in under twelve hours. In view of what might be in store at Dover, the helm was set for Sandwich, ten miles further up the coast. At this date Sandwich was one of the major ports of the land. It was an appropriate place for Becket's disembarkation since it was the property of the Church, having been given by King Canute in 1023 in compensation for the ravages committed at Canterbury and the destruction of the cathedral by his countrymen, mainly in the great attack of 1011. Rents and considerable profits from customs accrued from Sandwich to the monks, and would do so for another century, until King Edward I cut them off without, as the monks claimed, adequate compensation.

The township itself, with its wharves, warehouses and cranes, stood along the southern end of a great inlet where the River Stour coming from Canterbury mingled with the salt water of the Channel, forming a haven and fine anchorage sufficient to accommodate a fleet. Access to the open sea lay through a narrow passage flanked by the settlement of Stonar, backed by the rising ground of Thanet and the cliffs of Pegwell Bay. As Becket's boat turned into the harbour-mouth, it seems to have caught up with other vessels in the convoy and together they drifted southwards across the broad haven. Becket, with an ever-ready eye for drama, ordered his archiepiscopal cross to be raised in the prow of his boat to distinguish it from the rest.

The quayside of Sandwich was thickly crowded with townsfolk, particularly the poor. It seems that the tide was out and the ships could not make fast at the harbour front, for they grounded on the mud-flats. At once poor folk, tucking up their garments between their legs, waded out into the cold shallows ready to carry passengers dryshod to shore, a scene vividly depicted in the illustrated manuscript *Life of Becket* (and indeed in a parallel scene in the Bayeux Tapestry). One of the young people crying out a welcome to Becket was called George. He grew up to become a seafarer and benefited years later from a miracle of St Thomas when in difficulties on the ocean. The street flanking the harbour side at Sandwich is still called Strand Street and part of it bears the name Monken Quay, the special place where goods for Canterbury Cathedral could be unloaded. In a town so closely bound up with his church, Becket was not short of a place to stay.

The site of his lodging can with high probability be pointed out. Not many yards from Monken Quay there was a large building known throughout the later Middle Ages as the 'House of St Thomas'. It can be identified in the various rent lists among the archives of Canterbury Cathedral as affording income to the monks. At the Reformation it passed to the newly established Dean

Strand Street, Sandwich, *c.* 1930. At the end of the road from Canterbury, this dates from the fourteenth century. It runs along the 'strond' or bank of the river Stour which had been in Becket's time a much wider waterway. For centuries, until a bypass was built in the 1970s, this street was part of the main route between the two towns. (Kent County Library)

and Chapter who, in 1563, sold it to Sir Roger Manwood, the unscrupulous leading lawyer and native of Sandwich, who redeemed some of his sins by an enthusiasm for education. Here Manwood founded his celebrated school, Sir Roger Manwood's, which remained here until moving to another site in the nineteenth century. It seems highly likely that Becket's sojourn on the memorable occasion of his landing gave the house its medieval name. Indeed, it is precisely where it might be expected, close to the quayside and just within the Canterbury gate of Sandwich.

Becket decided to stay overnight at the port, anxious though he was to reach Canterbury. The hour must have been advanced, for thirty miles at sea, despite an early start, would have used up most of the winter daylight. Becket himself was still shaky at the knees from the crossing and (says the Saga) he had to wait for his horses which themselves probably needed a rest after being tossed about on the Channel. The party entered their lodging, but hardly had the baggage been brought in and undone when a great commotion arose. Back at Dover, where the three prelates were lurking and where the sheriff, together with Reginald of Warenne and Rannulph de Broc, had been keeping watch and ward, realization had dawned that Becket and his party had dodged that port and were making landfall at Sandwich. After a short conference, the sheriff and his companions came galloping up the road. The way was direct enough, for they had before them the dead straight Roman road linking Dover to Richborough, which is close to Sandwich. Under their cloaks they wore their armour and were all set for violence. They had sworn, says Guernes, 'by the Son of Mary', to slay Becket. Had they used force there would indeed have been trouble, says the chronicler Gervase, for like the men of Dover the townsfolk of Sandwich were all ready to take up arms and do battle for their archbishop.

However, John of Oxford, Becket's guardian, rushed forward on horseback to confront them. 'What are you doing? You must be mad!' he cried. 'This man is under the king's protection.' He said he would himself see to it that the archbishop was kept safe, but added that if they had any orders from the young king then they could see Becket, provided that they laid aside their weapons. The warriors complied, were duly admitted into the house and stood before Becket. He was seated as they came in and did not bother to rise for, as William of Canterbury says, there was no occasion for him to rise in the presence of people like these.

They affirmed that they had been appointed keepers of the land. They were suspicious of any French clerks who had been brought into the country, particularly any who might be involved in religious questions and troubles and had come without a proper passport from the Crown. They intended to exact an oath of loyalty. Reginald of Warenne specifically demanded whether there were any such in the party. They were particularly provoked by the sight of Simon, Archdeacon of Sens, who had landed with Becket's group, accompanied by at least one servant (who would sustain injuries at the murder, three weeks later).

It must be conceded that the barons were quite justified in their demands. The current legislation on the subject was incorporated in the revised issue of the Constitutions promulgated in 1169, according to which Archdeacon Simon, coming without proper entry documents, was an illegal immigrant. The sheriff and his companions would have been failing in their duty had they not objected. Becket defended the archdeacon, saying that all in the party were men of peace and that Simon had done him many good turns in exile. He added that demands for oaths were only required from spies, and he certainly had no intention of allowing any of his clerks to swear any. However, as Becket himself disclosed in a letter to Pope Alexander, an oath was in fact extracted from Archdeacon Simon, whereby he swore fidelity to King Henry against all other folk. The sheriff now told Becket that he had come with fire and sword and had excommunicated or suspended the bishops and the Archbishop of York for no more than doing service to the king, and that if he did not take better counsel something might happen which they would all regret.

Becket said he did not wish to deprive the young king of his crown. Rather he would wish him to have four crowns, but the coronation had been performed unjustly, against the dignity of God and of the Church of Canterbury. Due justice must be done for the sins of the prelates. He was ready, he said, to stretch out his own neck for justice, thus managing to confuse the issue. The clearly bewildered barons quietened down, but then they rallied and insisted that absolution should be extended to the bishops. Becket said that nothing could be done just at this moment and that he must consider the matter the next day, when he had reached Canterbury. Upon this the barons made off back to Dover, mouthing threats.

Meanwhile news of the archbishop's return flashed across the Kentish countryside. At Canterbury hasty plans were finalized for a dramatic reception. The cathedral was decorated and bellringers stood by. The next morning the travellers made the twelve-mile journey to the cathedral city. The day was Tuesday 2 December 1170. That date was entered into the cathedral calendars as the Regression of St Thomas and kept as a special feast day for the rest of the Middle Ages. Quite a large cavalcade set out from Sandwich through the Canterbury gate. There were many clerks including Alexander Llewelyn the crossbearer, no doubt riding at his appointed

Becket's triumphal ride from Sandwich to Canterbury is depicted on this stone mould for making pilgrim badges. He is shown riding a dappled stallion, led by a groom, and turning to give his blessing. (British Museum, MLA 90, 10-2 I)

station before the archbishop. Somewhere in the offing was the guardian John of Oxford, on the look-out for trouble. There was a good deal of luggage to be taken along the road. We hear mention of *superlectile*, literally furniture. There were certainly vestments and altar vessels, no doubt in their special leather containers. Then there was the precious load of half a ton of books. Perhaps a waggon followed with the luggage, though the most convenient way of carrying goods to Canterbury was by ship up the river from Sandwich to Fordwich, only a mile or two away from the city, so perhaps the luggage was not unloaded at the sea port.

The Kentish peasantry made a great holiday of the occasion, swarming up to the road to watch their archbishop go by. From each parish layfolk streamed out, headed by their priests in vestments with the processional cross, while garments were strewn before

Mercery Lane (*Merceria*). The building on the left is part of the pilgrims' inn known to Chaucer as 'The Chequers of the Hope'. The scene today differs little from this print of 1850, except that the cathedral gate has been restored and recently the figure of Christ replaced in the central niche.

Thomas with chants of 'Blessed is he that cometh in the name of the Lord'. Becket, his face flushed with pleasure, made his triumphant progress through the villages of Ash and Wingham (one of his own great manors), through Littlebourne (likewise one of his estates), and so over the crest of St Martin's Hill, where he could look down on his cathedral and city after his long absence, and past the ancient church which gave the hill its name.

The day was already far spent when the party descended the hill, entering the suburb of Longport. A procession of chanting monks emerged from the city gates, accompanied by crowds of citizens, all wild with excitement. Becket responded to the tumultuous welcome by handing out largesse in the shape of shoes, clothing, meat and cash to widows and orphans. The monstrous instruments in the cathedral belltower were set swinging (one bell was so great that thirty-two men on rockers were needed to set it in motion). Fanfares of trumpets blasted and the powerful Canterbury organ thundered.

Becket may have entered the city through the Burgate or may have chosen to ride in through Newingate and so down through the main street, turning into Mercery Lane to the square before Christchurch gate (the present Buttermarket). At all events, we know that he came into the cathedral precincts through this gate, not then standing on the site of the present entrance but some yards eastward, through a narrow alley between the houses. It is possible that some of the words sung in greeting can be recovered. It was customary to welcome a bishop with a liturgical 'acclamation'. One such 'acclamation' was actually repeated later that evening to Becket by Herbert of Bosham, who might still have had it running in his head after the excitements of the day. It is therefore very likely that as Becket came into his city and cathedral the choirs chanted the ancient refrain *'Christus vincit; Christus regnat; Christus imperat'* ('Christ conquers; Christ reigns; Christ commands'). On entry to the precincts Thomas removed his shoes and barefoot, amid chants from the brethren, was received into the cathedral itself, undoubtedly through the great western portal as became an archbishop. Here he stretched himself flat on the pavement, and then walked humbly the length of the great church, all adorned with hangings for the occasion, up to the high altar, where he again prostrated himself for some considerable time.

There were some among the monks who were probably less than enthusiastic about Becket's return. To begin with, there was Odo, the acting prior who had been put in charge during the exile following

Prior Wibert's death in 1167. Becket altogether disregarded Odo's existence, as one irregularly instituted. Then again, many monks were tainted by contact with the hated and excommunicate Brocs, administrators of the see of Canterbury during the exile. Odo, to all intents and purposes Prior of Christ Church, although snubbed by Becket, was no unworthy occupant of the office. He was a man of much popularity both with monks and layfolk, and an admirable preacher of great clarity in the three languages of Latin, French and English. He was furthermore much esteemed by the king – hardly a recommendation in Becket's eyes at the time.

Becket made his way to his archiepiscopal throne, sited behind the high altar, and standing there received the brethren one by one, from the least to the greatest, with the kiss of peace; all were overcome with emotion, with sobbing and tears. The archbishop then proceeded to the chapter house of the cathedral and there delivered 'a brilliant sermon' using for his text: 'Here we have no abiding city, but rather seek one to come,' no doubt inspired by the sight of Canterbury as he had approached down St Martin's Hill from the direction of Sandwich. The wordy Herbert of Bosham was much moved and said to Becket, 'Lord, now we do not care what hour you leave this world, since today the bride of Christ, the Church, has conquered in your person. Indeed, Christ conquers; Christ reigns; Christ commands.' Becket, however, gave him a look but said nothing.

Many of those present, who had known Becket in his heyday, would have been shocked at the change in his appearance since they last saw him in 1164. In the numberless pictures of the martyrdom he is depicted as the still-youthful-looking hero, confidently facing death. The great mosaic portrait at Monreale in Sicily shows him as the tall, black-bearded, serene, apotheosized saint, a vision based on the memories of those who had known him as chancellor and in his early days as archbishop, such as the entourage of Queen Joan of Sicily, daughter of King Henry II, or one of Becket's own nephews who lived in Sicily.

But we have another portrait, showing him as he was at the end of his earthly career, which must rank very high among accurate and expressive depictions in the whole of the Middle Ages. In the great glossed psalter from Canterbury now at Cambridge, written and illuminated by the versatile Herbert of Bosham, stand two tinted figures, one of the artist himself, and the other of an archbishop long claimed to be William, Archbishop of Sens, Becket's friend and supporter. Under ultra-violet light an obliterated inscription can

Mosaic portrait of the saint in the apse of the cathedral at Monreale in Sicily.

now be read: *Sanctus Thomas martyr et pontifex*. Herbert draws a portrait very different from that of Becket in his great days. It shows a man tensed with controversy, with gloomy and ravaged countenance, who had for years been under appalling strain and who had undergone crisis after crisis, burdened all the while with pain. On the forehead are deep furrows converging on the nose, while the

Archbishop Becket and
Herbert of Bosham, from the
'great glossed psalter', written
and illustrated by the latter.
(Trinity College, Cambridge)

mouth is turned grimly down. The once splendid black beard has
turned snow-white. This, then, is the real appearance of the man who
came back to England to die; not the smooth-skinned champion
calmly facing his assassins, endlessly depicted in portrayals of the
martyrdom in frescoes and illuminated manuscripts.

On the day following the landing, Wednesday 3 December, a
party of clerks representing the censured bishops came up from

This late twelfth or early
thirteenth-century stained-
glass portrait of Becket can be
seen on the north side of
Trinity Chapel, close to the site
of his shrine. (Photograph: Dr
Sebastian Strobl; the Dean and
Chapter of Canterbury)

Dover to register appeal. They had no success in arguing with the archbishop. Some royal officials, including Rannulph de Broc, managed to reach his presence. The clerks and the knights assailed Becket in turn with their arguments. He told them that only the Pope could lift the sentences. Rejoinder was made that Becket had secured condemnation from the Pope by misrepresentation. The clerks affirmed that their masters had actually come down to the coast to greet the archbishop in procession, in company with the cathedral body, but that, after the way in which they had been treated, they were reduced to mourning garments. Becket replied with taunts, saying that if the Pope declared war, then it was quite all right to break a false peace.

The knights then addressed him about the suspension and excommunication of the bishops. 'You have authorized this in contempt of the lord king and in violation of the dignity and customs of this realm. We have come to find out what you intend to do since you yourself fixed today as a date to give answer [referring to undertakings made at Sandwich the previous day]. If you don't restore them to office, some unheard-of evil, something pretty wonderful to relate, will come of it. What kind of security do you promise when to all intents and purposes you are waving the axe about, when you should be doing what you can to keep things peaceful? The king's supporters and advisers are being eliminated all the while. All you have left to do is actually to take the kingdom itself away from him. Think hard what you are doing and ease up a little.

'Anyone with any sense would give way on his rights and keep the peace for the time being. Don't break everything now that unity and grace have been re-established. Absolve them. We are warning you and in fact giving you orders from the king. Take action now or you may leave it too late.' Rannulph de Broc came in with, 'You won't be able to take the crown from anyone actually seated upon the throne.' The archbishop answered that the Pope had taken the action and he, as an inferior, could not release the bishops. 'What Rome has bound, we at a lower level cannot undo.'

William of Canterbury credits Becket with a long and ceremonious speech at this juncture, dwelling upon the spiritual sword, but it seems doubtful if it could have been delivered or, if delivered, recorded in such detail. He went on that he was prepared to relent to some extent, relying on the Pope's clemency and depending on advice received from the Bishop of Winchester and some others of his brethren. Herbert of Bosham says, in effect, that Becket would have been prepared to arrogate to himself some of the Pope's authority if the delinquents would give undertaking to abide by the judgment of the Church. Otherwise, he would do absolutely nothing in the matter. The archbishop affirmed that they were all thirsting for his blood. 'Let them drink it,' he said. Loud-voiced among the knights was Rannulph de Broc. So, fuming with wrath and uttering proud, insolent and abusive remarks, the party left Canterbury and returned to Dover, where the clerks of the episcopal party reported the unsatisfactory interview to their masters.

The three prelates took counsel together. Gilbert of London and Jocelin of Salisbury lost their nerve and were ready to make submission but Archbishop Roger of York talked them out of it. 'I have got the Pope and the king in my pocket,' he claimed. 'In my treasury', he said, 'there is eight thousand pounds and if necessary I will spend every penny of it to suppress Thomas's pride and arrogance. Come on, let us cross over to the king. Peace will never be made now after such hostile behaviour.' As the king was on their side, he said, 'If you give way and side with him, you will only be regarded as turncoats; and if the king decides to deal severely with you, then he could turn you out of all your possessions. And then where will you be? You would be destitute beggars. Stick it out. What more can Thomas do after condemning you? He has done all he can do and has given sentence against you on false grounds.' So they took ship and sailed over into Normandy to find the king and recount their tale of trouble.

About now, Becket sent off a long and woeful letter to Pope Alexander describing his hostile reception. It must have been received with dismay, for it dispelled the high hopes of reconciliation and opened up all the old wounds. Ill-composed, wild in language, repetitive and at times almost incoherent, the letter went into great detail about offences whose perpetrators could often have been no more than names to the Pope. It enumerated grievances – empty barns, plundered stock, unfulfilled promises of restitution and so forth – which must have seemed utterly trivial to a Pope who had himself suffered similarly, but on a much larger scale, on his return from exile only four years before. Certainly points of principle were involved, such as the sustained illicit occupation of churches, or plots to search luggage for letters sent by the Pope, but given a fortnight of amicable discussion and restraint, Becket could undoubtedly have got his way.

Becket had a great desire to see the young king, who was now installed in his own court, currently at Winchester. Prince Henry was in theory commissioned to govern England in his father's absence, but at fourteen years of age he was heavily controlled by a group of tutors and councillors who seem to have looked all the while over their shoulders at the older king, with a consequent stifling of initiative.

Richard, the Prior of St Martin's at Dover, was selected by Becket as envoy to pave the way for him. His arrival at the young king's court had a dramatic effect. A group of churchmen assembled there to consider elections to vacant bishoprics, without any reference to their archbishop, a group which included the suspended Archbishop of York and the excommunicated Bishops of London and Salisbury, instantly melted away. Prior Richard was interviewed by the young king's guardians, who asked him about his mission before they would take him to King Henry. They told him that the young man was under their control. 'He does what we do, and says what we say.' They did not want any trouble. They observed that Richard had sealed 'letters close' and wanted to know what was in them. Sealed letters gave the impression of trouble because, if they were peaceful, then they would have been sent unsealed or at least accompanied by a note of their contents. Past experience warned them that Becket had caused disturbances before, and they were apprehensive now.

Prior Richard affirmed that the archbishop had come back in peace and was not scheming trouble. He assured them all of Becket's sincerity and that he was certainly not wishing to incur a charge of treasonable activities. The argument went back and forth. The tutors complained that though peace had been promised, the archbishop's return had brought nothing but suspension, excommunication and so on, which was not likely to generate confidence. The archbishop had struck blows at the kingdom and, they argued, was trying to snatch the sceptre from the ruler. The prior replied in a long speech (if William of Canterbury is to be believed) that just as secular magnates were themselves subject to the Crown, so in the same way bishops and archdeacons were subject to archbishops. The baronage was expected to do its military duties, and so likewise clerics ought to fulfil their obligations and not try to take over from those above them. If a monarch found one of his knights sitting on his throne, would he take it lightly? In the same way a metropolitan could not be expected to stand a suffragan adorning himself with an archiepiscopal pallium, or undertaking his administration for him.

Was not the primate justly angry if he found another archbishop setting the crown upon the young king's head and undertaking a consecration which did not belong to him? Anyone would despise such a primate for not asserting his rights.

The councillors went into the king and had discussion with him. At length Prior Richard was allowed in. Bowing low before the throne where the young man was seated, he launched into another long speech (according to William of Canterbury). The first words sound like the start of an official letter: 'To his Lord and King Henry, Thomas Primate and Legate of the Apostolic See, greeting.' In fact the oration probably reproduces the body of the letter Richard had brought with him, with an occasional interpolation. Prior Richard spoke of the archbishop's return to England, praying that those whom God had joined together, no man should put asunder. Lying tongues must not intervene: 'Trust not in every spirit.' With much citation of holy scripture he explained that Thomas had but one grief on behalf of the Church of Canterbury, which was that it had not been he who had crowned the young king, and that his right had been snatched away by others. Richard fell silent while some around criticized the archbishop, making suggestions that he was not in fact a papal legate as he claimed to be. The young king remarked that although Prior Richard of Dover had not gained much credit for undertaking this mission, at least he was grateful to him for his good entertainment two years before of his mother, Queen Eleanor, and his sister, Princess Matilda, on their way through Dover to Matilda's marriage with Henry the Lion of Saxony.

Decision was postponed about receiving Becket until the young Henry had taken advice from the two archdeacons, Geoffrey Ridel and Richard of Ilchester, who had long opposed Becket and who had also been with the party of clerics which had beaten such a hasty retreat from Winchester when Becket's envoy arrived. They were now waiting to cross over into Normandy. Messengers were sent to them at Southampton, and Archdeacon Ridel sent back word: 'I know the opinion of King Henry senior. I will not be party to letting him [Becket] see the king's son when he is at work trying to disinherit him.'

Present in the young king's council was Reginald, Earl of Cornwall. William of Canterbury puts another long speech into his mouth. It is a reasonable and reasoned argument that Becket should be granted access to the young king. The archbishop had returned to England with due authorization. He had not brought an armed band with him, but just a few members of his household. He was armed only with his pastoral staff. 'I cannot see any reason why he cannot be heard now that he has been authorized to return. He just wants to come and greet his lord.' However, although certain of those present gave limited support to this view, the consensus was that the king overseas would not want Becket to be admitted by the young king's advisers. Prior Richard was therefore ordered to go back and was told that instructions would be sent by special messengers in due course. Herbert of Bosham says that both the boy and his tutors were very frightened of the older king, which was why the mission failed. Prior Richard rode back to Canterbury and reported his lack of success and his generally contemptuous reception at Winchester.

Undeterred, Becket remained determined to go and see the younger Henry. After that he planned (says Bosham) to make a circuit of his Province of Canterbury (despite the time of year) and to put right what had gone wrong in his absence. He also wanted to go to London, where he could expect to receive a splendid welcome.

Thomas, who had once had Prince Henry in his tutelage and knew his tastes, organized a splendid gift in the form of three mighty, magnificent and swift chargers, adorned with trappings rich in flowery devices and colours. These steeds had probably been picked up during Becket's passage through Flanders, then a great breeding ground for horses. As William FitzStephen says, the archbishop had much affection for the young king, not only as his new lord, but as the former protégé of his house when he was chancellor to his father. FitzStephen indicates that it was on or about Thursday 10 December that the archbishop and his party set off towards London, fifty-five miles away, which they apparently reached in a single day. With Becket there rode a small group of five vassals, happy to turn out in support of their lord after so long an absence. However, their attendance upon him was soon to be represented to the old king as armed insubordination to the Crown.

Even though it was a crowded day, the archbishop found time to stop at Newington, twenty miles from Canterbury, where he dismounted and performed the rite of confirmation, with proper ceremony and not in the perfunctory manner of some bishops. Miracles were claimed to have been performed on six blind men and some layfolk at Newington, later commemorated by the erection of a cross. At Rochester, twenty-eight miles along the London road from Canterbury, the archbishop was received with due veneration by Bishop Walter and his monks in procession. As he drew nigh to the capital a fresh procession came out to greet him, composed of the canons of St Mary in Southwark. It was swamped by the vast crowd which, wild with joy, poured out of the city now only three miles distant. There was also a group of the poor scholars of London, and priests of the churches. As Becket came in sight the chant was raised 'Te Deum laudamus'. Becket bent his head in recognition and, thrusting a hand into his purse, scattered largesse into the crowds.

Quarters had been made ready for him in a house belonging to the Bishop of Winchester (in whose diocese he now was), standing hard by the Church of St Mary in Southwark. He dismounted from his horse while the canons of Southwark escorted him in procession to the church door, chanting 'Blessed be the Lord God of Israel', the crowd joining in. Among all the joyous shouts, the voice was heard of a well-known local neurotic named Matilda who cried out 'Archbishop, beware of the blade!'

During his short sojourn at the Bishop of Winchester's house in Southwark, there came to him on the next day two emissaries from the young king's court, Jocelin of Arundel and Thomas de Turnbuhe. They forbade him in the name of the young king to set foot in any of the king's strongholds, towns, boroughs or castles. If he did so, they insisted, he would have reason to regret it.

'What,' said Becket, 'does he repudiate my allegiance?' 'No, certainly not,' said Jocelin, 'but the king has sent you this message because you have opposed him so often. You are trying to do away with the laws and customs of his realm and to take the Crown from the young king. You take armed knights up and down his land, and bring into it clerks from foreign countries. You have cut off his prelates from their functions. King Henry requires you to absolve them now. In this matter and in others you have done him great wrong.' Becket rejected their allegations. 'That is not right. What has been done by a superior', he said (referring to the excommunication or suspension of the bishops), 'cannot be undone by an inferior. All the more then, what is done, confirmed or commissioned by the Pope cannot lawfully be annulled by anyone lower than him' (meaning the archbishop himself). To this the knights retorted, 'If you don't obey the king's orders he will make you pay for it, and dearly too.'

Becket answered courteously and said that if the Bishops of London and Salisbury would go to him and swear to stand fast in peace and by the rights of Holy Church, he would undertake and bear the heavy responsibility of releasing them. If he could rely upon the advice of the king, of Roger, Bishop of Worcester, and of the other bishops whom he ought to consult, he would, in honour of the Pope, behave to them with all kindness and humility. They would be most dear to him. Jocelin repeated the order already given. 'Since you refuse to absolve the king's prelates, he now forbids you to enter his boroughs, his cities, towns and castles. You enter them at your peril. Go and get on with your work at Canterbury.'

With such a restriction on his movements, the archbishop complained, he would be unable to do his work properly. 'How can I visit my diocese?' he demanded. 'In such case I cannot dedicate any churches, consecrate any nuns or do any preaching.' Said the others, 'We have come here to give orders, not to argue about them.' As Jocelin went out he met a citizen of London who was known personally to him. 'Well,' he asked his acquaintance, 'have you come to visit the king's enemy? I'll give you a bit of advice. You clear off at once.' The citizen replied: 'If you consider him to be the king's enemy, well then, we don't know anything about it. We have seen the letters from the king over the water going on about peace and restitution. If there is anything else, we are unaware of it.' Thomas de Turnbuhe and Jocelin of Arundel finally departed, grumbling that Becket's travelling companions had come all equipped in war-like manner. These were the knights, vassals of the see of Canterbury, who had ridden with the archbishop to London.

Appalling news was then brought to Southwark. The shipload of wine commissioned by Becket before leaving France had been intercepted by Rannulph de Broc. In a burst of characteristic savagery he slashed the rigging, stole the anchors, murdered some of the crew and thrust others into prison at Pevensey.

Despite the stormy encounter with Jocelin of Arundel and Thomas de Turnbuhe at Southwark, Becket had not given up hope of making contact with the young King Henry, nor of having a rational discussion with him. News had reached the archbishop that the young man was on his way to Woodstock, north of Oxford. He decided to move in that direction himself, first to his manor of Harrow, ten miles from London, and then to St Albans, about eleven miles further on, which would place him within striking distance of Woodstock.

There were certainly inducements to go to Harrow. It was the property of the archiepiscopal see and needed inspection after Becket's absence of more than six years. He had last seen it in 1164, on the day when he set out for the conference at Northampton, when the wooden buildings sweated in clear weather, presaging the evil to come. It was at Harrow that young Thomas Becket had thrown in his lot with the Church and had joined the talented group around the person of Archbishop Theobald, some seventeen years before. Moreover, Harrow was one of the festering grievances in Becket's mind, for here King Henry had intruded into the living his clerk Nigel de Sackville, who had put in a curate of his own and was as yet still holding on to the church keys, and stood excommunicate for the offence.

The obvious way to Harrow lay across London Bridge and along the present Holborn and Edgware Road, but Becket was unable to enter any town after the flat prohibition he had received and he must therefore have crossed the Thames westward by a ferry near Westminster or Lambeth. Memories of the visit remained in the Abbey of St Albans and were set down by the great chronicler Matthew Paris, who remarks that one of Becket's objects was to go hither on a journey of pilgrimage and prayer. Matthew had access to documentary evidence in the shape of an archive called 'the ancient roll of Bartholomew the clerk'. This man had acted as business assistant to the very competent if unlettered Adam, cellarer of St Albans Abbey, who, as will be related, took an active part in events connected with Becket's visit to Harrow.

The small party which set off for Harrow included Becket, Prior Richard of Dover and an unnamed clerk of London. Matthew Paris says that on the way to Harrow Becket was accosted by certain royal officers who demanded in the name of both kings that he should grant absolution to those whom he had excommunicated or suspended, and bitterly reproached him for making so much trouble after his return to England. There is nothing unlikely in such an encounter, for Becket would certainly be watched, all the more so if he set off from Southwark in any direction other than towards Canterbury. Certainly if Jocelin of Arundel and Thomas de Turnbuhe thought he was making for Woodstock and the young king then they would be likely to try to head him off.

Becket was upset at the failure of the young king, his old pupil and protégé, to offer him a welcome. 'I had it in mind,' he said, 'to visit him at Woodstock where they say he now abides, and to go through St Albans tomorrow.' God knew, he said, how much he wanted to see him, 'and that I cherish and embrace him in the bowels of my loving kindness'. The royal officials glared back with the words, 'Why do you trouble both him and his father? It is hard for thee to kick against the pricks' (some of them knew their Bible).

Becket did not answer and the encounter ended with a prohibition against any journey beyond Harrow.

News of Becket's arrival at Harrow quickly flashed across the nine miles to St Albans Abbey. Very soon an ample load of provisions for the stay came to the gates of the manor, sent by Abbot Simon, whom Becket had known long years before when he was prior. The archbishop was unusually affected for, as he said, St Albans had bestowed on him when he was young and poor the living of Bramfield (about twelve miles from the abbey), and now the same abbey had come again to his aid at this late stage. Grateful though he was for this 'present' from Abbot Simon, he would be overjoyed to have his 'presence'. In this he was gratified for one of the abbey servants who had come with the load cried out, 'My lord, he is even now here at the door.' So Becket, in the French language common to both of them, was able to say that he had *sun present et sa presence*. The two met with kisses after the custom of the time. Abbot Simon was overjoyed, believing that all was now well between Thomas Becket and the king. But Becket disillusioned him, and pulling the abbot's hand beneath his cloak, he said to the other's great distress that all was far from well.

Simon was known as a man of eloquence and persuasive tongue, and Becket determined to make use of him. He asked him to go to the young king at Woodstock and make another effort to secure an interview. Prior Richard of Dover joined forces with the abbot and the pair set off, in company with a clerk of London, probably around Monday 14 December. Their journey, amounting to about fifty-five miles, would take them past St Albans and the abbot generously enjoined Adam, the cellarer there (whose servant, Bartholomew, recorded the story preserved by Matthew Paris), to go over to Harrow every day with bountiful provisions for the archbishop.

It seems as if news of the young king's removal to Woodstock must have been faulty, for the usually reliable William of Canterbury records the encounter between Becket's representatives and the royal court as taking place at Fordingbridge in Hampshire, some twenty-five miles west of Winchester. Abbot Simon and Prior Richard made contact with the royal entourage, but failed to get past them to see the boy himself. When the interview started with the tutors, the messengers set out a familiar list of complaints in a numbered list with tedious quotations from canon law and the Old Testament: 1. the clergy were oppressed beyond all measure; 2. the property of the see of Canterbury had not been restored; 3. the archbishop's wine had been looted; 4. churches in the archbishop's patronage were detained (this with reflections upon Sennacherib the Assyrian); and 5. clergy were forbidden to travel overseas. A hint was added, no doubt coming directly from Archbishop Thomas, that the clerics were agents of God and would do whatever their sacerdotal duty required.

Reginald of Warenne (who had intercepted Becket at Sandwich) remarked, probably making use of a contemporary saying, 'Bows are bent on every side.' Reginald, Earl of Cornwall, added, 'Before mid-Lent we shall do something quite dreadful.' He did not say this on his own account, for he was a man of clear conscience, but he well knew about the plotting and angry talk prevailing at the young king's court. The messengers were told that the archbishop's petitions which they had brought could not be considered while he continued in his obstinate conduct towards the king and the court. As the meeting broke up, one of the courtiers uttered threats to the unnamed clerk of London, saying that but for the presence of the young king this clerk would have been severely punished for trying to intimidate them instead of showing proper respect. One point at least was satisfactorily resolved. Restitution was ordered by the young king of the shipload of wine seized by Rannulph de Broc.

The two monks now made their way back to Harrow and reported to Becket, whose mind by now was running on the sufferings of Jesus Christ just before the crucifixion. 'This sport will not endure for long,' he said, 'it is the Mockery.' Abbot Simon did not understand the remark until the murder had taken place a fortnight later. Becket thanked him for his efforts and gave him an affectionate look, saying 'Lord abbot, I give you hearty thanks for your labour, even if it has proved ineffectual. It is not your fault that the young man has not relented,' adding prophetically, 'He himself shall soon be brought to judgement and his life shall be cut off as by a weaver's shears,' a prophecy that was fulfilled when young King Henry predeceased his father, dying twelve years later in 1182.

The abbot, clasping his hands together, beseeched Becket to come back with him to St Albans and there celebrate Christmas and the 'feast of Stephen' on the following day, while Becket tried to persuade the abbot to go back with him to Canterbury. Abbot Simon said it was essential for him to be present in his own church at such a feast time. 'So you fear for your skin,' said Thomas, 'and I must face the peril of death,' which gave Abbot Simon cause for bitter regret when he heard of the murder shortly afterwards.

The journey there and back to the young king's court probably took no more than three days so that the two clerics, Abbot Simon and Prior Richard, were again at Harrow by about Wednesday 16 December. That Becket was at Harrow so long we can tell from other evidence, for Matthew Paris claims that he celebrated the Great Antiphons there. These were the seven anthems under the beautiful names *O Sapientia*, *O Adonai*, *O Radix Jesse* and so on, sung on successive days from 17 December. But Becket can hardly have stayed for the whole series of seven, for we know that he was back at Canterbury by the weekend, conducting ordinations in his own cathedral.

The archbishop, no doubt enlightened by Prior Richard, realized that he had an ally in Earl Reginald of Cornwall. He called to a member of his household named William, a man clearly with medical qualifications. This is likely to be Master 'W. *medicus*', who had been resident physician in the archbishop's *familia* for long years, ever since the days of Archbishop Theobald, and is fairly certainly the same William who had operated on Becket's festering jaw during the exile at Pontigny. The archbishop told William that the earl was afflicted with the *fistula* and had been asking for a doctor (which Becket probably also heard from Prior Richard on his return).

'You go along,' he told him. 'You can save his body and our lives and his life.' The doctor did not want to go at all, but at length got up his courage and, after a long ride, found the earl at Breamore in Hampshire (about eight miles south of Salisbury and a couple of miles from Fordingbridge where the court had been residing). The earl received him and, in the course of conversation and in front of his servants, said of the archbishop that 'he has created a lot of disturbance in the country, and unless God intervenes, he will bring us to eternal shame. We shall all land up in hell through him within a little while.' The earl was repeating his own words, more or less, uttered at the meeting at Fordingbridge a few days before.

The next day a messenger came over to Breamore from the young king bringing greetings and a present of venison, welcome no doubt since Christmas was close at hand. The messenger took a look at the earl's attendants standing around and exclaimed, 'Here, that's William that I can see, one of the archbishop's household.' 'No,' said the man he was talking to, 'that's just the doctor attending the master.' Said the other, 'I used to know William all right, a long time ago, when he was one of the archbishop's household.' Earl Reginald, valuing his credit with the court before anything else, took William aside and said to him, 'Clear off at once and get as far away as you can. Tell the archbishop to look after himself. Nothing's safe. They have only one idea about John of Salisbury, John of Canterbury, Gunter and Alexander the Welshman. Wherever they are found they will be put to the sword.'

The earl extracted a promise from William the doctor not to give him away, and then urged him to go. William slipped away in the night and covered as much ground as he could. At length, tired and exhausted, he came to the archbishop, evidently at Canterbury. John of Salisbury came in and, hearing what was said, burst into tears. Becket, however, merely stretched out his neck and lightly tapping it with his hands said, 'Here, here, the lads will find me.'

Whether Becket went back to Southwark after the Harrow trip is unclear. It may be imagined that he avoided London as one of the great boroughs he had been forbidden to enter. It is not very likely that he went into Southwark as this too was a populous centre (as we know from the language of William FitzStephen in his description of the capital). It is most probable that he crossed the Thames above London and struck out across the Kentish border.

That night he slept at Wrotham, a few miles from Maidstone. At Wrotham he was approached by a poor priest named William, who ministered in the church at Chiddingstone, some twelve miles away across country near Tonbridge. The priest had got wind of Becket's coming and had brought with him an impressive collection of relics, alleged to be those of SS Vincent and Cicely with St Laurence who had, so he claimed, made a nocturnal visit to him and had assured him of the authenticity of the items. Becket, as a man of the world, not unnaturally asked how this country priest was so sure that these were in fact true relics. The other was ready with his answer. He had, he said, asked St Laurence for a convincing sign. He told the archbishop that he (Becket) had just put his hand inside his garments and discovered that his hairshirt was torn and that, while he was wondering whether to sew the rent up or put on a fresh one, it had mended itself.

Since no one was supposed to know about Becket's self-mortification in wearing a hairshirt, except his more intimate acquaintances and servants, even less so about the tear, this was indeed an indubitable sign. Becket forbade the priest to tell anyone while he was himself yet alive. Exemplifying the unhappy state of

The Westgate through which Becket entered the city was still the Roman gateway of 900 years earlier, surmounted by a chapel. Two centuries after his death, this was replaced by the present gateway, with Holy Cross Church (now the city council's chamber) alongside. (Photograph: Jack Whitaker)

those who did the actual work in parishes while the nominal incumbent, like Becket himself in some cases and many of the higher clergy and the monastic houses, took the main bulk of the income, the priest went on, 'I am a poor man and minister in someone else's church. Think about me.' The archbishop answered, 'Come to me within four days of Christmas and I will provide for you.' At that the priest departed.

On the return journey to Canterbury, the archbishop kept with him the group of five knights armed with lances who had ridden up to Southwark with him, for there were by now very many presages of evil, with ambushes a real possibility. News of this modest escort reached King Henry overseas, exaggerated into a picture of Becket amid a large force armed with helmets and chainmail, ready to occupy towns and expel the young king.

The next port of call for which we have evidence is again Newington, on the London road between Rochester and Canterbury. With the prohibition from the young king against entering any town, Becket and his company must have found difficulty in crossing the Medway at such places as Rochester or Maidstone, and it is not easy to see how the party reached Newington from Wrotham. Edward Grim remarks that on the return journey the archbishop administered the sacrament of confirmation to children and that, in later days, miracles were effected at the places concerned. But perhaps Grim is thinking of the outward trip. If Becket made his last entry into Canterbury from Newington, then he approached the city down the London road, round the corner of St Dunstan's in the suburbs (where King Henry would start his barefoot approach in penance three-and-a-half years later) and so in through the Westgate. That night he slept in his own palace, showing every sign that he was aware that his time was drawing near. As Dom David Knowles says, he was 'fey'.[1] The five knights who had acted as escort to the archbishop were now dismissed and sent home.

Meanwhile back in London the Broc gang and their accomplices were pursuing their venomous hatred of Becket. Rannulph de Broc and Gervase of Cornhill, acting as king's officials and claiming to act upon the orders of the king himself, had summoned the heads of the monasteries and the more important citizens of London and others who had gone out to welcome Becket to the capital. Their names had been noted secretly, with a view to bringing them to court as enemies of the king. Many citizens put in appearances on the appointed day, but claimed that they had never seen any letters of the king authorizing the action. They declared that they were the loyal subjects of the king, not trouble-makers, and there the matter rested.

The Ember Days were at hand, following the feast of St Lucy the light-bringer in the dark midwinter days. Of remote and obscure origin, they were used as the occasion in the Church for ordination of the clergy. The archbishop, indefatigable as ever, conducted the ordination of monks from local monasteries and men destined for churches in his diocese. Of the monks of Canterbury Cathedral one subdeacon was ordained, and three priests. William of Canterbury the chronicler was the deacon ordained on this occasion, even though he had been admitted to the cathedral priory after Becket's departure in 1164. The archbishop made difficulties about other candidates for ordination on the grounds of irregular admission to the monastery, and ordered their exclusion from chapter for the time being, so that no bad precedent should be established.

Christmas, the season of goodwill, was now very close. Archbishop Becket relaxed his rigour over the irregular admissions to the monastery and issued permission for petition to be made afresh for admissions to orders. 'Beloved, we bestow upon you this mercy', he said, heaving a sigh, 'beyond what might be expected or thought fitting.' He rubbed in their humiliation and his own condescension, adding, 'You are our creatures and are to keep in remembrance, as you are bound to do, all that we have so piously and generously conceded to you. May the Lord grant His grace and blessing to you.'

CHAPTER TWO

The Plot

In the meanwhile the Archbishop of York and his two fellow sufferers crossed the wintry sea to Normandy. According to William of Canterbury they sent on ahead a letter setting out their tale of woes. They were not the only ones to cross, for the two archdeacons Richard of Ilchester (of Poitiers) and Geoffrey Ridel (of Canterbury) likewise tempted the waves. They travelled apart on this occasion and Richard of Ilchester arrived first, while Ridel's ship was still plunging in the Channel. Richard recounted to the king the story of suspension and excommunication. The letter sent on ahead by the prelates of York, Salisbury and London reached the king before its senders. Henry's reaction to the contents of the letter was violent indeed, beyond even what was to be expected from a monarch of his temperament. Infuriated beyond words, he retired to his private apartments. After a while he cooled down a little but was still very much enraged. It may be inferred that he did not at first tell his barons what the trouble was, but went round in a rage, crying that he had nourished a crowd of cowards and weak-kneed people, not one of whom would avenge him. The royal household became very concerned, knowing that he was speaking about them.

'What is it all about?' they asked each other. The king, so they said among themselves, could hardly be more upset if he had lost his wife and sons or half his kingdom (perish the thought!). Would not the king tell one of them, who could then pass it on to the rest? 'We are not able to do anything without specific information,' they complained. 'Here we all are, ready to undertake sieges of castles or cities, or to deal with enemies, putting both life and limb in peril! What indeed is the matter? We can see that he is upset but do not know why. If we were peace-lovers or dodgers when it came to making any effort, cheerful enough in easy times but unreliable in adversity, then the king would have something to complain about.'

At length they summoned up courage to ask him directly what he wanted done. He answered, 'You have known very well for a long time what I wanted, to the point where it is making me positively ill. One man, who has eaten my bread, now kicks up his heels against me. One man, contemptuous of what I have done for him, brings shame upon the whole royal family and goes trampling across my kingdom while no one avenges me. One man, this low-born clerk, came pushing his way into my court mounted on a lame pack-mare. Now he is turning out the proper heir and sits in triumph on the throne while all you lot, who were companions in his rise, just stand watching.' It must be remarked in passing that there is one expression missing from contemporary records, the famous line 'Will no one rid me of this turbulent priest?'

The king's nobles took seriously what was said. Were they in fact being cowardly, not taking notice of their lord's injuries, ignoring them all for the sake of peace and quiet? Tempers rose, and one and all became inflamed against the archbishop. The three episcopal complainants worked on these emotions. They came to the king's feet and made deep obeisance with dismal faces. The king bade them get up. 'My lord,' said Roger, Archbishop of York, 'I am the only one who may even whisper anything to you. The use of fire and water is forbidden to my two companions.' He meant they were excommunicate while he himself was merely suspended. Anyone they talked to would incur the same sentence which that ungrateful man who, 'forgetting your permission granted to him to return, has showered upon anyone consenting to the coronation of your son. He has put himself in control of the land and is making very sure he will not get into trouble again. He goes riding around with forces of horse and foot, posting them here and there for his own security' – wildly exaggerating the modest force of five vassals of the see of Canterbury who had been escorting Becket along the London road.

The prelates vehemently assured the king of their own loyalty to him. 'Just as if we had committed some terrible crime,' they wailed, 'we are judged guilty and are made into a public spectacle when we have completely clear consciences.' The king answered, 'If everyone who consented to the coronation is guilty, then by the eyes of God, I myself am not excluded. You must bear the storm in patience. For the time being, see if you can ignore this fellow who is trying to do you damage.' Henry asked the three prelates what they would advise. Answer was given, 'Take counsel from your barons and knights. It is not our place to say what should be done.' At length someone (was it one of the bishops?) remarked, 'Look, my lord, all the while Thomas is alive you never will have good days, nor a peaceful kingdom, nor any quiet times.'

The next day all the members of the court who could be found were summoned to hear read aloud the letter sent by the bishops. All who heard it were outraged. It seems, from the accounts of both William FitzStephen and Guernes de Pont Ste-Maxence, that the question of Becket's recalcitrance was discussed at two meetings of the court. Guernes tells of an angry scene at Bur, probably at the first conference, which he assigns to Thursday, Christmas Eve. It sounds as if the actual papal letter (or letters) served on the three prelates was produced in council, provoking the barons to fury. They swore on holy relics and pledged each other that wherever in the world they might find Becket, they would pull his tongue down past his chin and dig both his eyes out of his head. Neither the Church nor even the sacred season of Christmas should protect him. Guernes goes on to say that the room at Bur had a strange destiny for it was there that Rainild, the daughter of Duke William who died young, had been given in promise to Harold, and there in 1066 that the army destined for England took its pledge to William the Conqueror. Now in this same place, he says, the death of St Thomas was plotted by the best men of the court – but he would not set down their names as they had all long since repented and God had forgiven them.

In his bedchamber the king gave vent to his fury. Becket, he said, had come back like some tyrant into his land; he had suspended or excommunicated the Archbishop of York and others for doing their duty; he had disturbed the whole kingdom and intended to deprive his son of the crown. Furthermore he had secured the legateship over his (the king's) head and had extracted from the Pope rights of presentation to churches, to the exclusion of himself and the barons. Those who heard him vied with each other in their condemnation. Robert, Earl of Leicester, said that his late father and Becket had been close friends, but since all the trouble he had had no contacts. Engelram de Bohun, paternal uncle to the Bishop of Salisbury and described by William FitzStephen as 'that inveterate of evil days' and excommunicate, 'with the mark of the beast upon his forehead', said that with a man like Becket there was nothing to be done except to string him up on the gallows. William Mauvoisin, nephew of Eudo, Count of Brittany, said that on the way back from Jerusalem he had stopped at Rome where his host told him that one of the popes (possibly Lucius II in 1145) had been slain for his insufferable insolence and conceit.

Drastic action was decided upon. Henry determined to arrest Becket and nominated a party to carry the seizure into effect. Three very senior barons were commissioned: William de Mandeville, Earl of Essex, Saher de Quincy and Richard du Hommet. These three men had a record of long service to the king. Richard du Hommet was Constable of Normandy and leader of the royal forces there. He had conducted business on behalf of the Crown on previous occasions. With Archdeacon Richard of Ilchester, he was sent to Louis VII in 1166 to give Henry's excuse of severe illness for failure to attend a conference, thereby thwarting Becket's plan to excommunicate his own monarch at Vézelay. In 1168 he was involved in negotiations with King Louis. His loyalty to Henry had suffered severe trials at times. It was he who provoked the famous scene in 1166 when he made a generous remark, imprudently early in the day, about the prowess of King William the Lion of Scotland. Most people's tempers are short before breakfast time, but Henry surpassed himself on this occasion, screaming with rage, throwing his limbs about, tearing up his counterpane and ending up on the floor stuffing the contents of his mattress into his mouth.

William de Mandeville had succeeded his brother as Earl of Essex in 1166. The two were sons to Geoffrey de Mandeville, the formidable first earl. William had been knighted by Philip, Count of Flanders, and had been brought up in his court. He remained faithful to the king during the revolt of 1173–5, and was to serve as ambassador to the Emperor Frederick Barbarossa in 1182. Not long before his death he was made Chief Justiciar by Richard I. Obviously he was already a competent, tried and trusted counsellor to the king. The third commissioner was Saher de Quincy, another leading baron, found in service with the Crown for the whole of Henry's reign on both sides of the Channel. Within the tight circles of court and army Becket must have known the commissioners personally; the names of at least two of them appear as witnesses of charters issued over the royal seal when he was chancellor.

Whatever their courage and enterprise, the three must have faced one alarming certainty: it was most unlikely that Becket would 'come quietly'. If approached by would-be captors, he was virtually certain to resort to excommunication, the weapon he had repeatedly used against all who crossed him, even in non-spiritual matters. Any attempt to arrest him would lead to a furious anathema, something still taken seriously by almost everyone despite the way in which the archbishop had debased its currency.

Two of the commissioners did not venture to cross the Channel but assigned themselves instead to watch ports of possible arrival, should Becket attempt to make for the Continent. These were Saher de Quincy and Earl William de Mandeville, who before long is discovered on guard at Wissant. Richard du Hommet made the passage over into England and made contact with two of the guardians at the young king's court, Hugh de Gundeville and William FitzJohn, giving them orders to set out for Canterbury but to say nothing to the young king. They went on their way, but had the good fortune – to the immense relief of their master – not to reach the city until after the murder had taken place.

But there were four men in the court who decided to take action on their own account. These were William de Tracy, Richard le Bret, Reginald FitzUrse and Hugh de Morville. They quietly went aside, joining forces with Roger of Pont l'Evêque, the suspended Archbishop of York. He told them that Thomas was troubling the whole kingdom and he did all he could to incite them to evil. If Thomas were dead, he added, peace would be restored. He set out the arguments and expressions which they afterwards repeated at Canterbury to Archbishop Thomas. After briefing them he came to practical matters. Money was no object for him, as he was loaded with the treasure of the Church of York and had sworn to use it to break his enemy. To cover their travel costs he handed out the large sum of 60 marks to each knight, enough to enable them to hire shipping and to transport their crowd of henchmen over the water.

One record says that when they left the king's presence, they got together under a certain tree plotting to kill Becket, and that the tree, like the barren fig tree in the Bible, stood accursed and never bore leaf or fruit thereafter. Gerald of Wales even goes so far as to assert that the four knights made an oath to Henry to slay Becket. The monastic chronicler Gervase of Canterbury claims that the knights slipped secretly away from the court on Christmas Day itself, and went to the waterside to find shipping. Channel tides and winds are ever a menace to sailors and the conspirators, expecting their two boats to lose contact in the dark and wintry weather, decided on a rendezvous at Saltwood Castle, near Hythe in Kent, where they would be certain to find a welcome from Rannulph de Broc, its custodian, who was holding it in despite of its legitimate lord, Archbishop Thomas Becket.

On the day following their departure, says FitzStephen, King Henry held a council in his chamber. It was probably after this

The ruins of Saltwood Castle, Kent, depicted *c.* 1820.

second session that the king sent off to Pope Alexander a furiously worded letter by the hands of his trusted clerks John Cumin and Master David. Wild with rage against Becket (whom he does not bother to name), the king told the Pope: 'I have been devoted to you from the moment of your elevation, a point which may have slipped your memory [*elapsa forsitan a memoria*], but at least bear in mind that I have complied with your recent requirements [meaning that he had allowed Becket back into the country]. This man is an insufferable enemy to me and it is impossible to live in the same kingdom with him. He is hard at work all the time setting traps and scheming to do me down. Then there are those men of his who have been going round all over the place slandering me behind my back. I submitted to you and let him come back in peace, protecting against injury the very people who have caused injury. It is up to you', he added, 'to make sure that I am not rewarded with evil for good.' He concluded with an appeal for release of the prelates who had been either suspended or excommunicated.

At the same time Bishop Giles of Evreux and Archbishop Rotrou of Rouen also dispatched letters to Pope Alexander, on behalf of

Henry, while the ever-scheming Bishop Arnulph of Lisieux could not forbear from putting his oar in too, criticizing Becket's behaviour and sanctimoniously enlarging on his own efforts to establish peace.

Who, then, were these men who were making their way to Saltwood?[1] Thomas Becket was certainly not assailed by some unknown group of assassins emerging from obscurity. He knew them all. When he was chancellor three of them (Tracy, FitzUrse and Morville) had rendered homage to him on bended knee. Although one chronicler uses the term '*bachelers*', implying that they were young, they all seem to have been mature men of around forty.

One of Reginald FitzUrse's ancestors may have been the Urs named at Corby in Northamptonshire in the age of Domesday Book. By the reign of Henry I 'FitzUrse' seems to have become a surname. By 1129 Reginald's father Richard held lands in Northamptonshire and five other counties in the Midlands and south of England. He is a frequent witness to charters, especially in the reign of King Stephen, whom he supported against the Empress Matilda. In 1141 he was captured after fighting valiantly for the king at the battle of Lincoln.

His son Reginald can be found confirming grants of land in a charter, now preserved at Eton College, which bears the family emblem of a bear and is witnessed by, among others, Simon *Brito* (or le Bret), the father of another of the murderers, Richard le Bret. Little can be recovered of Reginald's character and career, except that he was an exceedingly ready talker, as demonstrated by the way he was to dominate the conversation at Canterbury during the last hour of Becket's life.

Of the four knights who slew Becket, Richard le Bret is the most elusive. The name in its latinized form *Brito* is very common, and thus brings with it the danger of wrong identification. It may be claimed, however, that the family has left a mark on the map of Somerset in the placename Sampford Brett, the village near Watchet on the Bristol Channel, close to Williton where the FitzUrse family lived. As a modest landowner with few pretensions to wealth or influence, le Bret seems none the less to have moved in elevated circles, for he appears as a witness to a grant by Henry II to the Abbey of Fécamp in 1155; another witness was the new chancellor, Thomas Becket. He invoked the memory of the Lord William, King Henry's brother, as he clove the head of the archbishop fifteen years later. Years after that his daughter Maud became a benefactress to the Priory of Woodspring in Somerset, for the souls of her father (the murderer) and others, and in due course her daughter confirmed Maud's grants 'so that the intercession of the most glorious martyr Thomas might not be wanting'.

Hardly less difficulty arises in identifying William de Tracy. The family seems to originate from the hamlet of Tracy-Bocage near Caen, some ten miles south of Mount Pinçon, the vast hill overlooking the plain of Bayeux, so hotly contested in 1944. Around 1066 one Turgis de Tracy is found involved in transactions relating to the provision of knights for the prospective invasion of England, and he may be the 'cil de Trac' who is mentioned by the English poet Wace as being in action at Hastings. At all events, whether or not Turgis was the murderer's ancestor, it is more certain that William de Tracy was the son of John of Sudeley and Grace de Tracy. If that is right, an ancestry can be adduced for William de Tracy (who chose to take his mother's name) which stretches far back into pre-Conquest England. Such a genealogy contradicts the theory advanced in old-fashioned histories and modern drama that Becket represented an English resistance movement against the Normans. In fact Becket himself was exclusively of Norman blood, his father hailing from Rouen and his mother from Caen, whereas English blood flowed in the veins of Tracy.

Hugh de Morville's family took its origin from the hamlet of Morville in the Cotentin some twelve miles south-west of Cherbourg. Members of the family are found in Dorset, the Isle of Wight and Yorkshire, but undoubtedly the most successful of the clan was Hugh de Morville who penetrated to Scotland and by 1140 became occupant of the prestigious office of Constable of Scotland. His son, also called Hugh, transferred his loyalty in 1158 from David, King of Scotland, to Henry II, who was then in process of wresting Westmoreland from the Scots. For this he was rewarded with the castle of Knaresborough in Yorkshire and became a leading member of the Anglo-Norman baronage, a man of great wealth and influence. After the murder he, like the other assassins (although he himself struck no blow), was excommunicated by the Pope. He was able to achieve absolution only by making a pilgrimage to Rome and then going to the Holy Land on crusade.

The last and most dreadful wound dealt out during the murder of Archbishop Thomas was inflicted by Hugh, the 'evil clerk', alias of Horsea. Even in a well-documented age it is hard to find out much about him outside the chronicles, or even to be sure which of the various places called 'Horsea' or 'Horsey' refers to him. Certainly none of the chroniclers is very clear about his identity. The historian Anonymous I mentions him twice. In telling how the knights followed Becket into the cathedral, he says that they brought with them a 'certain clerk, named Hugo *malus clericus*', and that after the blow by Richard le Bret which severed the top of the skull, this 'most evil of men' put his foot on Becket's neck and scattered the brains, afterwards calling to the others to come away.

Some of the other chroniclers differ as to who actually did this deed, and some do not even know his name. But Edward Grim and Guernes de Pont Ste-Maxence tell the story in much the same terms as Anonymous I, while Guernes adds a scrap of information not offered elsewhere, that Hugh Mauclerk was 'a clerk of Robert de Broc, full of wickedness'.

CHAPTER THREE

Christmas at Canterbury, 1170

The city of Canterbury was no mere adjunct to the monastery, as in so many abbatial boroughs, but was a thriving community in its own right, with plenty of manufacturing trade and retail commerce based on scores of shops. More is known about Canterbury in the twelfth century than any other English inhabited centre, owing to the fact that the monks drew rents from great numbers of dwellings and from time to time compiled detailed surveys, especially following the devastating fires (like those of 1161 and 1198) which periodically swept through the wooden structures. Names of occupants and of other landlords are known. Some of them find a place in the story of Thomas Becket, such as the borough reeve, John son of Vivian, commanded on the day of the murder to bring out the citizens on the king's behalf, and the goldsmith William, whose brother Arnold the monk (also called goldsmith) came back early to the scene of death. Also to be found in the surveys are the names of William, the priest of Bishopsbourne who secured Becket's bloody cloak, and William of Eynesford, the feudal lord who had several, and unfortunate, contacts with Becket.[1]

In Becket's day the cathedral consisted of a great Romanesque structure originally built under Archbishop Lanfranc and extended by 1130. There were two cross-aisles. Becket was slain in the north-western wing, which therefore requires some description. This cross-aisle projected at the eastern end of the nave, and was flanked by the chapter house. A door led in from the cloister on the western side, while opposite there projected the chapel of St Benedict. Above the chapel there was poised a tribune, a curious feature of great churches of this date, supported on a massive central column, as may still be

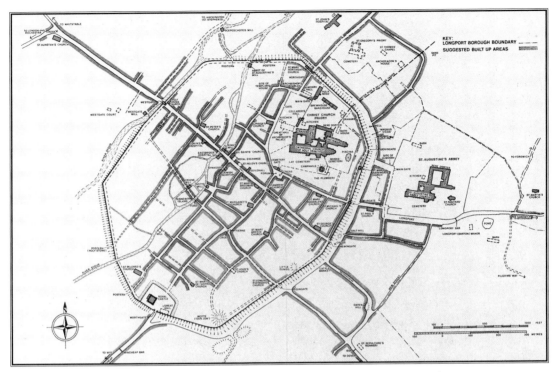

Canterbury, *c.* 1200.
(Canterbury Archaeological
Trust)

seen at Winchester and Caen. Beyond the column (as observed from
the entrance doorway) was a staircase of stone leading up to the choir,
while to its left a short flight gave access downwards into the vast
crypt, the greatest of its class in Europe. In a corner rose a winding
staircase leading to St Blaise's Chapel above the tribune, and thence
to the space beneath the roof. At the eastern end of the nave aisle,
close at hand, stood the altar of St Mary, the back of the reredos of
which must have been visible from the transept.

The monks of Canterbury (as wanting in sentiment as the builders
of the Church of the Holy Sepulchre at Jerusalem, who gouged away
the very hill of Golgotha) drastically changed the configuration of
the north-west transept during the ages. The great shaft, at the foot
of which the saint was slain, with the tribune above, was demolished.
The steps to the choir, mounted by Becket at the last moments, were
brought forward in a greatly different layout. The chapel of
St Benedict and the door from the cloister were drastically
'modernized', the latter twice.

Of Thomas Becket's archiepiscopal palace very little is now to be
seen. A hypothesis must be adopted that his residence conformed in

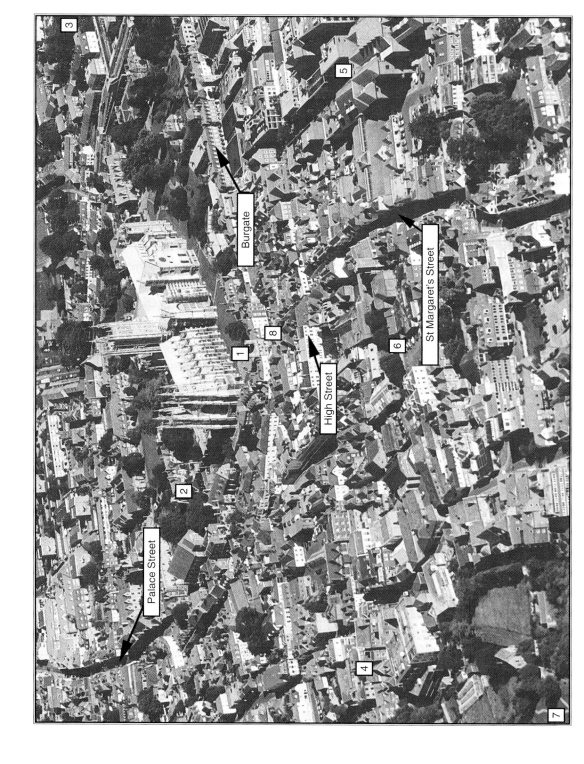

Palace Street

Burgate

High Street

St Margaret's Street

Opposite: This aerial view of Canterbury, with its annotations, is modelled on one prepared by Dr Urry in 1966 to illustrate his article 'Cantorbery au temps de Saint Thomas Becket', published in *Archaeologia* (Paris), which gave a foretaste of his *Canterbury under the Angevin Kings.*

Canterbury today: some sites associated with Becket

1 The main gateway to the cathedral, Christ Church Gate, was built in 1200 and rebuilt in 1517. Its predecessor, by which Becket entered on his return from exile on 2 December 1170, was about 40 metres to the right.

2 The archbishop's palace. Only fragments remain of the palace built here by Lanfranc (and mentioned in the Domesday Book) from which Becket went to his death.

3 St Augustine's Abbey, where the knights met abbot Clarembald on the afternoon of the murder. (The visitors' entrance to the abbey ruins is in Longport.)

4 King's Bridge: on the north side was the king's mill from which Becket's sister, Rohesia, drew profits after the king's penance in 1174. Her own house was a little farther downstream (i.e. northwards). On the opposite side of the bridge Eastbridge Hospital, dedicated to St Thomas, was established about 1180.

5 Site in Rose Lane of Town Prison established in 1166, according to the Constitutions of Clarendon. Becket's nephew, Ralph, was imprisoned there in 1188.

6 Site in Hawks Lane of the property of Magister Feramin, Becket's doctor, who set up a practice in Canterbury after his master's death. Two visions he had of St Thomas in glory are recorded in contemporary chronicles.

7 Riverside plot of land owned by Robert de Broc, possibly the site of his house made of wood stolen from the archbishop's forests.

8 Merceria (Mercery Lane).

(Photograph: *Kentish Gazette*)

plan more or less to the great structure set up in its place from about 1200 onwards, and indeed all the evidence of the numerous chronicles points strongly in this direction.

[Editorial Comment
Excavations and building recording work carried out since Dr Urry's death have changed our understanding of the topography of the archiepiscopal palace and its surroundings in Becket's day. As Tim Tatton-Brown has written: 'Dr Urry thought that Lanfranc's Great Hall was on the same site as the later thirteenth-century Great Hall but . . . there can now be no doubt that the original Great Hall was well to the south of the later Great Hall, and was within a range that ran west from the north-west tower of the cathedral.' The diagram of the palace and cathedral in Frank Barlow's biography of Thomas Becket ('compiled with the help of information kindly supplied by Tim Tatton-Brown') is in keeping with this newer knowledge. No attempt has been made to bring Dr Urry's text into line with what is now known of the site of the palace.

Professor Barlow's diagram shows the routes followed by Becket and the knights on the afternoon of the archbishop's murder as being along the south side of the cloister, which leads directly from the site of Lanfranc's palace to the north-west transept of the cathedral where the murder took place. Dr Urry's description of events below (which he represented diagrammatically in one of the maps attached to his book on Canterbury under the Angevin kings), based as it partly is on another understanding of the topography, favours a different route between palace and cathedral, along the north and east sides of the cloister. Some of the evidence from the chronicles, such as the sally into the chapter house on the way into the cathedral, lends support to Dr Urry's view that the approach to the site of the murder was more likely along the east rather than the south cloister, because the chapter house leads off the east cloister. However, as Dr Urry says in the concluding paragraph of Chapter 4, 'Which way the knights came through the cloister is not really clear'. The same can be said of the route followed by Becket and his party.

None of this affects Dr Urry's account of what happened in the cathedral itself.[2]]

In the enceinte of some four acres lying north-west of the cathedral church, there was a great hall standing across its southern end. The hall was cut off at its eastern end to provide living quarters for the archbishop, at a higher level than the main hall, and mounted on a vault or basement. A door gave access to the dais and high table. There was a porch (as in the thirteenth-century layout, in this case still surviving) on the northern side leading out into the great yard of the palace. At the western end stood the kitchen, probably detached from the main building for fear of fire.

South of the hall there was a private garden where bushes grew, some close to the kitchen. The eastern side of this garden was closed by the long cellarer's building of the cathedral monastery, itself

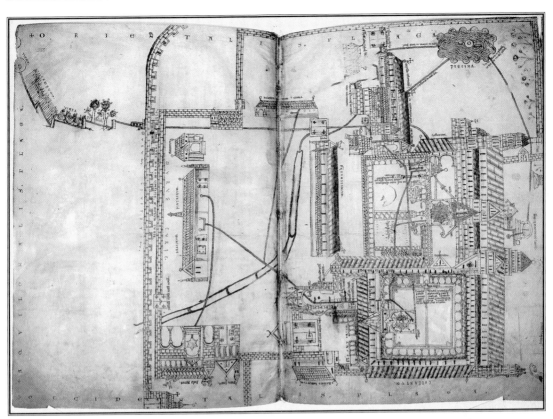

The mid-twelfth-century 'waterworks' plan of Canterbury Cathedral Priory, showing the choir and nave surmounted by towers with gilt angels. This was the cathedral Becket knew. (Trinity College, Cambridge; Ms R.17.1.ff.284–5)

flanking the western wall of the cloister. Abutting on to the private quarters at the north-eastern corner of the garden there appears to have been an annexe containing steps which led down from the private quarters at their high level. There was another set of steps, made of wood, which allowed direct descent from the private rooms into the open air, allowing the archbishop and his staff to take strolls in the garden without passing through the hall and among its occupants. This wooden stairway finds conspicuous mention in the story of the murder, for it was out of action on the fatal day.

To the north of the great hall lay the open courtyard, entered from the city of Canterbury by a gateway, probably on the same site as the existing sixteenth-century portal. Around the yard there would have been storerooms, sheds and latrines. Somewhere in this area the domestic knight William FitzNigel had an abode. At the far end of the courtyard was a gate to the street, on the other side of which stood a detached stable block where Becket kept his much-prized steeds. The name survives to this day in shadowy form as

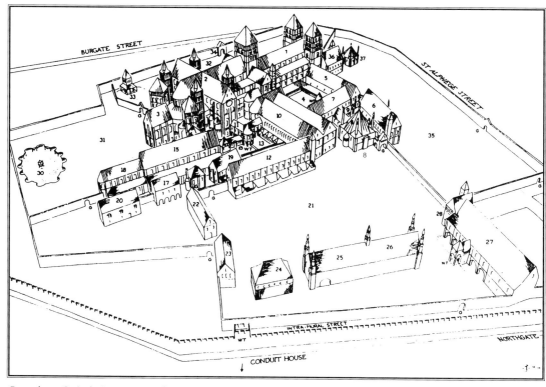

Canterbury Cathedral Priory, *c.* 1160, a reconstruction by John Bowen for the Canterbury Archaeological Trust.

1. nave; 2. choir; 3. Trinity Chapel; 4. great cloister; 5. cellarer's range; 6. guest hall; 7. refectory; 8. kitchen;
9. locutory; 10. great dormitory; 11. night passage; 12. necessarium; 13. herb garden; 14. vestry/treasury;
15–18. infirmary: hall, kitchen, necessarium and chapel; 19–20. prior's old and new camera; 21. outer (Green) court;
22. bathhouse and camera; 23–6. barn, granary, bakehouse and brewhouse; 27. north (new) hall; 28. court gate;
29. almonry; 30. fishpond; 31. monks' cemetery; 32. lay cemetery; 33. bell tower; 34. cemetery gate;
35–7. Archbishop's outer court, great hall and kitchen. WT = Water Tower; G = Gate.

'Staplegate', or more accurately 'Stablegate'. From the narratives of the murder it sounds as if Becket's clerks likewise kept their mounts in these detached stables.

The palace was a city within a city. Unhappily the artist of the splendid tinted monastic plan of Canterbury drawn up in such detail a few years before Becket's death stops short at the cellarer's building along the side of the cloister and gives no indication of the layout of the palace, but he does show the long structure separating palace from cloister.[3] Today there is a door from the palace into the cloister at its north-western corner. It seems quite certain that in Becket's day there was a tunnel beneath the cellarer's department from the annexe mentioned above, adjoining the private quarters. There was a long-disused door, closed by a faultily attached lock, leading into the tunnel. At the cloister end of this tunnel there was a second door, bolted on the eastern, or monastic, side. Next to it there was, and still is, a strange and ancient orifice, evidently serving as a speaking hole or tube to call for the bolts to be undone by anyone finding himself in the tunnel. All these topographical details play a significant part in the course of events just before the slaughter.

By the time Archbishop Thomas had returned from his trips to London and Harrow, Christmas was imminent and foodstuffs were being brought in from various manors and farms of the church and archbishopric of Canterbury. Along one of the roads towards the city (tradition said at Strood near Rochester), there was plodding a pack-mare laden with supplies destined for the palace kitchen. Quite by chance, one day just before Christmas, the beast and its driver were encountered by Robert de Broc who seized the opportunity to humiliate Becket and to ingratiate himself with the king. Either he cut off the animal's tail himself or he urged on a nephew John de Broc (otherwise unknown) to do the deed. This John de Broc is mentioned only by William FitzStephen and he finds no place in the plentiful records relating to the family group. It seems not unlikely that he had no real existence and that the cruel insult was perpetrated by Robert de Broc, nephew of Rannulph. Edward Grim says that more than one horse was mutilated and that the servants of the archbishop, evidently the drivers, were wounded. The unhappy animal was led to Canterbury and brought into the presence of Becket himself. The incident was to have a very long life, living on into comparatively modern times in a tradition that Kentish inhabitants were afflicted with tails.

There were further annoyances. The Broc clan issued out of Saltwood Castle and set up roadblocks on the highways around Canterbury. They went hunting in the archbishop's woods and took a deer. One news item provides the surprising information that Becket's pack of hounds was still in being or had been reassembled soon after his return from exile. The Brocs encountered and rounded up the animals.

Robert de Broc had a house in Canterbury built of timber filched from the archbishop's woods during the exile. It probably stood in St Peter's Grove, within the south-western quadrant of the city walls, not far from the Westgate.[4] Becket directed messengers to go to find Broc and denounce him as excommunicate, requiring satisfaction.

The speaking-tube in the north-west corner of the cloisters. (The Dean and Chapter of Canterbury)

A contemptuous answer was given by a knight named David of Romney, who reported that Broc said that he would carry on just the same, excommunicated or not. So far had the archbishop debased the currency of the supposedly dreadful weapon of anathema that some laymen no longer feared it. To add insult to injury, David was one of the archbishop's own vassals who held ground at Romney and in the nearby marsh for which he had undoubtedly sworn homage. So the next day the excommunication was enforced in solemn terms, as will be seen.

In the night before Christmas the archbishop went to the cathedral to participate in the service. He himself read the Gospel which was the long genealogy from St Matthew: 'the book of the generation of Jesus Christ, the son of David, the son of Abraham. Abraham begat Isaac; and Isaac begat Jacob; and Jacob begat Judas and his brethren,' right down through thrice fourteen generations to 'Joseph the husband of Mary, of whom was born Jesus, who is called Christ'. On Christmas morning itself Becket mounted the pulpit and preached to the layfolk of Canterbury assembled in the cathedral nave. It was a splendid sermon, says William FitzStephen, based upon the text 'Peace on earth to men of goodwill'. The archbishop talked about the holy fathers and confessors of the Church of Canterbury. Alexander Llewelyn the cross-bearer was of course there, and at the end of the sermon the archbishop remarked to him, loudly enough for those around to hear, that they had one martyr already, St Alphege, and would soon have another, himself. Herbert of Bosham recounts this as if it were part of the sermon itself, and says that Becket disclosed that the time of his own death was near at hand and that he would very soon migrate from this world. Thomas started to cry and the whole congregation was carried away on a wave of emotion, while the nave resounded to sobs and weeping as the people moaned 'Father, why are you forsaking us so soon? Whom are you going to leave us to, all desolate like this?' – a question they might well ask, with the lawless Broc gang ravaging round Kent.

The archbishop's mood changed. He abandoned consideration of anything that might edify, and talk of his impending departure. His tears dried up and then, grotesquely in the light of his own text, he started up again on his grievances. There and then, on the very feast of love and goodwill to men, he launched a new series of excommunications. The lighted candle, without which no scene of anathema was complete, was passed up to him. A book he certainly had, to read the formula, and it may be guessed that a handbell completed the equipment necessary to the occasion. The victims of excommunication on this Christmas Day are variously defined. The royal clerk Nigel de Sackville, excommunicated already long before, was damned afresh for retaining the Church of Harrow, in the gift of the archbishop. Geoffrey Ridel, another royal clerk and Archdeacon of Canterbury, was anathematized for holding on to the Church of *Thierlewda*, an unintelligible name occurring where one would expect Otford, and probably caused by some scribal aberration.[5] Ridel had long been in illicit possession of Otford Church and had suffered excommunication on that account in the days of Becket's exile. Indeed, the archbishop, in his long and angry letter to the Pope sent since his landing at the beginning of the month, had complained of the alienation of Otford by Ridel, who had been commanded by a papal commission to disgorge it together with the profits he had reaped from it.

Rannulph de Broc, an old offender from the days at Northampton, now six years before, was bracketed in excommunication with his kinsman Robert, newly in trouble over the mutilation of the pack beast. Rannulph had exploited the archiepiscopal estates and had hounded Becket's kin out of the realm in the winter of 1164. He still held Saltwood Castle, a fief of the see of Canterbury, and had aggravated his accumulated offences by the mad act of seizing the shipload of wine on its way to Becket, sent through Henry's continental domains by the king's special leave.

Becket could not forget his festering grievance against Archbishop Roger of York, Jocelin, Bishop of Salisbury, and Gilbert, Bishop of London, so he published their names yet again, telling the people of their offence in connection with the coronation of Prince Henry. Then the archbishop cursed all those who had been the cause of his falling out with the king and who had unjustly brought him or should bring him into trouble with his 'protector'. 'Christ Jesus curse them all!' he cried, and dashed the lighted candle down on to the pavement 'as a sign that their memory should be erased from the Book of Life and that they themselves should be expelled from the kingdom of the elect'.

During this display Thomas Becket altogether lost his spirit of Christmas goodwill and, according to Herbert of Bosham, became wild with indignation. He burned with anger 'against the stiff-necked, the proud of the land, the unclean, as it were flourishing a sword against them. If you had seen him,' says Herbert, 'you would have thought him to be that beast of the Old Testament, with the

Herbert of Bosham's dream was of a creature like a centaur, a familiar figure in medieval mythology – half beast, half man, usually vicious but ocasionally benign. This one is from Hildesheim (thirteenth century). (Metropolitan Museum, New York)

body of a lion and the face of a man.' Even if you discount much of Herbert's flamboyant language, it certainly appears that the archbishop lost control and worked himself up into a violent state of rage. After this orgy of anathemas, Archbishop Thomas proceeded to lead the Christmas High Mass, after which he went to Christmas dinner where he allowed himself some indulgence in meat dishes, like the rest, against his own scruples. It was a Friday and therefore, properly speaking, a fast day.

On Saturday, 'the feast of Stephen', the morrow of Christmas, the archbishop celebrated the Mass proper to that saint, the first of all the martyrs of the Christian Church. Becket was now getting messages from his own people and contacts at court that schemes against his life were afoot. He decided therefore to send messages to supporters and sympathizers overseas to announce what had happened so far since his return, and to disclose what kind of shaky peace prevailed. He took Herbert of Bosham aside and told him that he had destined him to go to King Louis in France, to Archbishop William of Sens and to other leading men, to inform them that the peace he had found was not peace at all but only turmoil.

Herbert could not restrain his tears. He told his master that he would never see him again in this world and that he desired to stay by his side and share his martyrdom. No doubt he spoke sincerely, for whatever his shortcomings, he had shown at Northampton that he was a man of courage. Becket, also shedding tears, replied to his protests, 'Not so, my son, not so. You will not be cheated of your reward if you fulfil the orders of your father and carry out his advice. Indeed, you will never see me again in the flesh. But I want you to go, principally because the king thinks of you as one of the more suspect characters in this business of the Church.'

On Sunday 27 December (the feast of St John the Evangelist), under cover of darkness, Herbert slipped away from Canterbury and England, taking final leave of Becket with lamentation and more tears. Another messenger sent off to France was the loquacious Welshman Alexander Llewelyn, the cross-bearer. To Pope Alexander at Rome was destined another of Becket's clerks, Gilbert de Glanville, while John called *Planeta* and Richard the chaplain were sent to the Bishop of Norwich with commission to absolve the clerks of Earl Hugh, who had knowingly performed divine service for some whom Becket had excommunicated. Even this gesture of peace was qualified by the condition that the guilty clerks were to make their way within a year to Rome to seek papal absolution, or send a couple of their number to deputize for the rest.

That Sunday night a written message from a sympathizer among the king's own servants arrived at the palace, warning Becket of death. He slipped the missive into his clothing between the hair-shirt and his skin. He was now well aware that his end was nigh. In these days, when talking to his clerks, he remarked that his cause could not end without bloodshed, and that he himself would stand until death for the sake of the Church.

On his final journey back to Canterbury, Becket had been intercepted by William, the hard-up priest of Chiddingstone, who appealed for a church of his own instead of his underpaid curacy. Thomas told him to call on him within four days of Christmas. In spite of all the stresses and strains he was under, the archbishop had not forgotten his promise. The inclusive reckoning which seems to have been used would bring the fourth day of Christmas to Monday 28 December, and it was probably on that day that Becket sent out one William Beivin who knew the priest (he was possibly a member of the citizen family of that name living close to the cathedral in Burgate Street) to see if the priest had come to town.[6] He could not find him, so Becket caused a special grant of the chapelry of Penshurst, in western Kent, to be made out to William of Chiddingstone, with excommunication written in against anyone who attempted to expel him from the post. Later on the priest gained possession of the church with the support of the young king who, having heard the terms of the charter and the story of a miracle (probably the priest's preternatural knowledge of Becket's hairshirt), was unwilling to incur the threatened excommunication.

Moves against Becket were afoot. The garrisons of certain castles in the south-east were now called up to take station, as at Hastings, Canterbury, Dover, Rochester and Saltwood, and even at the distant Bletchingley Castle, fifty miles away beyond the Kent–Surrey border. This action was taken in case Becket and his adherents were to barricade themselves in Canterbury Cathedral to withstand a siege, or the citizens and other local people rose to protect their archbishop. If he tried to flee instead, there would be forces well based at strategic points to cut him off.

After the various messengers had been dispatched, there still remained to the archbishop many of his familiar staff. On the day of the murder, there was the nervy John of Salisbury who had rejoined the household after years of comfortable exile at the monastery of St Remi at Rheims, together with the worldly William FitzStephen. These two were to write accounts of their master's death in due course. The cross-bearer was now Henry of Auxerre. He might have been a long-standing acquaintance of Thomas Becket who had been a student in that town when he went on a course in law there long years before. Auxerre is within riding distance of both Pontigny and Sens, and so Becket might have got to know Henry during his exile.

Heading the lay staff there was the seneschal, William FitzNigel, with another man of knightly status in attendance called Ralph Morin. William FitzNigel occurs at intervals during the story of Thomas Becket.[7] He was contacted by the archbishop's emissaries who had come over from the Continent before his return in an attempt to take possession of sequestered archiepiscopal estates. He was clearly one of the archbishop's vassals, but also had other lords, for one of his name is found holding ground in Bedfordshire from

Simon de Beauchamp. That he is the same man is certain, for he is bracketed with Robert de Brai who can hardly be other than the courageous young squire who appears in Becket's service at Northampton in 1164. William FitzNigel had property likewise in Derbyshire, where he is named in conjunction with his son Robert. Guernes de Pont Ste-Maxence, who might have had the chance to notice FitzNigel around Canterbury during his own sojourn there, goes out of his way to say that he was a tall, handsome knight, possessed of many fiefs.

Ralph Morin's name can be found in the list of knights of the see of Canterbury drawn up soon after the murder. He held ground from the archbishop at Boughton between Canterbury and Faversham, and may well be identical with the Under-Sheriff of Northamptonshire of the same name in 1183.

There was a considerable crowd of domestic servants in the palace, attending to the creature comforts of the archbishop and his senior followers. Not many of these domestics are known by name. One assistant in the palace kitchen named in the narratives of the murder is Robert Shinbone (*Tibia*), the scullion. Two others in the humbler ranks are also given names: Algar (not assigned to any particular office), and Osbert or Osbern, the archbishop's brave and faithful personal attendant in all the days since the Council of Northampton.

Certain outsiders can also be named. One was Simon, Archdeacon of Sens, whose presence as a 'foreign clerk' had caused trouble on the quayside at Sandwich on Becket's landing earlier in the month. Archdeacon Simon had a personal attendant of his own with him. The other principal outsider was Master Edward Grim, who had come on a visit to see Becket and by that chance became not only an eyewitness to the murder but one of the best recorders of that event. Edward is given a place among the *eruditi* by Herbert of Bosham, though admittedly he was only a casual visitor. He has been called clerk and monk, and although some have seen him as a somewhat shadowy figure, a fairly simple explanation of who and what he was can be offered.

With his title of 'Master', Edward seems to be a graduate of one of the nascent universities. He is regularly said to be a native of Cambridge. Not yet a university town itself, Cambridge supplied two distinguished teachers to Oxford towards the end of the twelfth century. These two, the brothers John and Geoffrey Grim, are highly likely, in view of their surname and profession, to be kinsfolk to Master Edward. After the student riots at Oxford in 1209 there was a dispersal of teachers to such places as Maidstone and Reading, while the brothers Grim went back to their native Cambridge. On reassembly of the University at Oxford, so it has been suggested by a Cambridge scholar, they 'came to Oxford and their friends no more', but set up as teachers at Cambridge, starting a tradition which has continued to this day.[8]

The busy and shifty Bishop Arnulph of Lisieux could always be relied upon to write out a testimonial for someone. At this very late moment before the murder he was helping out two of Becket's foes, Bishop Jocelin of Salisbury and Bishop Gilbert Foliot of London, by writing to Pope Alexander with some sharp reflections upon Thomas Becket's own conduct. Among Arnulph's correspondence is a letter addressed to the archbishop on behalf of the bearer, Master Errardus, who had once (it is explained) received Saltwood Church by grant from the Abbot of Bec and 'of your official'.[9] This Master Errardus had been ejected 'by the violence of evil men' from the church and wanted to have it back. The 'evil men' are readily identifiable as the Broc clan established in Saltwood Castle next door. It is not impossible that Master Errardus can be identified with Edward Grim, which makes his presence at Canterbury entirely intelligible: he was perhaps seeking the archbishop's help in getting back his old benefice, the patronage of which was indeed held by the Abbey of Bec and its dependency, St Philibert.[10]

A man with the title Master and the capacity to write admirable Latin (as shown in his *Life* of Becket) is not likely to have hidden his talents in a remote and windswept parish like Saltwood, with its tiny church. Clearly Edward Grim was yet another of the pluralist clerks, like John of Salisbury and Becket himself in earlier years, who put in a poorly paid priest to do the actual work and, pocketing the balance, went off to serve a bishop or some other highly placed official.

Full of deep foreboding, knowing that hostile forces capable of violence were established at Saltwood no more than a dozen miles away, the archbishop and his attendant clerical staff retired to bed on the night of Monday 28 December. Artificial light was poor. The night was long and the company probably asleep by 7 or 8 p.m. They arose around midnight as was customary to say the offices of Matins and Lauds in the bedchamber. Becket had one of the window shutters opened and, when orisons were ended, moved over to it and looked out into the night. There he stood for some time in prayer and meditation. He had heard that the knights had landed in warlike guise, and a struggle was clearly going on within him. The flesh urged him, while chance offered, to avoid the death which now stood before him. On the other hand, he knew he must not flee any further and must offer himself as a bulwark to the house of God and be ready to shed his own blood on behalf of his flock.

After some while he turned from the window and asked his household how much was left of the night and whether anyone could get to the port of Sandwich before dawn, 'seven leagues' (about twelve miles) away. Answer was given that quite a large part of the night was still left, and that it would be easy to reach there before daylight. But Becket remarked, 'Let the will of God be done upon me; Thomas will await God's decision in the church under his charge.' Again they addressed themselves to a few hours of sleep.

As the night came to an end Becket no doubt embarked on his usual round of Maundy ceremonies and charitable works. He heard Mass and made a circuit of the cathedral altars, vehemently invoking the prayers of the saints. Thrice he underwent his customary flagellation. He lingered a long while in the chapter house, right until dinner time, when he confessed his sins to Thomas of Maidstone, the 'venerable man' who had been commissioned by Becket when still overseas to absolve the brethren contaminated through contact with the excommunicate. Now the archbishop undertook with a great show of humility to abide by any penance which might be enjoined by his inferior in rank. It would be surprising and shocking to learn of the penances undertaken, says William of Canterbury.

The conspirators had the devil's own luck, for the Channel crossing, made at midwinter, was fair and calm with favourable wind. However, despite the welcome conditions, the two vessels veered far apart and by the time they made landfall, one (according to Guernes) was at Winchelsea on the Kent–Sussex border, and the other at Dover, well over thirty miles away. Edward Grim and Gervase both say that the whole party disembarked at the 'port of Dogs', wherever that might be. No such placename can be identified today, but perhaps there was some now-lost inlet near either port which bore such a title. Some notice should be taken both of Gervase and of Grim, for the former was a local man and the latter had been parson of Saltwood, albeit an absentee.

If we follow Guernes' version, those who had landed at Dover had a straightforward ride of a dozen miles over the high ground behind Dover cliffs, while the other group had a more circuitous and difficult trip of over twenty miles, crossing streams and avoiding inlets of the sea around the Rother levels. Nevertheless both parties rode up to the castle gateway at the same moment, to be met by Rannulph de Broc who was already well aware of their coming. How the news had reached him is not evident, although on some winter days the Channel is astonishingly clear, and from a vantage point like Hythe cliffs he could easily have seen a ship beating towards Dover. As soon as he heard the travellers' purpose he sent out orders to royal officials and supporters to 'come under arms and do service for the king'. The de Broc gang lied to people, affirming that they had orders from Henry's own mouth. The archbishop, they declared, was to be seized or slain. The chronicler Anonymous I states that 'castles in the neighbourhood' (Dover, Lympne?) supplied recruits, though these were ignorant of what was really afoot.

Night drew on, and the conspirators settled down to plan the next day's activities. Candles were put out, and plotting, muttering and whispering went on in the darkness. The group had sworn an oath of mutual support, but one passenger in the ships (called in the Saga *miles*, meaning soldier or knight) had begun to develop misgivings. Though he had sworn an oath of complicity, he slipped away from the crowd and rode up to Canterbury where he had an acquaintance, Richard the cellarer, an assistant in that department in the cathedral monastery. The knight found him and told him what he knew, warning him of the arrival of the party at Saltwood. Richard at once went and told the archbishop, who exclaimed, 'These are dreadful threats.'

There was another informant. One Reginald, a citizen of Canterbury, had occasion to ride to another town on business and picked up news that a force had come from the south and from overseas and was even now scheming in Saltwood Castle. He said that Rannulph de Broc and his following were there, having ridden around with such din as to shake the dwellings of folk living by the coast. Reginald made his way into Becket's presence to make his report, saying that there was no concealing the fact that their minds were bent on blood. Becket started weeping profusely, either concerned for the fate of those around him or shaken from his calm for a moment by his own prospects. When the tears abated, Becket said to the citizen, 'My son, we think we know for certain that we shall be slain by weapons. But they shall find us ready to suffer pain and death for God's name. Let them do what they want. But certainly they shall not slay me outside my own church.'

William pushes back his helmet so the troops can recognise him. (The Bayeux Tapestry; eleventh century. By special permission of the City of Bayeux)

When it was light the four knights made ready to lead their followers to Canterbury. It was the morning of 29 December, the morrow of Holy Innocents. In his anxiety to get at Becket, de Broc stripped the strategic site of Saltwood of all its fighting force, leaving only a couple of servants to occupy this forward stronghold in the country's system of defence. Quite a large party rode out of Saltwood Castle on that day. There were the four principal knights and their followers, who had been numerous enough to need two ships. There was Rannulph de Broc with the castle garrison, and local knights summoned ostensibly in the king's service. Further calls were sent out around the district to sergeants-at-arms and knights, 'to come and avenge the shame of the King of England'. Resolve was made that if anyone were to try to hide Thomas Becket or to get him out of reach, they would besiege the cathedral the next morning, set fire to it and bring it all down to the ground. By the time the party got to Canterbury there were some twelve extra knights, though how many joined up at Saltwood or how many came in along the way to Canterbury is not clear.

We have some idea of the appearance of the various *milites*. There are many pictures of knights available in that age, such as the

Barfrestone Church, Kent: the south door. Armed knights stand guard at each end of the outermost band of decoration, which shows a variety of people of the manor, from its lady (left) to a peasant digging (top). This church was built soon after Becket's death, and possibly the figure just below the digger represents the archbishop. (Beric Tempest)

dramatic sculpture of a fully equipped warrior in a vignette among the carvings on Barfrestone Church near Dover, more or less contemporary with the murder. The knight is shown in chainmail open at the front to facilitate riding, with the same conical helmet with a nose-bar to be seen so often in the Bayeux Tapestry. Below the hauberk shows a pair of baggy shorts looking like ill-cut *lederhosen*. The shins are covered with stockings or gaiters. Shields might have

St Augustine's: the great gateway built in 1308 to replace the earlier one of Becket's time.

borne a design (as on the tapestry), but fully developed family heraldry was then only in its infancy.

The dozen extra knights mentioned above must be part of the crowd which hung about in the archbishop's courtyard the same afternoon, said to have been wearing tunics over their chainmail. Of

the four principal knights, three were likewise clad in chain covered with tunics, though they would cast off the tunics to do the murder. The fourth knight was Tracy, who wore no defensive armour but went in a green jerkin with a multi-coloured cloak. All four principal knights wore gloves, which find a mention in the narrative of the angry scene in Becket's private quarters later on in the day.

Little more than an hour's brisk ride along the ancient Roman Stone Street would have brought the knights from Saltwood to the outskirts of the city, with their attendants, laden with their masters' warlike equipment, following unobtrusively at a distance. The precise line of entry into the city is uncertain, as the road divides four miles from Canterbury, yet we know that the first objective was neither the cathedral nor the archiepiscopal palace, but the Abbey of St Augustine, standing outside the eastern city walls. Consequently it may be supposed that the party of knights and followers wound its way past Streetend and Nackington towards the cluster of buildings at St Laurence's Priory on the Dover road, from where they could ride (probably along New Street, now Chantry Lane) to the abbey's great

The city wall and cathedral, seen from the great gateway of St Augustine's. The present Queningate (fourteenth century) is high in the wall, at the top of a flight of steps, but the Roman arch of its predecessor, still in use in Becket's time, can be seen at ground level, adjoining the bastion on the extreme right of this picture.

gateway. Orders were meanwhile sent out into the city of Canterbury that the citizens should come armed in the king's service. According to FitzStephen, these orders were met with a flat refusal although a contingent of local men, whether through compulsion or inclination, joined forces with the newcomers and was present in the cathedral cloister at the last moments.

At this time there presided over St Augustine's Abbey at Canterbury the remarkable figure of Abbot Clarembald. He had served Henry II as clerk and negotiator and the king, completely disregarding his want of suitability, rewarded him with presentation to the abbacy of St Augustine's. He had paraded himself, still in secular attire, before the newly consecrated Archbishop Thomas Becket for blessing. This was deferred since the monks put in a series of appeals, with much justification, for the newcomer was a man of notorious private life. He was, however, no mere ignorant roué, but an experienced negotiator and a sufficiently good Latinist to serve as emissary to the Pope who, so he boasted, would go over Becket's head and supply him with the necessary blessing into his office. Seven years later, nothing had been done and Clarembald had not even bothered to assume the monastic tonsure.

The abbot fell foul of the archbishop by acting as King Henry's agent at the papal curia and, on a special mission in 1168, secured assurance that Becket would be restrained from censuring the king or his men. There was not much love lost between the intruded abbot and his monks either. At first they would not let him into the chapter house, but he built up a party for himself and managed to get hold of the abbey seal which was used to ratify all sorts of unauthorized conveyances. Monastic buildings were allowed to go to rack and ruin, and rain seeped in all over the place. Clarembald's shameful personal habits continued and a shocked papal commission, which eventually ejected him, set on record that he was little better than a circulating studhorse, having had as many as seventeen illegitimate children in one small township alone. The four knights and their followers could certainly count on a sympathetic reception from Clarembald.

On arrival at the abbey the party from Saltwood was taken into the abbot's private dwelling and made at home. A discussion was held as to what should be done. Dinner was served, with quite enough to drink. As the knights sat eating at the abbot's table, Archbishop Thomas was consuming his last meal a quarter of a mile away in his palace at the far end of the cathedral. The four consulted with

Clarembald about the action to be taken. It must have been 3 p.m. or after, by our reckoning, that a move was at length made. The knights were in the abbey precinct, well outside the city fortifications. Opposite the great gateway to St Augustine's, the cathedral church towered up over the city walls, as it still does. Quite how the knights entered the city is uncertain. They could have gone off left from St Augustine's to the Burgate, or right to Northgate, or indeed through the Roman portal opposite the abbey called Queningate, from which a lane led round inside the wall to a point near the archiepiscopal palace. Their party meanwhile received reinforcements, for as they rose from the table a crowd of abbey servants decided to join forces with them. This group was headed by 'G' *marescallus*, who may readily be identified with Walter (*Gualterius*) the marshal, a lay official of the abbey and occupant of some of its ground near Canterbury, and named at much the same date in the abbey records. Another recruit was a knight in the service of the abbey named Simon de Crioil, a member of a well-known Anglo-Norman Kentish family.

After penetrating into the city by one of the gates, the party found itself at a large house occupied by one Gilbert, a citizen, 'close to the gateway of the palace', where an advance headquarters was set up and followers crowded in. Since the house probably had a yard at the front, as did many city dwellings at that date, it may be imagined that this yard was full of lounging followers awaiting events, with the street crowded with tethered horses.

The various histories differ about the knights' time of arrival. FitzStephen says that it was the tenth hour; Anonymous I about the ninth hour; and Benedict around the eleventh hour. If the day was calculated to begin at 6 a.m., then these accounts cover a range of two hours from 3 p.m. until 5 p.m. But in the absence of mechanical clocks, and late on a midwinter day when sundials gave no help, precision can hardly be expected. At all events, it was becoming dark. As contemporary – and much earlier – calendars observe, in December 'Night hath eighteen hours, and Day but six'. Perhaps the knights arrived at the archbishop's palace in the twilight towards 4 p.m. Herbert of Bosham remarks that the archbishop usually dined at about the ninth hour, and allowing about an hour for the meal on this particular day, we again arrive at about 4 p.m. It seems inconceivable that there can have been elastic hours, long in summer and only forty minutes long in midwinter, as envisaged by Dom David Knowles.[11] No individual or community could have conducted life upon such a scheme.

The scene in the archbishop's hall on the fatal day can be reconstructed. Becket sat at high table on the dais across the eastern end, flanked by clerks and monks. If his usual practice as recorded by Herbert of Bosham was followed, the monks sat on his left and the clerks on his right. There would certainly be a lector (temporarily Henry of Auxerre, the stand-in cross-bearer deputizing for Alexander) reading out a portion of the scriptures, of Lives of the Saints or some other improving piece of literature. Down in the body of the hall at another table sat the lawyers and other professionals not admitted to high table, such as William FitzStephen and perhaps William the doctor. At yet another table sat lay members of staff and the knights, just out of earshot of the lector. Other layfolk sat at the tables along the hall while waiters moved back and forth from the kitchen at the west end, the whole activity superintended by William FitzNigel, the tall household seneschal.

Other details may be added. Quite certainly the archbishop's high table was supplied with the table-cloth seen in so many contemporary works of art, such as the great engraved Last Supper which winds its way around a broad pillar in the eastern crypt at Canterbury. Gerald of Wales has put on record Becket's last dish. It was pheasant, which he ate with some show of appetite and jollity. A monk sitting there remarked that they were glad to see him dining happily on this day, to which he replied that it was proper for any man about to go to his God to appear happy. It was only a few days since Christmas, and across the land every baronial hall and humble dwelling would have been decorated with evergreens brought in by Christians to shelter pagan spirits from midwinter cold, so imagination may readily add clusters of holly hung from walls and pillars, with the ashes of the Yule log still on the central hearth. Becket was not indeed very Christmas-minded, but it seems unlikely that even he could have suppressed the feelings of his numerous lay staff.

As the meal ended and grace was sung, the occupants of high table moved out up the steps behind them into the private quarters of the archbishop, he himself making his way through into his bedchamber. There he settled down on the edge of the bed with his immediate entourage around him, most likely sitting on the floor, as indeed senior people would do today in many affluent households across much of the eastern world. It was now the turn of kitchen staff and waiters to eat, and accordingly they came in and sat down at vacated tables in the body of the hall, a scene which can still be observed today in more than one Oxford college. The seneschal, his duty done, now addressed himself to his own meal, probably at the knights' table.

William FitzNigel the seneschal was in a very difficult position. In a small city the news cannot have escaped him that the party of knights had ridden up from Saltwood and was even now being entertained at St Augustine's Abbey, just outside the city wall. In any case the cathedral cellarer's assistant had been contacted by one of the party the previous night and the archbishop had been informed. The seneschal had had time enough to consider his own predicament. He was Becket's liege man but also the liege man of the king, for William the Conqueror had made it very plain that no allegiance to any lord, however great, could interfere with allegiance direct to the King of England.

As their followers were establishing themselves in Gilbert's house, William de Tracy, Reginald FitzUrse, Richard le Bret and Hugh de Morville rode through the palace entrance gate into the wide courtyard and dismounted outside the door of the great hall, close to the mulberry tree growing there. They decided not to enter the presence of the archbishop fully armed (thereby showing better manners than Reginald of Warenne and the Sheriff of Kent with their followers at Sandwich three weeks earlier), though three of them (other than Tracy) wore their chainmail beneath their tunics. Swords and other weapons were now apparently deposited at the mulberry tree, since the knights returned to that tree to re-arm themselves half an hour later, just before the murder. They made their way to the entrance, attended by an archer named Rannulph (or possibly a man in the service of Rannulph de Broc).

At the tables in the body of the hall sat the servants at the second sitting, who were now finishing their own meal (according to Anonymous I, though Guernes says that they had already eaten and got up). There was movement down at the hall door as the knights entered. In the small world of court and army everyone knew everyone else and William FitzNigel and the domestic staff recognized the visitors. Greetings were exchanged in quiet tones, with FitzNigel at the foot of the steps leading down from the archbishop's private quarters. He greeted the party with a kiss as was customary at the time. Food was offered to the newcomers but they had already dined at St Augustine's Abbey and, as was noticed, were somewhat the worse for drink.

It was clear now to William FitzNigel that the time had come to part from Archbishop Thomas Becket. No man could serve two masters, especially such exacting lords as the archbishop and the king. The choice was now forced upon him. He had already discussed his position with Becket and had been given the advice that it would be best for him to depart. He went up the steps into the private quarters, and so into the bedchamber, to put the issue to his master. 'My lord,' he said, 'would you please listen to me for a moment? I have decided to take your advice, my lord, and go to our king's court and stay there, for you are in such disfavour with the king and all his men that I dare not stay with you any longer. The king may hold it against me if I do.' The incident and the language used hardly qualify FitzNigel for Bishop Stubbs' harsh judgement of him as the 'faithless steward who had deserted S. Thomas in the hour of his last peril'.[12]

Becket generously allowed him to go, saying, 'Of course you may leave, William. I do not want to make you stay here if you want to go to the king's court.' The seneschal turned and went back down the steps into the hall where the knights were waiting. They ordered him to announce their arrival to the archbishop, so he went up the steps yet again and told Becket: 'My lord, there are four knights here from the king's court and they want to speak to you on his behalf.' He did not give their names. 'Show them in,' said the archbishop and the seneschal returned to bring them up into the chamber.

CHAPTER FOUR

The Interview at the Palace

The afternoon of 29 December, says Dom David Knowles, is covered by a group of reporters more completely than any other moment of medieval history.[1] Four of the biographers whose names are known (John of Salisbury, William of Canterbury, William FitzStephen and Edward Grim) were present and it seems from the subject matter of the so-called Anonymous I that he was in close contact with eyewitnesses and auditors of events. Other chroniclers who arrived at Canterbury very soon after the murder, such as Guernes de Pont Ste-Maxence, clearly drew upon the still-vivid body of memories of the participants in Canterbury and the cathedral monastery. The extent to which a given chronicler made use of another's material presents a complex mathematical problem almost impossible to disentangle.[2] They all supplement each other to a remarkable degree, and, where they overlap, the variations are not considerable. Different men recalled words in different forms, while in some cases (such as William FitzStephen) translation into Latin and the urge to adopt a classical style and presentation has removed the language a degree or two away from the original French.

Any attempt such as the following to reconstruct the conversation and incidents of that afternoon must be very much an individual interpretation. Snatches of talk recalled by one contemporary sometimes correspond closely with recollections of another, but sometimes the divergences are more notable than the similarities. There may be repetition in the evidence, but it would be unwise to reject automatically words that have occurred before, since angry conversations are often marked by repeated attempts to drive home a point. Sometimes there is a remark which seems to be an answer to some challenge flung out from one side or the other which has not survived, as for instance where Becket affirms that Holy Church has been quitclaimed of obligations.

The lapse of time and geographical distance must have affected the various renderings. Herbert of Bosham was writing many years later, and readily admits that, since he had left Canterbury a couple of days before Thomas's death, he was obliged to rely upon other people's memories. Benedict the monk and his colleague William of Canterbury were each close at hand, both to the archiepiscopal palace and to the murder site, and were thus able to check with each other when they came to write down their memories – apparently soon after the event. Guernes de Pont Ste-Maxence, who wrote at Canterbury within a year or two of the murder, drew on the memories of actors in the drama and of Becket's own kinsfolk, and made himself familiar with the sites of the events. It is indeed unfortunate that the version made by Benedict survives only in fragments, for its quality, had it been complete, would have assured it a dominant place among the various accounts.

Timing offers difficulties. Different chroniclers will occasionally assign a given remark to different stages or different participants, and a decision which may appear arbitrary has had to be made as to the order of events and the identity of speakers.

The narrative which follows is offered as a conflation of the various accounts. It may be claimed that nothing of consequence has been left out and nothing invented, but it is readily conceded that other students may interpret the materials differently. It must constantly be borne in mind that the whole conversation that afternoon was in French. Consequently, Guernes de Pont Ste-Maxence's version is of particular value, as he recounts words as actually spoken. It is also probable that, even in the cathedral when Becket had sharp exchanges with the monks at his entry just before his death, the language was French rather than Latin.

Here in these accounts we have the record of a contemporary conversation, long, angry and uninhibited. There is more than one instance where the parties throw out ejaculations current in that age. Clearly the interjection 'threats!' – *'manaces . . . manaces!'* – so frequently heard during the quarrel in the bedchamber, was common usage in that contentious society. In frustration and rage FitzUrse shouts out *'Avoy!'* at one point in the altercation, precisely the exclamation uttered by Aucassin, hero of the contemporary romance, as he was defending Nicolette.

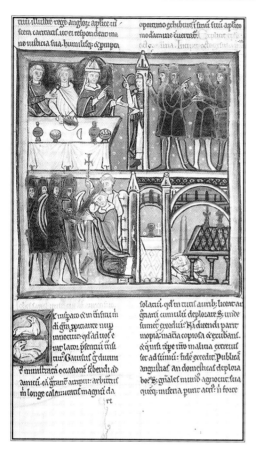

This illustration of *c.* 1180, prefacing John of Salisbury's letter describing the martyrdom, shows (top) the knights arriving while Becket dines. In the lower half there is the earliest known representation of the murder scene, and (right) the tomb with pilgrims crawling into its underspaces. (By permission of The British Library; Ms Cotton Claudius BII f.341)

To resume the narrative. In accordance with orders, William FitzNigel the seneschal conducted the new arrivals up the steps into the private quarters. Followed by the archer, the four knights came trooping into the archbishop's bedchamber, promptly squatting down on the floor while the archer likewise sat himself down behind them. Becket was sitting on his bed, with his clerks and monks seated around him, some probably on the floor in the rushes, discussing various items of business. The lawyer William FitzStephen (who records the conversation on that day and was present at the final scene in the cathedral) must have joined the group. Guernes and Anonymous I show that Becket was talking to the monks and clerks and that he was leaning over on his arm towards one of the monks who was evidently sitting on the edge of the bed. At first he studiously ignored the newcomers, then turned and surveyed them 'pitifully', says Guernes. He looked closely at each face along the line, then greeted one of them, William de Tracy, by name.

For a few moments there was a tense silence. Becket wondered why the newcomers would not speak. At length the knights lowered their gaze. They exchanged glances with each other, and suddenly FitzUrse broke out with the contemptuous ejaculation *'Deus t'ait!'* ('God help you!'), bringing a deep flush to Becket's cheeks. The knight added, 'We have been sent to you from overseas by our lord the king and we have some of his orders for you. Now then, we want to know whether you want it all said in private or in public.' 'I will leave that to your own choice and decision,' said Becket.

Guernes inserts a short altercation in the original language at this point, as with over-elaborate courtesy the archbishop argued with the knights who was to decide whether to include or exclude his followers. *'Tut a vostre talent,'* said Becket. *'Mais al vostre,'* they replied. *'Mais a voz,'* responded Becket. 'All right, then,' said FitzUrse finally, 'let us have it in private and let all these people be sent out.' So at Becket's motion the crowd of clerks and monks got up and trooped out of the chamber into the larger room outside, leaving the archbishop alone with the four warriors and the archer.

The doorkeeper left the portal of the inner chamber standing open so that everyone could see and hear what was going on. It was just as well, for a common idea shot through the minds of the knights (as was afterwards disclosed) to kill Becket forthwith, battering him to death with the only weapon in view (since they had come in unarmed) – the shaft of his own much-venerated archiepiscopal cross. Certainly, says Guernes, if they had had a blade anywhere upon them and if the members of the household had not come back so quickly, the archbishop would have died there and then.

Becket's intuition suddenly told him that there was no vestige of peace and goodwill anywhere in the knights' minds. Sensing danger, he said 'We can't have this kind of talk kept quiet.' He called out to the doorkeeper, 'Leave the door,' and told him to recall the monks and clerks of his *privé conseil*, who straightaway filed back into the bedchamber. Any layfolk other than the knights and the archer were excluded. When the company had reassembled, Becket addressed himself to the knights. 'Well sirs, with these people all here you may say what you want to.'

FitzUrse started up again, 'If you have decided to have it all in public rather than in private, we will go ahead and let them know all about it. The lord king sends to tell you that he established complete peace in all good faith with you but you have not kept to your side; for he has heard that you have been going through his cities and castles with a large crowd of armed men. Also, you have excommunicated the Archbishop of York and other bishops taking part in the coronation of his son, and have turned out other faithful servants of his from churches. All that is suspicious enough. And on top of it all it is quite clear that you want to take away the crown from his son and are working in every way against him. The lord king therefore wants to know if you are prepared to come to his court and make answer about all this.' Said the archbishop, 'Have you any more to say? If so, say it.' FitzUrse answered, 'First we hear *your* answer.'

Becket replied, 'I do not want to take the crown away from the son of the king or in any way at all to diminish his honour, but on the contrary to exalt his kingdom and glory in every way. I have come back to his kingdom and my church with his licence and under his safe conduct, and the lord king ought not to object if the laymen of our church ride alongside me for a short distance through cities and towns, doing their proper duty.' They had not seen each other, he said with slight exaggeration, for some seven years. 'As for the bishops that you are talking about,' he continued, 'well, it was not I but the lord Pope who excommunicated them, not only because in the coronation of the young king they usurped rights not their own but also because, when summoned to make answer, they ignored the summons. Not I but Pope Alexander is the source of their suspension and its cause is the anointing of the young king (God give him his blessing!). They did wrong without reason and would not come and make satisfaction.'

According to Benedict's narrative, FitzUrse, after remarking that the discussion was not to be in secret (following the return of the clerks and monks), started off, 'We bring you an order from our lord the king overseas, to go to the new king here on this side of the water (at Winchester) and to do unto him whatsoever you are supposed to do to him as your lord and king.' Becket demanded, 'And what am I supposed to do to him?' 'You ought to know that better than ourselves,' was the rejoinder. 'If I *did* know,' retorted Becket, 'I would not say that I did not. Anyhow, I truly think I have done absolutely everything towards him that I ought to do,' a not unreasonable claim considering Becket's vain attempts to gain an interview after his return from overseas, not to mention the handsome, rejected, abortive gift of three richly caparisoned chargers. FitzUrse contradicted. 'Not a bit of it. There is still a great deal to be done and a lot to be put right.'

Becket answered yet again that he did not know what he was supposed to do in due deference to the royal estate unless they would have the goodness to tell him. FitzUrse came back with, 'If as you say you have no idea at all, well, we are going to explain to you what ought to be done. Our lord the king orders you to go at once to his son the young king over here on this side of the water and swear an oath of fealty to him and put right any offence you have committed against the dignity of the Crown.' 'I would be ready to go to his court,' said Becket, 'but he has forbidden me entry to his towns and castles. I would enter at my peril.'

William FitzStephen sets out Becket's answers to the tirade of accusations made by Reginald FitzUrse in the form of a long monologue. The Archbishop of York, he bitterly complained, had carried out the coronation of the young king in Becket's own province without calling him, without his knowledge and without his consent, to the prejudice of the rights of Canterbury. It was the Pope who had given sentence, and he himself could not interfere with the decision of a superior. However, let the coronation of the young king remain firm, stable and unassailed. The king had given him permission to act on the day when peace was re-established.

'I was all set', he affirmed, 'to go to see him and congratulate him when I was ordered to return. The king has quitclaimed Holy Church,' Becket remarked, using the technical term for absolution from any obligation. He then asked, 'And why do I now have to confirm my oath upon the Bible; and anyhow in what way have I been guilty of offence against the dignity of the Crown?' The knights brushed the second question aside, going back to the former with, 'About your barony, which you hold from your lord the king, you ought to do fealty upon oath for it. And those clerks whom you have brought into the country with you, if they want to stay here they will also have to swear an oath for security.' Becket answered, 'As for the barony, I am quite ready to swear to the lord king whatever law and reason require. But there is no question whatsoever, and let him get this quite straight (*pro certo teneat*), that neither from me nor from any of my clerks will he be able to extort an oath!'

The language is wildly defiant, not to say rebellious, suggesting that Becket was beginning to lose self-control. He went on, 'Too much has already been extorted and there are already too many perjured, forsworn people and excommunicates about' (a strange remark to come from Becket!). 'Already, thank God, I have absolved a lot of people from charges of perjury and from excommunication and intend to release others from the same perils when God gives the chance.' 'We quite realize,' said FitzUrse, 'that you are not going to carry out anything which we have put to you. Furthermore, the lord king gives you orders to absolve the bishops you have excommunicated or suspended without his licence, both from damnation and the bond of silence, and to obey the law in this or anything else which he has to object against you.' Becket responded, 'I have neither suspended the bishops nor yet have I excommunicated them. It was the lord Pope, whose power comes from God, as everyone knows. If you want to take up that cause, well then, it stands between you and him. It is not for me to account to you for it.' FitzUrse came back with, 'Well, at any rate, if it has not actually been done by you in your own capacity, then it was done through you and at your motion.' He received answer, 'If the lord Pope has seen fit to take notice and to vindicate me and my church against grave injury, then I must say I am not sorry for it.'

Close to this point in the altercation, the chronicler Anonymous I includes a passage between FitzUrse and Becket, which may be a slightly different version of what has gone before or follows afterwards. But, as already pointed out, any true rendering of an angry discussion is prone to repetition. 'If indeed', said the archbishop, 'I have gone too far (*in aliquo excessi*), I am prepared to come to the king's court, or anywhere else he likes, to make satisfaction as far as is just,' to which FitzUrse responded, 'The bishops were excommunicated by you and therefore the lord king orders that you speedily release them.' Becket said that he did not deny that the excommunications were effected by the Pope through him, the archbishop. 'And indeed,' he went on, 'unless they go in all humility to the Pope, ready to make amends, they will have little chance of absolution through me.'

FitzUrse was now getting beside himself. 'The king orders you to get out of his land without any delay, together with your foreign clerks and anyone else belonging to you. If anyone stays here, you won't be able to protect him.' Guernes de Pont Ste-Maxence renders the passage relating to the bishops thus: FitzUrse told Becket that the king wanted the bishops released. 'You are to absolve them at once, just as it was you who suspended and excommunicated them.'

'I don't deny,' said Becket, 'that it may have been at my instigation. But they won't get any help or comfort from me. They must go off to the Pope, all three of them, for they have fallen into his grip. Let them be obedient to him and do as he commands.' FitzUrse cried out, 'You're threatening in a fine old way. You're going to be guarded better than you've ever been. Don't go flying off as you did once!' Thomas was not alarmed. 'I will never be put to flight by any man henceforth,' he said, 'nor will any chase me out or push me out of the land.' 'What,' said FitzUrse, 'you won't go for the king's sake?' 'No,' said Thomas, 'I won't go overseas again, ever. No, not for anyone; you will find me here.'

From these inflammatory words of self-defence, Becket suddenly moved to the attack. 'You ought not to bring me such a message. My lord the king is so faithful and true that he would not send me such an order through your words. He would never confirm them or back them up.' 'Indeed he would,' came the answer, 'and we well dare to repeat them.'

After all his efforts to entrap Becket, FitzUrse (says Benedict) was just like some frustrated fowler who had failed to ensnare a bird in his net. He started up on a railing note, accusing Becket of wanting to do down the bishops in despite of the king, and to cut them off from Holy Mother Church after they had dared to crown the young king to whom succession rightly belonged, he being son to both the king and the queen, and bearing the sign of government upon his shoulder. (It is of interest to note that a knight knew at least a little of the Bible and was able to quote Isaiah.[3])

'You have carried on like this, rebelling against his elevation, and it is obvious that you want to take the crown away from him,' continued FitzUrse, who now launched an extraordinary and half-hysterical accusation: 'You have come across into this country to get yourself named as king. You will set yourself up as king and archbishop together! But God in his mercy forbid that you shall ever be a king.' This seems a remarkable suggestion indeed to fling at the archbishop, but it must be remembered that he had been for long years, when chancellor, king in all but name, and not long before King Henry had offered him a regency with guardianship of the young king. At this outburst, Becket managed to keep his own temper for the moment, replying quietly, 'Not at all, Reginald, not at all. I do not aspire to the name and dignity of king. I do not want to take away the crown but would rather bestow upon him (the young king) three or four crowns if I had the power. Nor can I believe that there is anyone in the whole world, except my lord the king, his own father, who loves him more tenderly than I do.'

Becket of course had had the young king in his tutelage for some time and *was* virtually a father to him. 'Nor indeed,' he continued, 'is there anyone who has more goodwill towards him. And I will try to do everything I can for him as long as my life lasts, please the Lord. As for the bishops, who as you say have been suspended or excommunicated by me or through me, well, you should know very well that this was done by the king's consent and counsel. When last St Mary Magdalen's day [22 July at Fréteval] peace was made between us, the king took me back into grace, and all was as before. I then made a formal complaint to him against those who had done me injury and violence, especially the bishops who had not feared to usurp my function, in despite of the Mother Church of Canterbury. The king then gave me permission by his own grace to seek vindication according to justice and equity from the lord Pope, not merely agreeing with me but ready to give me active support.'

Reginald FitzUrse gave vent again to the angry ejaculation '*Avoy!*' and was near to complete loss of control. 'Whatever are you saying? This is an unheard of piece of bad faith if indeed the king did actually give you leave to excommunicate or suspend the bishops who, at his own command, were there at the coronation of his son. You had better realize that you are implying something pretty dreadful if you impute that sort of bad faith to our lord the king.'

'Reginald, Reginald,' said Becket, 'I certainly do not impute bad faith to the king. We came to concord and agreement and there was nothing secret about it. It was all heard by everyone there, archbishops, bishops, high-ranking church people, with five hundred or more knights [or two hundred, as other chroniclers record it]. And you were there too, Sir Reginald, and you saw the letter which was composed there for the protection of our goods, far and wide.' The other answered 'Indeed I was not there. Nor did I see or hear anything of this.' Becket answered quietly again, 'Oh yes, indeed. God knows I saw you there.' FitzStephen says that Becket remarked that he had 'seen some of them there' at Fréteval and that they all seemed quite contented, as far as he could judge.

FitzUrse kept on swearing vigorously that he was not at Fréteval, adding, 'It is quite astonishing and quite outrageous that you keep on imputing bad faith to the king. He will not be able to put up with much more of that from you, and we here are his faithful men and we are not going to put up with it either.' At this, says Benedict, the other knights, who from the various records seem to have remained mostly silent all this while, started shouting and uttering threats, blasphemously crying again and again that, by the wounds of God, they had endured him beyond all measure. They flung out oath after oath, piling threat upon threat. FitzStephen notes that when mention of the meeting at Fréteval on St Mary Magdalen's day came up, John of Salisbury intervened with the nervous remark, 'My lord, let us speak more privately about all this.' Becket said to him, 'It is no good; they are making proposals and demands which are quite out of the question for me to agree to carry out, and which I cannot and indeed ought not to do.'

'From whom do you hold the archbishopric?' demanded FitzUrse. Becket came out with the ready answer. 'The spiritual side from God and the lord Pope, and the possessions from the lord king.' Reginald FitzUrse played right into the archbishop's hands with, 'Don't you admit that you hold the whole lot from the king?' 'Certainly not,' cried Becket, 'but we have to render unto the king those things which be the king's and unto God those things which be God's.' At this (says FitzStephen), FitzUrse and the others, as if Becket had said something quite unusual and preposterous, started raging violently, gnashing their teeth at him.

Becket himself then brought the conversation to a less elevated level by starting off again with, 'All the while since I came back to these shores with safe conduct, in full peace with God and king, I have had to put up with abuse and insults, and with many losses too. For example, my men have been thrown into prison and property carried off. And then there are my horses, off one of which Robert de Broc has cut its tail. And again there is my wine which Rannulph de Broc has violently kept back, wine which the lord king sent to me from over the seas. My churches are held sinfully and by force. And I have had all sorts of other injuries and insults to put up with, even though the king has said in writing to his own son, and by word of mouth through messengers, that I should have firm peace. And now, on top of all that, you have come here threatening me.' He added plaintively, 'You must realize that I take all this very badly.'

FitzUrse said: 'If anyone dared to do something which could cause you any injury, why did you not say so plainly and then you might have got compensation as far as law and reason demanded?' Becket asked, 'And with whom might I have registered my complaint?,' to which answer was returned 'To the king on this side of the water.' Anonymous I assigns a similar remark to Hugh de Morville: 'If the king's men committed any atrocity against you or yours, why did you not inform the king instead of taking things into your own hands and carrying out the excommunications?' 'Hugh,' Becket gibed, *'comme tu entres la tête haute*. If anyone does anything against canon law and will not make amends, I will certainly do justice and he may not hope to get away with it.' 'These threats are a bit too much,' cried FitzUrse.

'Look here my friend,' said the archbishop to him, 'I have made quite enough complaints and have set out my injuries plainly enough. I have kept on trying to get satisfaction. Day after day injuries build up. I am assailed by so many and such burdensome troubles. Complaints from poor people are ringing in my ears day and night, so much so that I haven't even enough staff to run round and deal with everything. However much I publish the wrongs done to me, there is no hope of reasonable redress. The king on this side of the water and his judges all depend on the king overseas and his advice, and they won't do anything just on their own. I myself cannot get legal redress while my people are denied the right of going across the sea to see the king. That is why so much trouble is brewing up against me. Anyhow,' he added defiantly, 'even if I cannot get right and justice, I will carry on with my work as archbishop to the best of my ability and won't fail to perform one single bit of it for any man living.'

'Manaces, manaces!' cried out one of them. 'Are you going to put the whole country under an interdict and excommunicate the whole lot of us?' Another exploded with, 'God help me, he shall never do that! He has excommunicated far too many as it is.' The chroniclers other than Benedict reproduce some variations, evidently occurring late in the altercation. Edward Grim, present there in the chamber, says that the knights told Becket, 'You will never have peace again from this day, as you have broken the peace.'

To their orders that he should lift the sentences upon the prelates, which they claimed came from the king, Becket answered, 'Stop your threats, stop this quarrelling. My faith is in the King of Heaven who died upon the cross for His own. From this day no one will find the sea between me and my church. I did not come back to fly away again. Anyone who wants me will find me here. It is not proper for the king to send such orders. I and my people have had more than enough insults from the king's agents.'

Both William and Guernes introduce about this point in the narrative a remark made by the archbishop. 'I can't go running off to court for every trifling matter. I am a priest and I will perform divine justice upon those misbehaving towards Holy Church. The sword will be drawn when and upon whom the priestly office requires.' '*Manaces*' cried the others, 'You will pay for it if you don't absolve the people who are under sentence.' 'Whoever it may be,' answered Becket, 'who violates the laws of the Roman see or the rights of Christ's Church and does not make amends, I will not delay to put ecclesiastical censure upon him.' The knights drew nearer to him. 'We tell you,' they said, 'that you have spoken like this in peril of your life.'

FitzStephen brings in a passage. 'You threaten me all in vain. If all the swords of England were hanging over my head, all your terrors could not move me from observing God's justice or from obedience to the lord Pope. Foot to foot you will find me in the battle of the Lord. Once I ran away like a frightened priest. Now I have come back, with the support of the Pope and in obedience to him, to my church. Never will I desert her again. If I am allowed to do my task as a priest in peace, then that is all right for me. If anything else, well, God's will be done upon me.' Benedict's parallel rendering of this passage includes the remark, 'What's this, do you really think I am all set to run away? I will never flee for the king or any other man living. I did not come back to run off again but, as it appears, to wait for the arrival of a gang of ruffians and to put up with spite from a lot of godless people. Under God's protection I don't care anything for your threats.' 'It won't be only threats,' they answered, 'but something else besides.'

Benedict half apologizes for the seditious observation about King Henry, glossing it as a sign of consistency rather than as contumacy against the Crown. To Becket's affirmation that he would never flee again the gang yelled back, 'You're quite right about that, you certainly won't escape.'

Tempers gave way. The knights leapt up, twisting their gloves in savage rage, gesticulating and shouting. The archbishop rose to his feet as they stormed at him. Benedict says that such a noise was going on, and so many venomous remarks were being bawled at Becket, that all track of what was going on was quite lost for the moment.

Becket told them, 'On top of all this you well know what the relationship is between me and you, and I marvel all the more that you dare to come and threaten the archbishop in his own house.' He said this (said FitzStephen) to remind them that when he was chancellor three of them, William de Tracy, Reginald FitzUrse and

Hugh de Morville, had done fealty to him on bended knee, though reserving their loyalty due to the king. Instead of quietening them down, this had just the opposite effect. They boiled up into uncontrollable anger, shouting, 'There is nothing between us that can work against the king.' And Reginald added, 'We very well dare threaten the archbishop and do more than that too!' adding, 'Let's go.'

William FitzNigel, the seneschal of the household, had now returned to the bedchamber. The four knights, it will be remembered, had encountered him on their arrival half an hour before, just as he secured release from Becket's service. His absence during the altercation can readily be explained. He was no longer under obligation to stand by Becket and if he proposed to move out, then it is highly likely that he had gone back to his quarters to pack. Someone led his horse out and saddled it for him, for it was available for him to mount out in the courtyard a minute or two later. On seeing FitzNigel, the gang now cried out, 'Here, you come along with us.' William's recent feelings of allegiance had not had time to wear off and he cried out to Becket, 'My Lord, can you see what they are doing to me?' It is easy to comprehend what was going through Becket's mind at this moment. 'I can see all right,' he said, continuing with 'This is their hour and the power of darkness', echoing the words of Christ in St Luke's Gospel as his followers were encountered by the arresting party in the Garden of Gethsemane.[4]

Becket got up and went over to the group while they were still in the bedchamber, and asked them quietly to let the man go. They ignored the request, still keeping him with them, and turned to go through the doorway out of the private quarters and down the steps on to the dais in the hall. To the dismay of John of Salisbury, who thought the action beneath the dignity of the archbishop, Becket went after them as far as the door of the bedchamber, and apparently even further, to the exit from the outer room down into the hall.

As the invaders were moving off, FitzUrse uttered the solemn formula breaking the feudal bond between a lord and his vassal, insolently addressing the Archbishop of Canterbury by his Christian name: 'Thomas, in the name of the king, I repudiate your fealty!', and the rest of the knights echoed the words. It seems that in the general uproar Becket only half heard the words or could not believe them. It was a matter of the gravest import, for possession of all the vast archiepiscopal estates (so recently recovered) depended upon the feudal tie. At the door he cried out to Morville as being of higher social standing than the rest and supposedly more civilized,

demanding of him what had been said. *'Huge, qu'tu dit? Di!'* ('What
are you saying? Go on, say it.') But answer came there none.

Becket called after the knights, 'Your threats don't make you any
the more terrible, even if you do come from the king. You can strike
me on my naked neck. There is not even a knife to protect it from
you.' So saying, he struck his hand several times upon his neck,
suiting his action to his words. They made to depart crying, 'There
will be more than threats.' In touching his neck, Becket repeated the
gesture made a few days before Christmas. The archbishop was
clearly quite determined that his death should happen by beheading.
'I know that you have come to kill me,' he said to the knights, 'but
I make God my protection.' He would have been quite content to be
slain then and there, in his own house.

Many members of the archbishop's household, clerks and some
knights, were now standing around, drawn by the noise and loud
voices. The intruders swore violently at them, telling them in the
king's name that anyone standing up for the archbishop would be
counted as an enemy and liable to be killed. Reginald FitzUrse cried
out to them, 'We warn you in the king's name, as you are his men
and lieges too, to abandon this man.' The four knights had warned
off the citizens out in the town and now they were concerned about
the household, in case they started a struggle on behalf of their
master. But the dazed crowd stood stock-still, so Reginald gave a
contrary command mainly directed at the clerks and monks. 'We
order you to keep this man here and not to let him get away,' or, as
Grim says, 'not to let him go off until the king has done full justice
upon his body.'

The knights came out with the customary cry of 'Threats, threats!'
'Lord monks', they added, 'in the king's name we order you to keep
tight hold of this man. If he escapes, you will be responsible.' Now,
says Benedict, they were actually trying to subvert the monks against
their own spiritual father. The archbishop said, 'I am quite easy to
guard and will not go away.' With fearful shouts and with flashing
and threatening eyes, the knights cried, 'To arms, men, to arms!'
Having already seized William FitzNigel the seneschal, the knights
now, as a further safeguard against armed resistance, took hold of the
other household knight, Ralph Morin, and carried him off too, going
down the middle of the hall and out through the porch to rejoin
their followers.

The captive William FitzNigel underwent a sudden change of
direction at this moment. Hardly a minute before, he had been

Becket's man at heart, calling him 'my lord', even though the feudal tie had been loosened, but now he went right over to the other side. 'A moment ago he was on his side, and now he was against him,' as FitzStephen says. He mounted his horse (standing waiting for his departure) and took up station within the gate as sentry, in company with the knight of St Augustine's Abbey named Simon de Crioil. The knights' objective was the mulberry tree, where evidently their equipment had been dumped. Fired with excitement, they chanted their war cry, '*Réaux, réaux!*' ('King's men, King's men!'), the Anglo-Norman battle-cry as opposed to the shout of French knights, '*Montjoie, Montjoie!*'.

At the sound of their shouting their followers, who for the last half hour or more had been occupying the house of Gilbert the citizen close to the palace gate, came rushing out across the street and through the archway, likewise shouting 'King's knights, King's knights!' Access was easy. Some of the party had already quietly slipped through within the palace boundaries, to ensure a way in when the inevitable trouble started. As the knights rejoined their followers, they cried out to them (in the words of the Saga), 'We think he is a doomed man by reason of that folly which is manifestly in him.'

The archbishop's own gatekeeper (probably still at this date William son of Pagan) was pushed out of the way in case he felt inclined to let in anyone from the city disposed to help the archbishop. The great doors were forthwith closed, though the small wicket was left undone. The crowd in the wide courtyard north of the hall was now considerable, consisting of the four principal knights, their followers, the dozen knights brought with them, and the crowd of servants from St Augustine's headed by Walter the marshal, not to mention some citizens of Canterbury who were either hostile to Becket or who had been compelled to come along.

At the mulberry tree, tunics were dragged off exposing coats of mail, and swords were girded on. Only eyes were left visible, so the chainmail flap was probably drawn across their faces. FitzUrse retired to the steps of the hall-porch, forcing the scullion called Robert Shinbone from the nearby kitchen to help him equip himself. Alone among the four, William de Tracy did not put on his chainmail, judging no doubt that the archbishop and his clerks were unlikely to carry earthly weapons. He wore, as we know, his green tunic and a multi-coloured cloak. Within a few minutes they were all ready for action, as were others in support, including Robert de Broc and the obscure and sinister Hugh of Horsea, alias Mauclerc. Some were bringing along bows and arrows.

Meanwhile, back in the hall, the domestic staff had not stood still. Some fled for their lives along the middle of the hall and down some steps, probably those giving access to the kitchen at the west end, and so out into the open on the southern or cathedral side of the hall, where the private garden lay. They were off to the cathedral itself, where they meant to seek sanctuary. Two servants, more faithful and with more presence of mind, pushed their way to the door opening into the north porch and set about barring it shut. These two were Algar, of whom nothing else is known, and Osbern, the tough and faithful chamberlain who had gone through thick and thin with his master since the day, six years and more before, when he risked his life to cover up Becket's night-time flight from Northampton. These two got the bar across the door leading into the porch (where FitzUrse was girding himself), and must almost at once have shut the western door of the hall leading to the kitchen (and so out into the open), as the one action would have been useless without the other.

At the same time the monks, clerks and other companions of the archbishop shut themselves in by closing the door leading on to the dais. They assembled in the inner chamber, the archbishop's own bedroom, anxiously listening to the clatter of running feet on the steps, as many of the servants fled before the doors were closed by Algar and Osbern. Now came home to them, says William FitzStephen, Becket's remark made before embarking at Wissant at the end of November, that it would soon be preferable to be anywhere other than in England.

The archbishop himself came back into the inner chamber and sat down on his bed. He started complaining about the king's orders and about the insulting and insubordinate language of the knights, and their threats. At that moment few of them can have realized that the murder was imminent. Becket certainly knew and so did the imaginative and apprehensive John of Salisbury. There were different opinions all round the bedchamber. Some were not very worried, putting the knights' behaviour down to drink, suggesting that they had dined not wisely but too well. They were drunk when they came in, they said. If they had not had their dinner they would not have talked like that. 'Anyhow, it is Christmas time and we are under the king's peace.' But some were worried that the gang might carry out their threats. They said, 'It looks very much as if there is going to be violence.'

It seems that there was sudden and general realization of the dire danger in which Becket and all of them stood. Looking out of the windows on the north side into the courtyard, some saw what was happening and cried out, 'My lord, they are arming themselves.' Just before the hall door was closed, some of the servants saw the knights picking up their arms at the mulberry tree and cried out the same warning. Becket merely remarked 'Who cares? Let them arm themselves.' John of Salisbury, who had already made one nervous intervention, was getting agitated. 'My lord,' he started, 'it really is quite amazing that you never will take any notice of our (or anyone else's) advice. You just make up your own mind, all on your own. Now, why did a man of your rank have to get up and go to the door, and make those evil people even more furious?' Becket asked, 'Well, what do you want, Master John?', to which he replied, 'Wouldn't it have been enough to have had words with us here ['to call your council', as Anonymous I and Guernes say], and then have given them a softer answer? They are just out to do you mischief, to get you all worked up and to catch you out in anything you say. All that these knights want to do is get an excuse to kill you. But no one can free you from your own obstinacy.' The archbishop let out a sigh saying, 'I have had all the advice I want. I know quite well what I ought to do,' to which John answered, 'Let's hope to God that it turns out all right.' 'We all have to die,' the archbishop went on calmly, 'and we must not swerve from justice for fear of death. I am more ready to meet death for God and for his Church than they are to inflict it on me.' John replied, his fright overcoming any regard for his master's rank, 'We are all sinners and not yet ready for death. I can't see anyone who wants to die without any reason, apart from you.' 'May the Lord's will be done,' said Becket quietly.

Above the conversation the clerks could now hear a confused murmur and wailing coming from the southern side of the hall, made by the townsfolk of Canterbury, of all ages, men and women, who had seen the arrival of the knights and had heard their proclamation, and were lamenting for the archbishop and his followers as 'sheep destined for the slaughter'. These townsfolk had probably gathered in Palace Street or around the west end of the cathedral. There was also the other band of a dozen warriors who had remained outside while the long interview had been taking place. These were wearing chainmail underneath their tunics, which they did not bother to remove.

William Urry's own sketch depicting the citizens learning that the archbishop has visitors.

All equipped and now followed by others, the four principal knights turned back to the hall and tried to burst in, but with the door in the porch effectively barred they could not get through, despite a fierce and noisy attack upon it. However, they had with them Robert de Broc, who had been occupant of the palace during the years of exile and 'knew all the ins and outs of the place'. He shouted out in his mother tongue, 'Follow me, noble knights! I'll get you in another way round!' Guernes has preserved the actual words: '*Or me siwez seignur franc chevalier! Je vus metrai laienz par an altre sentier!*'

What he had in mind was the short exterior wooden staircase leading up from the garden or orchard on the south side of the hall to a door into the private quarters at the eastern end (*oriol* as Guernes calls it). This would mean passing through or by the kitchen block, and accordingly the four knights, three of them shambling along in their heavy chainmail, burst out among the trees and bushes into the garden on the south side of the hall, heading for the short flight of steps. But the staircase was out of action. On his return from years of absence, Becket had, not surprisingly, found his palace in need of care and maintenance, and had called in the carpenters to effect repairs. One of the items requiring attention was the wooden staircase. The carpenters had taken it to pieces and had then knocked off for their dinner break. Now, when it was nearly four o'clock in the afternoon, and getting dark, they had not yet come back to resume the job. '*E li carpentier erent a lur disner alé,*' says Guernes.

Trustingly, they had left their tools lying around and at once the knights seized some of them as valuable instruments if it came to battering down doors or other obstacles in an attempt to reach the archbishop. At least five implements were appropriated at this

This drawing of 1683 shows the south face of the archbishop's palace. It had been greatly changed since Becket's time, but one medieval feature seems to have survived – the oriole or stair-tower on the left. This may well have been where the knights forced an entry on 29 December 1170. (Bodleian Library, Oxford; Ms Tanner 123 f.24)

moment. There was a small hammer (found later in the cathedral with the body just after the murder), three *cuignies* (*cognées*) or heavy-duty axes, with a *besague* (*besaiguë, bisacutum*), or instrument with two long heads, one terminating in a narrow straight edge and the other in a wider 'duck's bill'. This particular tool served a double purpose, making mortices and tenons for the new steps, and as an adze. It appears that the carpenters had brought bulk timber on to the site, to be split down by the heavy axes and then trimmed with the adze.

Robert de Broc immediately seized hold of a ladder conveniently left with the tools and set it against the first window of the hall proper, next to the private quarters. With one of the choppers he hacked at the wooden shutter at the bottom of the window and climbed in. Guernes says that he brought the knights in up ladders, with which William of Canterbury agrees, but William FitzStephen seems to imply that he opened a way to them from the inside, probably by the door at the west end of the dining hall leading to the kitchen block. To any twelfth-century knight trained in siege warfare, Robert de Broc's action was quite elementary. With a door open, the knights charged in, finding there servants of the archbishop who had not made good their escape, including Osbern and Algar, who had just barred the great door into the porch. Robert de Broc set about the servants, stopping short of actual murder yet severely wounding them.

In the bedchamber clerks and companions trembled in terror as they heard the sound of splintering woodwork, while Robert de Broc hewed at the shutter of the hall window, only a few feet away from them. They were decisively surrounded, for the garden to the south was occupied by knights trying to force their way in, while the great courtyard to the north was crowded with the knights' supporters and followers. At any moment the violent men now in the hall might turn to assault the door leading into the private apartments. Despite the din going on in the main hall and the increasing agitation among his followers, the archbishop sat serene and motionless upon his bed. It was clear enough to him that his hour had come. He was quite calm and the chroniclers agree that he was not only prepared for death but even in fact welcomed it, and would have been prepared to meet his end right there. He rejoiced that he had found a good cause to die for: justice and freedom and the welfare of his own Church. He longed to become one with Christ and was filled with desire for the liberty of the Church. Such were the thoughts credited to him by the chronicler FitzStephen at this moment of crisis.

And crisis it was indeed. 'My lord,' the monks implored him, 'go into the cathedral. These men are getting ready to take you prisoner or to kill you.' 'No, I will not go,' he answered. 'Don't be so scared. Most of you have lost your nerve. I'm not frightened of them. I am going to stay here and wait for whatever pleases God.' Now quite determined to meet his end, Becket decided to remain where he was. He feared that if he went to the cathedral, the knights would not dare to attack him there. Neither with prayers nor by tears could the monks induce the archbishop to make a move, until they jerked him into action by reminding him that it was now time for the evening service, and that he was due to hear Nones and Vespers.

In the ordinary way Becket and his entourage would have formed a procession at this time in the afternoon, and would probably have descended the wooden steps if serviceable. They would have continued down through the garden and most likely would have moved along the southern walk of the cloister, next to the cathedral nave, and so through the transept door to the choir, where two services of Vespers were held, one for the monks, followed by another preceded by Nones for the archbishop and his clerks when they were in Canterbury.

Guernes says (in the early draft of his poem) that the party could not escape by the garden (on the south) as there were knights there, nor did they dare open the hall door (on the north) since the courtyard was likewise occupied by the enemy. Escape seemed impossible, but then someone thought of the long-disused room at the east end of the private quarters, with its concealed access to the cloister. The monks made their way to it down some steps, and so reached the door to the tunnel running beneath the cellarer's hall. The door, however, proved to be fastened by a lock probably encased in a wooden block. In dismay and desperation, the assassins being so close, they wrenched at it with bare hands and managed to tear it off the door 'as if merely stuck with glue'. Evidently long years of neglect had rusted away any iron pins attaching it to the portal, although its easy removal was accounted a miracle by some.

Becket still resisted attempts to make him hurry or even move, so one of the monks cried out, 'Pick him up and carry him!' The party of clerks and monks, half-pulling, half-pushing or carrying the archbishop, urged him down into the disused room and so through the newly opened door into the dark tunnel. Yet they were still cut off from their objective, the cathedral church. But up in the cellarer's hall (flanking the private garden) the clash of arms and the general clamour had been heard by the staff including Richard (who since the previous evening had known what was afoot) and William, the cellarer's servant. These two came running along the cloister from the door leading from their hall. As they ran they must have heard frantic shouts coming through the speaking hole beside the door from the palace. Reaching the door, they at once drew back the bolt, at which the jostling crowd in the tunnel rushed into the cloister, carrying and hustling Becket along, *'u voille u nun'* ('willy-nilly') says Guernes.

Normally the archbishop's progress to church would have been by way of a slow and dignified procession, headed by himself with his cross carried before him by the Welshman Alexander Llewelyn. Alexander was by now far away on the road to Rome and his substitute, Henry of Auxerre, was standing in for him. Becket, despite all the jostling and pushing that was going on, managed according to the Saga to make himself heard and insisted that the decencies should be observed. Henry was to go before him with the cross, although the cross-bearer and the archbishop came at the tail end of the procession rather than at its head, as was usual.

Here William FitzStephen (with the Saga) is much at variance with the other chroniclers. Some notice should be taken of him for he was actually there at the time, and was clearly present at the emergence from the tunnel. He was a keen observer but, if he set down the story long years later, he might have forgotten precise details or written up the scene to make it more seemly than it actually was. He says Thomas urged on his flock like a good shepherd, while the other historians tell of the monks and clerks half-carrying, half-pushing Becket, now ready to accept death, along the cloister. Guernes says that they stopped twice in the cloister when Becket, with his feet firmly on the ground, pushed them all away protesting, 'Why are you dragging and pulling me along? Let me alone!' But pull and carry him to the cathedral they did.

The first Anonymous chronicler (regularly well-informed) says that one of the monks called out, 'Pick him up and carry him,' and that the archbishop was in fact carried all the way to the church apart from three stops, twice in the cloister and once in the chapter house when Becket, really angry by now, resisted and managed to escape from their hands. FitzStephen says that when they reached the cloister, some of the monks wanted to shut the door behind them, but that Becket would not allow this. As they went along the north alley, he turned once and looked over his right shoulder to see if the knights were following, or to make sure that no one behind him had closed and bolted the door.

Becket's appearance on his last short journey can be recovered. He had on his fine-woven white surplice in which he probably lived. He wore a skull cap to cover the tonsure. His forehead was puckered, and his countenance worn. His beard was now white. Thrown about him was his 'iron dark cloak' with black fastenings, unbound at the edges. On his finger he was wearing a ring with a green stone set in it.

The unsteady progress continued. What is so unusual for a medieval incident is that, in this case, the sequence of events can be followed yard by yard in the contemporary plan prepared for Prior Wibert five years or so before. They passed the door of the monastic refectory in the north wall, with the monks' washing-place on the right, and turned at the east end of the alley round past the entry

The martyrdom doorway (much altered in the fourteenth century, when the cloisters were rebuilt) through which Becket entered the cathedral. (Photograph: Buffy Tucker; the Dean and Chapter of Canterbury)

leading up to the dormitory. Then they went by the 'iron door' leading eastward, looking for the transept door and supposed safety in the cathedral. But they turned off short, and passing through the next door on the left found themselves not in the cathedral but in the chapter house. It is of course possible that Becket, anxious for death and fearing still that the knights would not venture into the church, was prepared to take up position in that marginally less sacred place. However, after a minute or so of milling around the new tomb of

Wibert, the lately dead and redoubtable champion and organizer of the Church of Canterbury, the party went out again into the cloister. With valuable time lost, the monks redoubled their efforts to propel the by now very angry archbishop. In a few seconds they were at the door of the north-west transept, where they let Becket go at last.

The first service of Vespers, intended for the monks, was now drawing to its close. Two monastic servants burst into the cathedral and ran, stricken dumb with fright, right up the middle of the choir, making it clear from their gestures that violent trouble was afoot. The mere fact of their intrusion into the sacrosanct choir during a service was enough to advertise a crisis. It seems very clear that these two must have been Richard and William, who had just pulled back the bolts on the door from the palace into the cloister. They had probably raced down the western and southern ranges of the cloister, easily beating the archbishop and his party to the cathedral.

Some of the monks went on singing despite the interruption, but others streamed out of their stalls and ran down into the transept. Inside the transept door the archbishop and his party could see directly ahead of them, in the deepening darkness, the altar of St Benedict within its apse. To the right was the mighty pillar holding up the vaulting of the tribune, and beyond that the two staircases, one descending into the crypt and the other leading up into the choir. At this moment the latter was crowded with those monks who had deserted Vespers up in the choir. Some were moving around in the transept and wept with joy to see their archbishop still alive, for some thought he had already been slain. Some were weeping through fear. One of them cried out, 'Come in, father, come in, and if needs be, let us suffer together and be glorified together. We have been frightened to death through your absence and are now comforted by your presence,' to which sententious remark Becket brusquely retorted, 'Go back and finish divine office.' He stood quite still in the doorway saying, 'As long as you block the way in I will not enter.' As they made way he came in but halted at the threshold again, trying to see what was going on, pushing back those who had crowded around him wanting to witness the excitement.

'What is everyone so frightened of?' he demanded. Someone said, 'Look, there are the armed men in the cloister.' 'I am going out to them,' he said. The monks stopped him, crying 'That you won't,' and he turned about on the threshold as they urged him to go on, against his will, up the stairs to the high altar, where the sanctity of the area would surely protect him. If Becket had decided to take refuge in flight, he could well have made good his escape at this juncture for the great church was by now full of shadows. Close at hand (as FitzStephen notes) there was the winding staircase, still there today, rising from the north-west corner of the transept and leading up to St Blaise's Chapel and thence to the dark space above the vaulting. Also close at hand was the vast crypt, offering a great number of places of refuge. 'He could easily have avoided death . . . for there are many hiding places in that church.'

There is evidence to show that in the few moments before his death, Becket twice started to ascend the steps leading into the choir. FitzStephen says quite clearly that he came down from the stairs to ensure that the door into the cloister remained unbarred, while it is clear that when the knights entered after it was unlocked he was again up on the stairs. '*Domini*,' Becket called to the monks who surrounded him and seized hold of him, 'I insist that you let me go. This is none of your business. Let God see to it!' And, perhaps for a second time, he ordered them: 'Go up into the choir and sing your Vespers,' and added, 'Go away you weaklings. Let those blind wretches do their worst.' In the struggle Becket realized that the door was being closed and that the monks were setting the heavy iron bar into position. Perhaps it was a door of double flaps, with the bar set on a swivel attached to one flap so that when turned horizontally it would secure both, as may be seen today on the fifteenth-century successor to the same door.

Becket eluded his captors and came down the steps, making at this moment his celebrated remark: 'I order you by the sacred obedience which you owe me not to shut the door. The Church of Christ is not to be made into a castle.' Or was there in his mind (as Dom David Knowles would have it) not so much the Church of Christ, but Christ Church, Canterbury?[5] According to Grim, Becket added: 'Even when not barred it ought to be a castle all on its own.'

Some of the people outside in the cloister announced their presence by terrified shouts. Becket threw off the crowd jostling him and went back to the door, now barred. 'Open up,' he cried, 'let my people come in.' He pushed his way to the door, thrusting aside those standing around it, and with his own hands removed the bar and opened the portal to disclose stragglers from the group of monks and clerks or staff who had been left outside, as Benedict says, 'like food for the wolves'. 'Hurry up! Come on in,' he cried, pulling them in bodily. At that moment he himself was again seized and pulled back while the doors were left swinging open. Tugged along across the transept, the archbishop was brought back to the stairs again and pushed and pulled up, perhaps this time mounting to the seventh or eighth step.

According to William FitzStephen, it was now that John of Salisbury and all the archbishop's clerks, except his confessor Robert of Merton, FitzStephen himself and the visitor Edward Grim, fled. Some of those in flight took refuge at altars, while others sought out secret hiding places. But there were certainly others who remained at Becket's side, such as the monk William of Canterbury and another brave but unnamed monk.

Meanwhile, back at the palace, the knights, using the carpenters' tools found around the demolished steps, had smashed a way through into the private quarters of the archbishop. In the bedchamber stood his treasure chests filled with gold and silver plate, his splendid golden chalice, with cash and books, together with precious cloth for vestments and the like. They would not leave this potential source of loot unwatched and called to Robert de Broc to guard it. He took up station there with some others, thus avoiding direct involvement in the slaughter a few minutes later. Once in the private apartments, they could follow the archbishop and his party through the tunnel beneath the cellarer's hall and so into the cloister, bursting out with drawn swords in their hands. Their passage through the private apartments might account for the second wave of refugees, composed of clerks or attendants, evidently flushed out by the knights, reaching the cathedral and clamouring for admission after the transept door had been closed and barred.

Reginald FitzUrse led the charge, shouting 'To me, King's men!' William de Tracy was in his civilian attire. The other principal assailants were covered in armour right up to their eyes. Guernes says that there were four other knights hanging around some way behind, but that they did not enter the cathedral. There were certainly other knights about on that day, for FitzStephen tells of twelve accompanying the four principals. Also there were some of the citizens of Canterbury, compelled to come along, who followed right up to the moment of the murder, and the St Augustine's contingent headed by Walter, the abbey marshal. All in all, there was a large mob of lawless men desecrating the normally quiet cloister at that moment. Also present were the retainers of the knights who, says FitzStephen, wore no chainmail but came armed.

Which way the knights came through the cloister is not really clear. They could have come, like Becket and his staff, along the north alley and so down past the chapter house, or through the western and southern alleys of the cloister, or again they could have come diagonally across the central space. Within a minute or two they had reached the transept door, now wide open to them.

CHAPTER FIVE

The Murder

Violently shouting, the four principal knights, followed by Hugh of Horsea, mounted the few steps into the cathedral transept, their clanking armour adding to the din. In the deepening gloom they saw monks and clerks standing around and cried out to them, 'Don't you move!' Coming through the cloister the knights were brandishing their drawn swords in their right hands, while three bore the carpenters' axes in their left hands and the fourth was in possession of the double-headed morticing-tool or adze. Having gained entry to the cathedral without trouble, they had no further need for the tools and discarded them. Someone was carrying a small hammer, likewise dropped. Could this have been the fifth warrior, Hugh of Horsea?

Tracy, Morville and Bret advanced to the left side of the great pillar standing in the transept. FitzUrse veered to the right side of the shaft close to the back of the altar of St Mary at the end of the nave aisle. All around were monuments to the dead and holy relics. FitzUrse probably could not see Becket on the steps beyond the pillar, and colliding with a monk in the gloom demanded, 'Where is Thomas Becket, traitor to king and country?' The knight studiously used Becket's middle-class surname, forcing home his family status about which he was so sensitive. There was no reply, and the demand was made again in different terms. 'Where is the archbishop?' Up on the steps Becket turned about and, at this more proper enquiry, condescended to answer, doing so with a slight movement of the head. 'I am a priest and an archbishop, and if you are looking for me, you have found me,' or 'Here I am, no traitor to the king, but a priest of God. Why do you want me?'

Meanwhile he came down the steps and arrived at the level of the transept floor. Turning to the right (and so to the north) he took up position by the wall running between the steps down to the crypt and the chapel of St Benedict, at a point where he had once seen a vision of himself crucified. Upon his left was his archiepiscopal cross, probably still held by the crucifer Henry of Auxerre. About this moment Hugh de Morville separated himself from his companions and moved past the foot of the stairs coming down from the choir. He stationed himself at the end of the nave, ready to ward off any rescue attempt which might be made by the citizens of Canterbury who were lurking there in the darkness, watching events. There was, too, no knowing if any advance might come from the direction of the choir if any among the monks decided to intervene.

Action opened as one of the knights, evidently William de Tracy, got behind Becket and gave him a blow across the shoulders with the flat his sword, crying out, 'Fly, you're a dead man,' and 'Come on, you're our prisoner. We can't stand having you alive any longer.'

The main altercation, before it came to actual bloodshed, took place between Becket and FitzUrse, who had been the ready talker back in the palace during the previous half hour. FitzUrse lunged out and flicked the skull-cap from Becket's head with the top of his blade, crying, 'Come along, you're a prisoner.' The knight reached out and grabbed him by the edge of the woollen cloak, with the idea of dragging the archbishop out of the cathedral. 'Reginald,' cried Becket, 'I have done you many good turns; why do you come armed like this against me in this holy church?' 'You'll find out,' said the knight. 'You're a traitor to the king, aren't you?' he taunted, with 'Come on, get out of here.' 'No I will not,' retorted the other. 'You find me here, and here you can do to me what you want. Get out of this place, you abominable man. I am not a traitor and don't deserve any such accusation.'

FitzUrse, with a hand on the woollen cloak, pulled Becket towards him with a vigorous jerk, which made him stumble. The archbishop, affronted by such behaviour from a feudal subordinate and a layman, cried out to him, 'You are my man and have no business to touch me.' 'You and your crowd have gone mad,' FitzUrse retorted, 'I don't owe you any faith or homage against fealty to the king,' and tried hard to drag him out of the church.

FitzStephen says that they laid hands on the archbishop either to drag him out of the cathedral or because they feared that the citizens (who were close at hand in the nave) might bring about a rescue. Becket cried out, 'I will never go. Whatever you want to do or whatever you have been told to do, you can do here.' There were monks still around who hung on to him. The Saga elaborates

An early miniature of the martyrdom. (By permission of The British Library; Ms Cotton Claud. BII, det. f.241v)

Becket's remark to, 'Hence I go nowither, and here you shall do to me whatsoever you please. I am now ready to give my life for the freedom of Holy Church, in the name of Him who purchased her peace in His blood. Think never that I shall yield God's right to your swords.'

Becket tugged the cloak out of FitzUrse's hands and gave him a heavy push in exchange, at which the warrior lost his grip and went staggering back two or three paces, nearly losing his balance and almost falling down on to the pavement. At the same moment Becket let fly the violent and unexpected insult, so unbecoming a supposed scene of meek and passive martyrdom, 'You pimp!' There was organized immorality at King Henry's court and perhaps FitzUrse had some connection with maintenance of the official detachment of prostitutes there.

FitzUrse was certainly about to strike Becket at that moment, says William of Canterbury, but something held him back, some memory of past acquaintance and the fact that Becket had been the one who had brought him into contact with the king. Guernes indicates that

Becket of his own accord moved to the great pillar, but he is slightly ambiguous at this point and also suggests that the knights jostled him to it. As the gang surged upon him they snarled, 'You're going to die, and now.'

'I'm not frightened of your threats,' said Becket. 'I am quite ready to die for the sake of God. But let my people go. I forbid you under pain of anathema to hurt any of my own.' Even now he was still the good pastor, concerned for his flock. 'What you have to do, do to me alone, here. I am quite prepared to embrace death if the Church can find freedom and peace through my blood.' 'Absolve the excommunicated people!' cried the others, joined by the insolent soldier-clerk Hugh of Horsea, 'and anyone you have suspended and cut off.' 'I will do no more for them than I have done already,' Becket responded.

Realizing that death was imminent, he composed himself to utter the first of his commendations. He made the sign of the cross, folded his hands in prayer before his face and stretched out his neck to receive a blow, uttering the words 'To God and to the Blessed Virgin Mary, to the blessed martyr Denis and to St Alphege, Archbishop of Canterbury, and to the patrons of this place I commend my spirit and the cause of the Church.'

But the moment had not yet come. The gang moved in closer upon Becket and, still unwilling to deal with him in the sacred building, tried to hoist him up on to William de Tracy's shoulders and so carry him bodily outside. Tracy, it will be remembered, was the one among them who had not put on his chainmail, and as he was carrying much less of a load he would naturally be picked out to transport Becket. In the general mêlée Tracy received a shove himself from the archbishop, as he afterwards disclosed to his diocesan bishop, Bartholomew of Exeter. But they could not move him away from the column.

Tempers were now quite lost. The effort to convey Becket outside the door had failed, and shouts arose, '*Ferez, ferez!*' ('Hit him!'). The monk William of Canterbury, who had stood by his archbishop until this moment, lost his nerve as he himself admits. He thought he would be the next to be struck with a sword blow; and all too conscious of his sins and judging himself unfit for martyrdom, he shot off up the flight of stone steps towards the choir, smacking his hands together in agitation. Others disappeared into the dark and flung themselves to prayer at altars and in hiding places.

But Edward Grim was still there, and coming forward he slipped in between Becket and the great pillar. His object was to prevent the

The death of Becket, painted
c. 1200. Edward Grim holds
the cross. Fitz-Urse can be
identified by the bear on his
shield. (By permission of The
British Library; Ms Harley
5102 f.32)

archbishop from being dragged out of the building and he threw his
arms about him. He cried out at the same time, 'Whatever do you
think you are up to? Have you quite gone out of your minds? Think
where you are and what the season is. Think about the crime of
raising your hands against your own archbishop.' But they cared
nothing for the Christmas feast or for the sanctity of the church.

William de Tracy started yelling again that Becket was a traitor to
the king. There is a difference of opinion as to who struck the next

131

A depiction of the murder from the Ramsey Psalter, *c.* 1200. Compare with the illustration on page 131. (Reproduced by kind permission of the Pierpont Morgan Library, New York; Ms 302, f.4v)

blow. The Saga, Guernes and FitzStephen say that it was Tracy, while others accuse FitzUrse, who is said to have lashed out at Becket, hitting him over the head, bawling the while, '*Ferez, ferez!*' The blade struck the tonsured scalp, made even more sacred by application of the holy oil on consecration as archbishop, slicing off some flesh which fell forward in a flap. The ill-aimed blow glanced off on to Thomas's left shoulder, cutting right through the cloak, through the many layers of garments and into the flesh itself. Edward Grim raised an arm to protect the archbishop; the limb was struck by the descending sword, according to Grim himself, and cut or cut off (*praecisum*). He goes on furthermore to say that his elbow was cut (or cut off, *praecisa*). If it were crooked at an acute angle when cut, then it could well have been virtually amputated. The chronicler Anonymous II shows that Edward Grim had wound his cloak about his arm to serve as some sort of shield (just as any Elizabethan swordsman would do).

Late twelfth-century fresco of the martyrdom, in the church of SS Giovanni e Paolo in Spoleto, Italy. (Scala, Florence)

In the mêlée, the unnamed monk still bravely standing at Becket's side was struck over the head with the flat of a sword, perhaps at the end of the same blow, and fell back concussed. Edward Grim, dismissed from the conflict, tottered off to where several of the monks were clutching at the altar of St Benedict in terror of their lives. William of Canterbury says that at that moment Grim did not know who had hit him; but writing up the story some years later,

This fifteenth-century panel was originally painted for the foot of the tomb of Henry IV, who was buried close to Becket's shrine. (The Dean and Chapter of Canterbury)

Grim himself said that his assailant was FitzUrse. It should have been easy to distinguish between FitzUrse and Tracy, for the former was in full chainmail and the other in civilian attire. However, as William of Canterbury and Guernes report, that night back at Saltwood Castle William de Tracy was boasting that he had cut off the arm of John of Salisbury, whereas in fact that worthy had fled before the violence began. Perhaps the report of the boast was inaccurate and it was after all FitzUrse who uttered it.

Becket felt the flow of blood and put up his arm to wipe his head. Seeing the gore upon his sleeve he knew that his hour had come. He made the sign of the cross, then put his hands together in an attitude of prayer, making a second commendation. 'Into Thy hands O Lord I commend my spirit.' Thomas dropped on to his elbows and knees, uttering what seems to be yet another (third) commendation (according to Grim), 'In the name of Jesus and for the safety of the Church I am ready to suffer death.'

FitzUrse dealt a blow but did not bring Becket down. The knight stepped back, whereupon Tracy came forward and, as the archbishop submissively stretched out his neck, gave him a blow upon the head; still Becket did not fall, so Tracy gave him a second blow, knocking him out. As the archbishop fell he managed, by accident or design, to arrange his clothing about him in a dignified manner, with his cloak in place right down to his ankles. He collapsed upon his right side with his face turned to the altar of St Benedict, 'as one about to set out for the right hand of God', says FitzStephen. Guernes affirms that Thomas suffered 'for the church of the north, in the north aisle at Canterbury, turned towards the north'.

Gervase gives a specific description of the place where Thomas fell. The body lay, he makes clear, beside the solid wall running between the stairs to the crypt and the choir aisle, opposite the door into the cloister, that is, close to the east wall of the transept. It does not seem possible to recover the exact alignment of the body from the evidence of the chronicles and all we know is that it lay on its right side.

There is no doubt about the next blow, well attested by various historians. Richard le Bret stepped forward to the prostrate body and raising his sword brought it down with all his might on to the head of the victim, yelling as he did so 'Take that for the love of the Lord William, the king's brother!', working off the bitter resentment felt by some of the baronial class at the heart-broken death of this William for the love of the Countess Isabella of Warenne, and the marriage interdicted by Archbishop Becket some seven years before

The murder as depicted in a late fifteenth-century Flemish miniature. (By permission of The British Library; Add. Mss 54782 f.55v)

as lying within the prohibited degrees. The blow might have been intended to cut off the archbishop's head (in accordance with Becket's own premonition) but if so it was clumsily aimed and landed not upon the neck but across the already damaged cranium, slicing off the whole bony structure from the *conus capitis*, as Gervase the monk explains, to the *cella memorialis*, that is from the very summit of the skull to a point close to the fourth ventricle of the brain, deep at the back, above the neck.[1]

The blade struck the pavement at the end of the blow and a length shivered off (half, says Anonymous I); it was found later and enshrined on this spot as a sacred relic for the rest of the Middle Ages. A hinge of tissue at the side and front was left from the archbishop's scalp. From the account of Herbert it seems that the forehead was undamaged, and a general inference may be made that Bret must have stood over and facing the prostrate figure and have

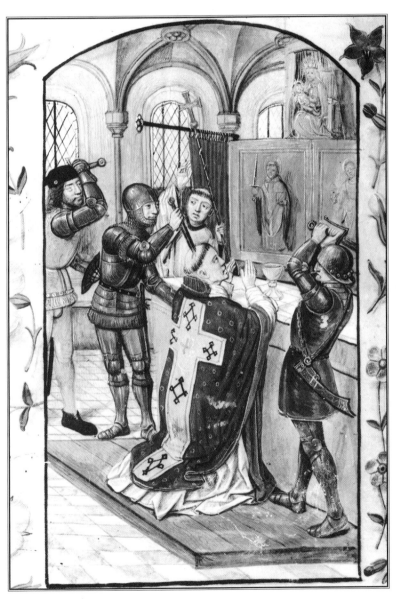

Edward Grim tries to ward off the fatal blow. A Flemish miniature of *c.* 1500. (By permission of The British Library; Add. Mss 17012 f.21v)

This painting by John Cross (1819–61) of *The Assassination of Thomas à Becket* was exhibited at the Royal Academy in 1853. It was purchased by public subscription after the artist's death and presented to Canterbury Cathedral, where it remained on view in the north choir aisle for many years.

delivered the blow standing in a position slightly clear of the summit of the head. He would have stood close to the corner where the wall turned into the chapel.

One of the four principal knights had never struck a blow. This was Hugh de Morville, who had posted himself on the flank towards the nave to ward off any attempt to succour the archbishop. He now withdrew from there and rejoined the other three, at which they all turned to go, bursting out of the transept door into the cloister.

A doubt suddenly arose. Was Becket really dead? The hanger-on, the subdeacon Hugh of Horsea, *alias* Mauclerc, Robert de Broc's evil soldier-clerk, turned back. It was he who, according to one version of Guernes' *Life*, had actually been ordained to his minor orders by Archbishop Thomas Becket himself. Still screaming threats, he went over to the body. Setting his foot on the neck to hold the head still, he thrust the point of his sword into the open skull and jerked the brains out on to the pavement, scattering chips of bone at the same time. He cried out (and again the actual words have survived), '*Alum nus en . . . ja mais ne resurdra!*' ('Come along, he'll never get up again!'), adding 'The traitor is dead.' Then he followed the others as they surged back through the cloister, swords in hands, shouting their triumphant war-cry, just as if in battle, '*Réaux, réaux!*' On their way they passed in the near darkness the other knights who had not entered the cathedral. Some of the crowd were making mocking remarks like, 'Well he wanted to be king and more than a king. Now let him be king; now let him be king.'

After action the normal procedure was looting, and a treasure house lay all ready for them to plunder. They had left Robert de Broc on guard in the archbishop's quarters to watch the chests of possessions; now they re-entered the palace, evidently going back through the door by which they had come at the far corner of the cloister. Hereabouts they found a servant of the Archdeacon of Sens who had come over the Channel with Becket about three weeks before. The fellow was weeping for Thomas, and they forthwith set about the defenceless creature, badly beating him up and drawing blood.

Guernes says that Robert de Broc, and others who stayed behind, started looting on their own account while the murder was in progress. He describes the booty pillaged from the strongboxes: woven stuffs and plate, silver and pure gold. They took Becket's good blade 'worth the price of a city', a remark which has puzzled many. Perhaps it had a heavy gold handle or perhaps Guernes has confused *cultel* (knife) and *cupel* (cup). Possibly, therefore, it was the great golden chalice which Thomas used at Mass to which he really alludes. This they took and defiled in secular drinking, as Guernes affirms, banging it and breaking it on the dining table. A ring with a choice sapphire set in it was taken,[2] and a piece of rich purple samite. They swept up vestments, clothes and anything they could find: spoons, cups, goblets of silver and refined gold, and at least £60 in silver coin.

They took Becket's jewels which he had always kept to himself and would not show to anyone. They seized writings and documents and had them sent over to the king in Normandy to see if there was anything incriminating in them against the Customs of the Realm. Gervase says that 'privileges and muniments' belonging to the cathedral were taken. William FitzStephen estimated that the total value in goods and cash lost through the depredation was over 2,000 marks. One discovery which astonished them was that of two spare hairshirts which, as they had no monetary value, they promptly threw away.

Some of Becket's clerks were rounded up and thrust into custody, so Guernes alleges. The chronicles are in agreement that horses were carried off. Guernes, however, makes contradictory statements, saying at one point that the knights went off with Becket's horses and later that on the next day Robert de Broc returned to seize two of the archbishop's best steeds. Meanwhile the household clerks had evidently managed to get their mounts across to the monastic stables which lay close to 'Stablegate', the archbishop's own stables, but de Broc (says Guernes) appropriated these too on the same occasion.

The load of loot must have been enormous, and pack animals must certainly have been seized, while the dead weight of some of the plunder (such as books, if taken) suggests that waggons were found. Eventually they made off. It must have been quite a large procession which wound its way out into the darkness through the palace gate. The servants of St Augustine's Abbey and the citizens who followed along in the train of the knights melted away. No chronicle mentions a return to St Augustine's by the knights, and it may be supposed that they left the city along the Dover road, soon branching off to Stone Street and at length reaching Saltwood Castle with their booty.

It is curious that there is one conspicuous absentee from the story of the murder, namely Rannulph de Broc, castellan of Saltwood. He had set out from the castle that morning with the rest of the party, but no mention of him is to be found in the course of the day in any of the narratives. It may be supposed that he either stayed at St Augustine's Abbey while the deed was done or, fearful for the stronghold which he had almost denuded of its garrison, went off back to Saltwood, where he was clearly established when the knights returned during the following night. Before long he had visited the king in Normandy and delivered to him some of the plunder in the form of writings.

Back in the cathedral, as distant shouts came from the pillagers across the cloister, the body lay for only a short while on its own. Perhaps it was never quite deserted, for the townsfolk of Canterbury had been lurking in the nave. Monks and clerks had disappeared into the blackness of the crypt or other recesses of the great church, apparently taking with them the wounded Grim and the unnamed monk, stunned in the mêlée. It was Osbern, the archbishop's chamberlain, who first came to the scene. He had to dodge looters in the palace and no doubt found his way through the cloister. He himself was certainly wounded when he was caught in the hall by Robert de Broc after taking part in the barring of the door. Bending down in the gloom, he found the corpse with its dreadful wound, the top of the head lying open ('like a dish' says Herbert of Bosham, gruesomely) and held on by the hinge of tissue. He tore a strip from his own shirt to make a bandage, and, replacing the cranium, bound it back into place.

The townsfolk emerged from the shadows of the nave, or from the streets into which some of them must have retreated. News of the deed flashed round the city, which at once echoed to howls of grief. Many, including the poor, attached to Thomas through his bounteous almsgiving, came crowding through the nave to the place of slaughter. Crouching down, they kissed the dead hands and feet, smearing blood upon their eyes and tearing off parts of their clothing to soak them in the gore. Hysterical cries rang through the darkened building. Some went and got bottles to secure a few drops, and those without some memento of this kind thought themselves very unlucky.

As the tumult and the shouting died away in the palace beyond the cloister, the monks came creeping out of the darkness. They waited, says the secular clerk William FitzStephen in a snide comment, until they were certain that the assassins had departed. The monks drew near to the body. It was necessary to get rid of the noisy and hysterical layfolk within the cathedral, bent on collecting souvenirs, and accordingly they were urged out through the doors which were then shut and barred. It was apparently while the body still lay on the pavement that, in the heightened atmosphere and darkness of the great church, the dead pontiff seemed to rise up and bestow the sign of the cross upon himself and bystanders, whereupon the corpse fell back again to the ground. Some went to find the cathedral bier and, as the corpse was lifted, there were disclosed beneath or beside it the small hammer and the carpenter's double-headed adze and mortice-tool, together with the broken-off point of Bret's sword. Someone found the skull-cap and set it in position above the bandages. The mouth was shut and the eyes closed.

The bier with its burden was now taken to the foot of the choir steps and carried at shoulder level up through the door at the top, up between the monks' stalls and so to the high altar. There it was set down. Canon Robert of Merton, Thomas's confessor and inseparable companion since his earliest days of ordination, who had slept in his room and knew all his secrets, was there. He pulled aside the clothing of the dead archbishop and disclosed the black garment, readily accepted as a symbolic or modified form of the Benedictine habit, if without a hood. Joy surged through the monks as they started to claim that Becket had really been one of themselves, a joy becoming overwhelming when they were shown the fearsome, infested, haircloth garments. They praised God, their lamentations turning to cries of delight. They bent down, kissing anew the hands and feet, calling him Saint Thomas, martyr unto God. They crowded around to look upon the mortifying haircloth, in such contrast to the so well-remembered, splendid chancellor in his purple and fine linen, and some no doubt recalled the reluctance with which he had abandoned his worldly array.

There was then a nauseating manifestation, repulsive to us today but at that time taken as an additional sign of sanctity. As the post mortem body temperature dropped, the army of lice infesting the garments started to leave their host, bubbling up like boiling liquid from the haircloth. The appearance of the face was singularly serene for one who had suffered such a violent death. There was a bloody diadem where the bandage was positioned, but the face was calm and unstained, apart from a thin line of blood running from the right temple down across the nose and down the left cheek. No discharge appeared from either the mouth or the nostrils. He lay 'just as if asleep'.

Soon one of the brethren named Arnold the Goldsmith, accompanied by some other monks, went back to the scene of the murder. Arnold was a local man whose family – including his brother, William, just beyond the palace wall – practised their craft in the city. The group of monks gathered up what was left of the blood and brains scattered across the floor and accumulated in depressions in the pavement into a bowl (in jars, says Guernes), and took the practical step of bringing benches (probably from the cathedral nave) into the transept and standing them around the scene of death to stop anyone trampling in the dreadful mess.

To add to the general atmosphere of crisis and tension, a blood-red glow appeared in the sky above Canterbury. As yet, few had adjusted to the idea that Becket had died as saint and martyr, and were not ready to seize upon this glow as a manifestation of the holy man's

The site of the martyrdom as it appears today. (Photograph: Thomas Neile; the Dean and Chapter of Canterbury)

soul mounting up to God. The first natural reaction of the monks was that here was yet another of the continual dangerous house fires beyond their boundary wall. It was only eight years since most of the city had been laid waste, the cathedral having a narrow escape, while their worst fears were to be realized less than four years ahead, when sparks from a burning workshop near their main gate lodged in the choir roof, resulting in utter ruin. So some of the monastic servants were sent out into the town to find out and came back to report that there was in fact a fire in progress. The glow would be reflected in the low cloud base. Meanwhile some sharp showers of rain fell, and there was a burst of thunder.

Quite early the next morning (Wednesday 30 December) a rumour raced round the cathedral that the Brocs were coming to drag the body out of the building, in some regret that they had been involved in a murder in a church. This was the first, if slightly perverted, sign of some misgiving. As dawn broke, Robert de Broc stormed into the monastery. No one had dared to bar any entry against him for fear of the king, and he no doubt came in through the portal to the palace in the far corner of the cloister. He cried out to the monks, 'This land is rid of the traitor who was trying to take away his lord's crown. He ought to be treated as shamefully as possible and deserves to be thrown into a rubbish pit or some filthy, stinking place. This man had little fear of God in him. It's a great blessing that this traitor has been killed. It's the best deed ever attempted. If St Peter himself had behaved as badly to the king as he did, then, if I had come along, by the body of St Denis,' he exclaimed (not the first time the patron saint of France had been invoked in the last twenty-four hours), 'my naked sword would have touched his brains!'

He ordered the monks to get the body out of sight, or else he would have it dragged around at the horse's tail. 'It ought to be tossed into a cesspit,' he claimed, 'or chopped up and thrown to the pigs.' The monks were terrified and decided to bury Thomas's body. They had with them for advice Richard, Prior of Dover, and the Abbot of Boxley, who had been summoned by the archbishop to discuss the appointment of a new prior at Canterbury, since Odo, who had acted as prior in recent years had done so during the exile and was not regarded as properly instituted.

First of all, despite de Broc's threats, they found time to examine the corpse and its raiment. Becket was not nearly as stout as they had imagined, for his bulk was due to the extraordinary amount of clothing which he wore. On top there was the 'iron dark' cloth lined with lamb's wool, having black fastenings but no edging. Under this there was a handsome white surplice of fine weave. Next was a lamb-skin coat such as was worn by regular canons as an outer habit. Then came two more items of lamb's wool in the form of two jackets, both short and roomy. Becket was subject to sharp attacks of pain in the side and abdomen and was always very cold, hence the load of clothes. Moreover, they helped him warm up after partial stripping for his daily flagellations, of which there was ample evidence on his back. He had received no fewer than three administrations on the very day of his death.

Under miscellaneous items of clothing there was still the modified monk's habit, with skirts and sleeves shortened to avoid revealing his way of life to all and sundry. Then there was a woollen shirt, and then the hair drawers and hairshirt, covered, however, with expensive white linen to avoid detection. It was furnished with special ties so that it could be undone at the back for flagellations. The drawers and hairshirt were still verminous and showed what a perpetual martyrdom was suffered by the archbishop long before his death. The drawers were so tight, they noted, that the seams had gouged a long trough upwards from his knees. There was renewed delight. 'Look, look,' they cried, 'he really was a monk and we did not know.' The archbishop had suffered torments enough from the haircloth underwear (they judged), without added torture from the vermin, some of which had actually burrowed into his flesh. Beneath the infested hairshirt, and next to his skin, was found the letter warning of imminent death which he had received from friendly-disposed people at the royal court on the previous Sunday night and had tucked away on his person.

It must have been at about this moment that the monks improvidently gave away some of the garments such as the jackets (which were cut off with knives) to the poor 'to pray for his soul'. They had still not grasped the idea that he had ascended to glory. The cloak, all smeared with blood, and the surplice likewise, both went. The recipients, equally thoughtlessly, sold them at once for little price. However, one item found a suitable home. William, a local priest, well known in Canterbury for his pleasant personality, bought the bloodstained cloak from its possessor and carried it off as a precious relic for exhibition in his church at Bishopsbourne, four miles from the city. It served not only as an impressive exhibit, but in due course was put to practical use, for William the priest wrapped the cloak round a little sick child at the point of death and so saved the infant's life. William the priest also obtained some of Becket's blood.

The funeral was conducted with maimed rites. The Abbot of Boxley and the Prior of Dover seem to have taken charge (since Odo,

Relics of St Thomas: (left) a small silver-gilt box, made as a reliquary within a few years of the murder scene depicted on it; (right) a gold pendant, called a phylactery, given to Queen Margaret of Sicily by Reginald FitzJocelin, bishop of Bath, before her death in 1181. It shows the queen receiving some relics of St Thomas – blood-soaked robes, a belt and a shoe – from a bishop, presumably Fitz-Jocelin himself. (Metropolitan Museum, New York)

acting Prior of Canterbury, was regarded by Becket as an intruder). They decreed that the body should not be washed; it had already been washed in its own blood. The corpse was to be interred wearing the hairshirt and drawers concealed by the seemly linen coverings, following removal and distribution of outer garments. The monastic habit was left in position as were his stockings. It was impossible to sing Mass and to work through all the elaborate ritual appropriate to the obsequies of a dead Archbishop of Canterbury, for the cathedral had been dreadfully profaned and must needs be cleansed physically and spiritually. But some things were ready. Becket, with death in his mind, had conserved the vestments in which he desired to be arrayed for burial. He had to hand, they found, the very garments in which he had been ordained eight years and more before, the alb, a simple 'superhumeral', his mitre, stole and maniple, and the chrismatic (the bandeau set around his head at his episcopal anointing to catch the sacred oil). They left on him the haircloth garments and the monastic robe as decided, and arrayed him in his priestly vestments. Then they added his archiepiscopal tunic, the dalmatic, chasuble and the pallium which they pinned into position on the shoulders. The gloves were drawn on to his hands. In his right hand they placed a chalice. On his finger outside

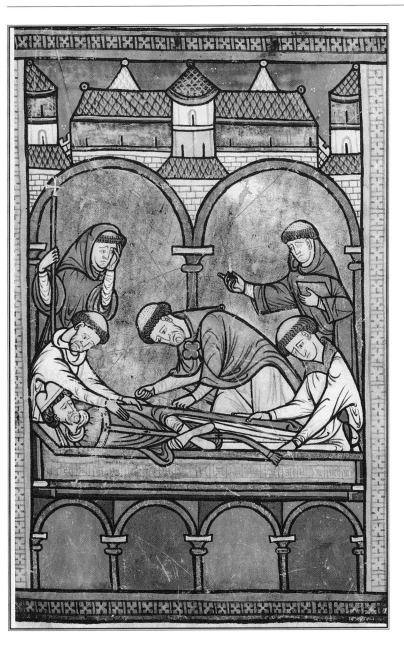

The burial of Becket, robed in the vestments he wore at his consecration, and wearing the palliun. From an English psalter of *c.* 1200. (By permission of The British Library; ms Harl. 5102 f.17)

the glove was set his archiepiscopal ring, and the fingers of his left hand were closed about his pastoral staff. The finger-ring with the green stone was removed and eventually found its way to the treasury of Glastonbury Abbey.

The appearance of the body, vested as if to sing Mass, can be recovered. It must have conformed almost exactly to the appearance

The eastern crypt of the cathedral, built in the early 1180s. Becket's tomb lay between the central marble pillars until its translation to Trinity Chapel in 1220.

of Archbishop Hubert Walter, who died in 1205 and whose tomb was opened in the Trinity Chapel at Canterbury in 1890, when vestments, with splendid chalice, paten and beautiful daisy-headed pall-pins were discovered. There was only one substantial difference. The mitre was now worn with points above the forehead and neck instead of over the ears, for episcopal fashion changed soon after Becket's death.

Ready too was a tomb in the eastern crypt. There is some mystery about this grave. It is spoken of as a new marble or stone tomb yet 'made some time before, in which no man had yet been laid' (Herbert of Bosham naturally cannot resist the Biblical allusion). It was certainly a tomb meant to receive the body of some prominent person in a place of honour before the two altars of SS Augustine and John the Baptist and between the resting places of two Saxon archbishops, Eadsin (d. 1050) and Ethelred (d. 889). Furthermore, it lay beneath the chapel of the Holy Trinity where Becket had spent much time in prayer. A tomb in such a place and in such company can hardly have been provided for anyone of modest importance, or indeed for anyone of lower rank than an archbishop. Surely it must have been intended for the next Archbishop of Canterbury to die and one may guess that between 1162 and 1164, when Becket was effectively in control of his cathedral and diocese, he commissioned the tomb in the eastern crypt. Being about seven years old and unused in 1170, it would answer the description both of 'new' and 'made some time before'. On the other hand, it could have been made in the interval after the archbishop's return from exile. Stone coffins were always available in a community numbering many elderly monks, and manufacture of a marble lid in that space of time would never be beyond the capacities of the cathedral works yard. There for the moment, but not for long, the body of Archbishop Thomas Becket was laid to rest on 30 December 1170.

There was soon to be a manifestation of the virtue of St Thomas, as he was now being called. While the murder was in progress citizens had watched in the gloom through the pillars. One of these had been among those who dipped their clothing in the gore. His shirt bore the stain. At home, relates William FitzStephen, he had a wife stricken with paralysis. He recounted to her everything he had seen, while neighbours stood around choking with sobs and shedding floods of tears, so that she could hardly hear the story. In an access of faith and inspiration on the night after the funeral she demanded that the bloodstain on the shirt should be soaked off into water which she thereupon drank, and rose up cured. This, claims FitzStephen, was the first wondrous sign from God manifesting the martyr's glory.

CHAPTER SIX

The Aftermath

News of the murder was soon flashing across the Continent. Certainly it was known on the other side of the Channel by the last day or so of December, for a party of monks who set off on the night of the 29th would by then have been well on their way to the Pope. It was probably on Friday 1 January that, just as discussions about the crisis caused by Becket's excommunications were about to start at Argentan, the frightful rumour started to circulate. Some of those present plucked up enough courage to tell the king. Henry said nothing at all. He went aside and shut himself up alone until the evening, stunned with grief and shock.

Travellers coming over from England quickly confirmed that the rumour was only too true. Henry was totally stricken. He remained three days in seclusion, taking no solid food but only some milk of almonds, a real penance for a man so used to French wines. It was not just an acquaintance that the king had lost, but an old friend, which made his despair all the deeper. There were tears at first for the archbishop, but before long all were in grave anxiety about the king himself, and started to wonder if the death of Thomas might also lead to the death of Henry.

Friends of the king, particularly the bishops, tried to calm him. Everyone would impute the crime to him, he said, and think he was a party to it. 'God Almighty is my witness,' he cried. 'This awful deed was not done by my will nor by my connivance.' David lamented at the deaths of Saul and Jonathan[1] but these were enemies, whereas King Henry wept for the death of an old friend. He said he would humbly submit to the Church and do what was required of him, and the bishops and others counselled him to seek guidance from the Holy See, with its great resources of spiritual experience and its accumulation of Christian wisdom.

One chronicler says that sorrow is usually most intense when first encountered and wears off after a little while. So it was with King Henry. Shame and grief gave way to opposite feelings. Some of those about the king when the news first arrived actually congratulated him, as if some big victory had been won. As he started to recover his nerve he threw off or concealed his grief. He sent over orders that no monk, clerk or suspect individual should leave England to go off to the Pope and announce the death – all too late, for the party of Canterbury monks had slipped away en route to Rome the very night of the murder.

In the first few weeks neither the king nor his court comprehended the immense forces unleashed by the archbishop's death. But waves of emotion swept across the ordinary populace. Wondrous miracles were already happening and the faithful started to travel down the road to Canterbury. The king refused to believe in the marvels and gave orders that anyone on the way to visit St Thomas (as he was already being called) should be stopped. After a while there was not much that the king could do about it since too many people were involved. Yet, urged on by 'wily instigators' whispering in his ears, he became sufficiently worked up to threaten to go to Canterbury and avenge himself upon the martyr's corpse. Good sense prevailed and he quickly retreated from such an intention, although on hearing of offerings being made at the tomb, he said he was going to make the prior and monks pay the cash over to him. Praise God, says the chronicler, the king's heart was softened and as time went by he

Pilgrims praying at the tomb in the crypt, before the relics had been transferred to the much grander shrine in the Trinity Chapel. (Photograph: Dr Sebastian Strobl; the Dean and Chapter of Canterbury)

became more and more penitent and started to believe in the martyr. But this did not happen quickly.

At all events the king decided that the monks of Canterbury were entitled to an official explanation for the sudden and dramatic removal of their head, who was both their archbishop and their abbot, and for the violent deed done in their midst. He therefore had an exculpatory document drawn up and entrusted to two clerks who were shortly dispatched to Canterbury. There they called the convent together (most probably in the chapter house) and delivered the king's statement, a standard model of civil service composition designed to excuse and cover up on behalf of a principal. The king, it is very clear indeed, was still a long way from the abject penance he was to display at Avranches in 1172 and at Canterbury in 1174.

William de Mandeville, Earl of Essex, was among the first visitors to Canterbury after the murder. He had, no doubt, very early news, for he was one of the official arresting party and had established himself at Wissant across the Channel ready to intercept Becket if he had taken flight. The party of monks which had left Canterbury on the night of 29 December for Rome must have passed him at close quarters, for Wissant was the usual port of call for cross-Channel travellers from Canterbury. His attitude when he came to the cathedral was very hostile. He told the monks that if they had been daring enough to conceal Becket, a traitor to the king, then all their hiding places would have gone up in flames and they would have been obliged to produce the traitor and suffer accordingly for protecting him. There were others who told them not to mourn a seditious fellow who had disturbed the whole kingdom, otherwise they might find themselves in like distress.

Two more visitors arrived shortly after the death. These were Hugh de Gundeville and William FitzJohn, two barons who had come across country from the court of young King Henry at Winchester. They had been detailed to give aid by Richard du Hommet, the one member of the official arresting party who had crossed into England and had gone to Winchester. Gundeville and FitzJohn were lucky to have arrived at Canterbury just too late, to the great relief of the young king when he heard of the murder. 'Alas,' he cried, 'but God I give you thanks that this was done without my knowledge and that none of my people were involved.'

It was necessary to apprise the Pope of Henry's official story of the murder, and of his grief for it, so another deputation was sent off on the tail of the first. The royal clerk John Cumin, who had been sent to the curia by Henry before the murder to try to effect release of the bishops from excommunication or suspension, was there when the fatal news arrived. He had almost succeeded in his mission (at an expenditure of 500 marks). On hearing of the murder, however, Pope Alexander shut himself up for more than a week, refusing to see even his own entourage, and ordering that no Englishman should be admitted to his presence. Letters came pouring in. Alexander Llewelyn and Gunter, Becket's clerks, had been sent by him to the Pope only just before the murder, bearing a list of bitter complaints. News of the murder caught up with them. They sent on dispatches to Alexander, to which were added fierce denunciations from the Archbishop of Sens against the bishops and against the king as the virtual murderer.

Certainly in the early months of 1171 King Henry failed to realize that, by his death, Becket had been elevated to the status of martyr throughout Europe. He wrote a letter to the Pope which was defensive in intent and offensive in tone. It spoke of the archbishop coming back to England not in happiness and peace, but with fire and sword, 'raising questions touching me and my kingdom,' as he said. Becket was an 'aggressor against his servants, excommunicating them without cause. . . . Such men were unable to put up with such insolence. Some of those who were excommunicated, with some others from England, attacked him, and,' said Henry, 'to my great sorrow in saying so, killed him.'

It was important for the emissaries sent by Henry to Alexander to contact and assuage the Pope before Maundy Thursday (25 March in that year) since it was on that day that the pontiff customarily pronounced major excommunications. The party reached the curia at Frascati (Tusculum) with less than a week to spare, on the eve of Palm Sunday. At first they could not gain entry to the consistory but at length two of the party, the Abbot of Valacé and the Archdeacon of Lisieux, were admitted as the least suspect. They caused uproar when they named King Henry as 'a devout son of the Church'. Later in the day they penetrated to the presence of the Pope himself, but Alexander Llewelyn and Gunter, Becket's clerks, had got there first, and the royal emissaries made little headway. There were some cardinals who were partial to King Henry, and it was perhaps through their influence that the dreaded excommunication of the monarch was not pronounced when the consistory came together at 3 p.m. on Maundy Thursday.

The royal messengers swore that Henry would abide by the decision of the Pope and would renew the oath in person. Emissaries of the Archbishop of York and of the Bishops of London and Salisbury were also there, and they gave satisfaction on behalf of their principals. Pope Alexander then pronounced as excommunicate the murderers of Archbishop Thomas. Meanwhile William, Archbishop of Sens, based safely in the domains of King Louis, launched a decree of interdict against all the continental domains of King Henry, notifying his action to the Pope. One anonymous chronicler asserts that King Henry showered gifts on the curia, while his skilled clerks and layfolk vigorously presented his case. However, it all had the effect of exasperating the Pope and his court. When the deputation returned, reporting ill success, Henry, apprehensive of what was to come, even dallied with the idea of going over to the then anti-Pope, Calixtus III. More remarkably still, he toyed with the idea of setting up a third Pope in his own domains, though he was dissuaded from this rash course by King Louis, who brought him back to his senses. In due course Henry gave intimation of submission, but without any intention of going to the curia to manifest it. The Pope was pleased, however, and named the Cardinals Albert and Theodwin as legates to deal with the matter.

At Canterbury anxiety and uncertainty marked the months following the murder. In east Kent Rannulph de Broc and his nephew Robert, both deeply implicated in the great crime, still ruled the roost. For a long time Henry himself was wavering between the ideas of Becket as traitor and Becket as virtuous martyr. No doubt the Brocs held the former view. Both Rannulph and Robert de Broc were close at hand, Rannulph with a vested interest in holding on to the castle at Saltwood, and Robert his wooden house at Canterbury, made of materials stolen from the archbishop's estates.

It appears that around Easter 1171 news was picked up that an assemblage of armed men was all ready to invade the cathedral and carry off the sacred remains. The organizers were some of those who had taken part in the murder. Clearly they were the Brocs, since the four principal knights were now far away. A warning dream was vouchsafed to a monk lying sick in the infirmary. He saw an angel on the pinnacle of the Temple, mystically surrounded by monks. A fiery rope with twitching ends appeared to try to encircle the precincts. In the event the would-be invaders were foiled by a mighty storm of rain and thunder which burst forth and dispersed them.

It was probably at about this time that the monks lifted the body (now surely in a state of putrefaction) from its resting place and concealed it in a hollow behind the altar of St Mary in the crypt. When it was replaced in its tomb, a solid low wall was erected about it, surmounted by a marble slab, the whole made secure with clamps of iron and lead. Two orifices were left in each side through which the devout might come into closer contact with the saint.[2] All the while the great church, one of the ancient shrines of Christendom, stood violated and defiled. The liturgy was suspended and services were conducted with maimed rites in the chapter house. In the silent cathedral, walls were divested of their hangings, crucifixes were shrouded and (according to a somewhat puzzling remark by Ralph of Diss) the pavement, soiled by muddy feet from the crowds, was taken up. No sound was heard from the great bells, and the crypt was sealed off, although news of miracles suggests that some of the faithful were allowed to penetrate to the saint's grave.

At length the Pope issued instructions for reconciliation. There was to be no actual reconsecration, but at least an asperging with holy water. The instructions were reinforced by Cardinals Albert and Theodwin in a letter to Prior Odo speaking of a petition he had submitted, and telling him to invite bishops and abbots to the ceremony. It was to be almost a year before Canterbury Cathedral was declared cleansed from the sacrilege. The day chosen was, most suitably, 21 December, the feast of St Thomas the Apostle, Becket's birthday. Bishop Bartholomew of Exeter was the chief figure and preached upon the theme: *For the multitude of the sorrows that I had in my heart, Thy comforts have refreshed my soul*. There was one conspicuous absentee from the service of reconciliation, namely the king himself, whose expressions of penitence had prompted hope that he would come. He was far away in Ireland, conveniently beyond the stormy seas, having decided that the best way to avoid trouble at the hands of the clerics who had him at such a disadvantage was to make himself scarce. Many years before, the English Pope Adrian IV (Nicholas Brakespear) had, so it was believed, assigned Henry a commission, signalized by the gift of an emerald ring, to invade and appropriate the verdant island and bring it under subjection to the Roman see.

Now was a suitable occasion to take up that commission, both to get away from the clamouring clerics and, by bringing a new province into the Church, to blunt the array of ecclesiastical weapons pointed at him. Gerald of Wales paints a picture of him dodging out of Normandy into England, out of England into Wales, and out of Wales into Ireland, where no papal decree had any force at all. Papal commissions and glittering tokens aside, Henry was drawn inevitably into the vortex of Irish history. The fierce peace-keeper of so much of the Continent could not have disorder at his back door. In particular, he found it intolerable that the Earl of Striguil, known to legend and history as Strongbow, had worked his way into a position of great power. From many and mixed motives, the desire to escape from the clergy, the need to reduce Strongbow to size and to impress the Irish with a sense of his own overwhelming might, he organized the expedition of 1171.

Happily for King Henry the winter of 1171/2 was stormy – so stormy in fact that Ireland was cut off from the outside world and little news got through. When it did, Henry found to his disquiet that the papal legates were in Normandy waiting to impose conditions if the king were to be relieved from complicity in the murder. They had been there for months and were now growing impatient and threatening him with the rigours of Church law. Henry made what arrangements he could for maintaining peace in Ireland and returned with inevitable misgivings to England.

There was now nothing for it but to face up to his plight. Henry, one of the mightiest secular rulers in Europe, met the legates, Cardinals Albert and Theodwin, at the Abbey of Savigny in mid-May. Agreement was hard to come by and at one point Henry announced bluntly that he had plenty to occupy him in Ireland, offering a strong hint of his intention to return there. At length an agreement was thrashed out, and Henry assented to a great public penance to be performed at Avranches. Accordingly on 21 May 1172, before the cathedral door overlooking Mont St Michel, Henry bowed before the legates. The forgiveness and peace he sought was accorded to him by ceremonial admission into the building, on terms which nevertheless ensured that papacy and monarchy might work henceforth in reasonable harmony.

All this time the English Church still lacked a head. Even after all that had happened, nomination was not left to the papacy nor to the uncontrolled decision of bishops and abbots. A meeting for election was called for 1 September 1172 in the demonstrably lay surroundings of Windsor, at which the young king presided. An unexpected contestant for the archbishopric was Odo, the Prior of Canterbury who had taken office during Becket's exile and suffered a severe snub on his return. After long argument, carried to King

Henry senior in Normandy, the choice fell on Richard, Prior of Dover, the able administrator who had served Archbishop Thomas conspicuously in the weeks after his return from exile. At an interval in the long-drawn-out proceedings Prince Henry decided to go on pilgrimage to the new martyr's tomb, setting out some time in September 1172. He was greeted with a procession. Arriving at the tomb in the crypt of Canterbury, he flung himself down on to the floor, uttering deep laments that he had consented to his father's enmity against the saint and that it was he who had ordered him to go back to Canterbury and stay in his church, 'under pain of death if he came out'. The young man gave handsome gifts, making promise of more, and issued a charter confirming his father's benefactions to the cathedral.

From the struggle between Crown and Church, one long-term victory for the clerics can be identified: *benefit of clergy*. In England it was not until 1827 that this privilege, by then a much mutilated and hardly effectual anachronism, was finally abolished. Yet in the centuries after the Reformation, many a condemned thief or murderer was able to call in court for a book and, on demonstrating that he could read and was therefore a clerk, escaped the gallows. When clerks and even monks formed much of Henry's judicature, the dividing line between the jurisdiction of the two sets of tribunals, lay court and court Christian, could not fail to be blurred on occasion, although with advantage, if anything, to the secular side. Alan, monk of Canterbury and later Abbot of Tewkesbury, and moreover historian and panegyricist of St Thomas and a great upholder of the rights of the churches where he ruled, managed to square his conscience on becoming one of the king's justices itinerant.

Probably Henry's greatest disadvantage in this sequence of events was loss of face, and this was severe indeed to a feudal monarch depending so much upon his own personality to maintain supremacy. He could count on a core of faithful supporters, but to a half-tamed baronage the mere sight of their powerful and overbearing master put so conspicuously in the wrong prompted an appetite for freedom. Henry's growing sons fretted at restraints and rebellious cliques gathered around them, while external enemies and rivals, the King of Scots, the Counts of Flanders and Boulogne, and King Louis of France, all waited upon events.

In 1173 there was the rumble of rebellion, largely engineered by Louis of France. He was aided and abetted by his own ex-wife, Eleanor of Aquitaine, who was now Henry's queen. She was captured and imprisoned in the tower of Chinon, and there remained for about a year. At Paris King Louis held a great council at which he and his nobles swore to help the young Henry against his father. Then the youth, multiple traitor to father and king, promised to give 1,000 marks of income in England, together with the whole of Kent, the castle at Rochester and the castle at Dover – the very key of England – to Philip, Count of Flanders. Similar wild offers were made to Matthew, Count of Boulogne, and Theobald, Count of Blois. Under his own seal Prince Henry made over Northumbria as far as the Tyne to King William of Scotland, and to Hugh Bigot the castle of Norwich.

Many remained faithful to King Henry, who surpassed himself in miracles of travel and energy. A force bent on penetration of Normandy, headed by Matthew, Count of Boulogne, was defeated and Matthew slain. A Breton rising in which Hugh, Earl of Chester, was implicated was crushed by Henry's Brabantine mercenaries, while the king captured the castle of Dol containing many prominent rebels. In late September an invasion fleet appeared off Walton on the Naze on the Suffolk coast. The commander of the force, which consisted largely of Flemings, was Robert de Beaumont, Earl of Leicester, traitorous son of the older earl who had started reading sentence against Becket at Northampton Castle nine years before.

Miles up the road towards Bury St Edmunds stood the castle of Haughley, which was held by the loyalist Rannulph de Broc, Becket's old enemy. He managed to hold out for four days but was at length overwhelmed by the Earl of Leicester on 13 October. William of Canterbury remarks that it was only divine justice that a castle put into the hands of a son of perdition like Rannulph should be lost. Any suggestion that this war was a gentlemanly tourney can be ruled out. The rebels and invaders occupied the fortress and destroyed it in an orgy of slaughter and rape. Rannulph somehow managed to escape with his life.

With Haughley eliminated, the forces of the Earl of Leicester and of Hugh Bigot, Earl of Norfolk, set off westwards towards Leicester, but their army did not get far. Near the great abbey at Bury St Edmunds, as they were picking their way across the marshes, there sprang out a contingent of Suffolk peasantry armed with farm implements, beneath the banner of St Edmund, headed by Humphrey de Bohun, Constable of England. Flails and pitchforks destroyed the rebels as a fighting force. Leicester himself was captured, together with his warlike wife Petronilla, who had joined in the invasion with her lord. The 'Leicester War' was over. Truces were arranged over the months of winter 1173/4, but as spring came the rebellion broke out afresh.

The King of Scots again came over the border and settled down to besiege Odelin de Umfraville's castle at Prudhoe, close to Hadrian's Wall. The Count of Flanders, allied with Prince Henry, got as far as landing another force of Flemings at the mouth of the Orwell close to Ipswich, and joined with the Earl of Norfolk in capturing Norwich. Henry, then in Normandy, received an account of all the bad news from Richard of Ilchester, now Bishop-elect of Winchester. Even the king's stout heart started to fail him. There was an obvious cause of his troubles: complicity in the murder of Becket. 'St Thomas,' he cried desperately, 'preserve my kingdom for me.'

What was required was a great gesture of repentance. Henry abandoned his campaigning and rode to Barfleur. He rounded up a group of female prisoners headed by his own queen, Eleanor, with Margaret, wife to his son Henry, together with the Earl and Countess of Leicester. A force of Brabantine mercenaries was embarked and the king himself set sail for England on 7 July 1174. There were gales in the Channel but Henry threw himself on the mercy of St Thomas as protector and insisted on making the journey, arriving at Southampton on the next day.

The king's movements are not easy to follow in the next day or two. He apparently went to London, for horses were hired for some of the ships' crews 'to follow the king to London'. Certainly Henry made contact with Bishop Gilbert Foliot of London at this moment, for a briefing must have been held when a prepared statement was worked out to be read by the bishop on the king's behalf and in his presence at Canterbury a few days later. Harbingers must have been sent to Canterbury to announce the king's approach and to stage-manage the dramatic penance which was about to ensue.

On Friday 12 July the king approached Canterbury from the west and reached the leper hospital at Harbledown about a mile from the centre of the city. The house had been founded a century before by Archbishop Lanfranc and still stands today as an almshouse for elderly citizens. We owe details of this episode in the story of the murder and its aftermath to Guernes de Pont Ste-Maxence. The king dismounted at Harbledown and entered the chapel and said his prayers. For all his evil deeds he asked God's pardon. For the love of St Thomas he granted 20 marks' worth of income to the poor house. There was another almshouse a couple of leagues away, says Guernes,

The leper hospital, dedicated to St Nicholas, in Harbledown, where Henry II prayed before completing his journey to the cathedral on foot. (Photograph: R.W. Pepper)

designed to harbour the poor. This was probably the obscure Hospital of Blean on the London road. To this house Henry assigned £5 per annum as a benefaction as part of his penance.

From Harbledown the king walked half a mile or more on foot to St Dunstan's, 'the first church you come to as you reach Canterbury', says Guernes, still true today. The church stands on the corner where travellers turned to pass the last quarter of a mile to the city's Westgate. Here in the church Henry stripped himself to his shirt. It was now raining and the king allowed himself the green cape 'such as he wore when hunting' to ward off the downpour. The lord of a large part of Europe now proceeded barefoot to the Westgate, watched by a wondering throng of observers. He walked up the High Street, through Mercery Lane where inhabitants like Solomon the mercer or Reginald the goldsmith must have gazed at him through their windows. At the cathedral the monks waited to receive him, as they had waited to receive Becket three-and-a-half years before in great joy on his return from exile. Normally a monarch would be received with the pealing of bells and with the solemn chant from the choir, called the *Laudes*, but there was none of that on this day.

At the entrance to the nave Henry knelt down, staying there a long time in tears and prayer. At length he rose and was led along the nave to the Martyrdom, as it was henceforth to be known, where Thomas had fallen on the fatal day. There Henry uttered the confession and kissed the floor where his enemy had lain. From the

Mazer (a drinking bowl, probably fourteenth century) belonging to St Nicholas Hospital. The crystal embedded in it is thought to be from Becket's shoe, which the great scholar Erasmus and his friend Colet, dean of St Paul's, were invited to kiss (to their disgust) when they visited the Hospital in 1512. The mazer is now on display in the Treasury of Canterbury Cathedral. (Courtesy of the Master and Trustees of St Nicholas Hospital)

Martyrdom he progressed into the crypt, evidently down the steps close by and through the adjacent and still existing portal. At the far end of the great vault he came to St Thomas's tomb, enclosed in its low wall with a marble lid. Again he flung himself into prayer, which lasted a long time, with grief and tears, an utterly contrite heart and deep devotion.

Bishop Gilbert, himself absolved from complicity long before, spoke on behalf of the king. 'He orders me', he said, 'to declare his unreserved confession on his behalf as I and others have heard it in private. He declares before God and before the martyr that he did not cause St Thomas to be slain, but freely admits that he did use such words as were the cause and origin of his being murdered. . . . He begs the saint to forgive his offence. . . . He returns all her holdings to this holy church, both to the archbishop and to the monastery. He asks you to pray to the true martyr lying here, beseeching him to lay aside all anger. The king has come here to make atonement.' Then the bishop went on to announce monetary compensation to Canterbury Cathedral, a benefaction of £10 per annum in addition to the £30 yearly already given at a previous date. King Henry then confirmed all that was said and the prior kissed him on behalf of the whole house.

Henry next removed his green cape and his shirt, and thrust his head and shoulders into one of the openings of the tomb, leaving his back all bare. The Bishop of London, Becket's old enemy, picked up a whip. The faint remains of a thirteenth-century painting survive today upon the crypt wall overlooking the site, and show the type of whip probably used, a short turned handle with a leather thong. The bishop gave him five cuts. The Bishop of Rochester followed, and then other bishops, and then the Abbot of Boxley. To the lashes from bishops and abbot there were now added three from each of eighty monks. The total is not certain, since the number of bishops attending is unsure, but must have approached three hundred. After the flagellation the king withdrew his head from the orifice in the tomb and stood up. He tottered to a pillar (most probably the central shaft supporting the quadripartite vault) and squatted down in the dust.

If the chronology of events in Guernes' account is reliable, it may have been about this moment that the widow Rohesia (Becket), sister to St Thomas, was brought to the king. She had been among the sufferers early in her brother's exile, when Rannulph de Broc had carried out Henry's cruel orders and harried the saint's kinsfolk into exile. Henry implored forgiveness. 'Pardon,' he said, 'Gentle sister, pardon and grace!' He gave her a 'goodly mill' and, says Guernes, she makes a good ten marks rent a year from that mill! The mill stood in Canterbury not far away at the central bridge over the River Stour, which still today bears the name King's bridge, after the king's mill which once stood here. Rohesia was indeed well rewarded, for the mill truly did bring in ten marks a year (enough to keep her in comfort), as recorded in the annual Pipe Rolls. This is another testimony to Guernes' accuracy as a historian.

Henry's self-imposed degradation was not over yet. There in the crypt he remained awake all night, not getting up for any bodily needs until after Matins (held in the small hours). Then he rose and made a circuit of altars throughout the church. When morning came, he caused Mass to be sung. When he put his boots on to go, he pulled them on to dirty and muddy feet. Exhausted bodily and mentally as he was, he set off for London, ignorant of the fact that on that very day, as dawn broke, salvation had come to him in the far north, and that the bad weather which he had experienced in Canterbury had dispersed his enemies on the seas off Flanders, where his traitorous son was ready to lead a naval invasion of England. The king was sufficiently apprehensive about such an invasion that before he left Canterbury he told the citizens to move their goods beyond the River Medway for safety.

Eastbridge Hospital in the late eighteenth century, from the King's mill opposite (the road is shown still unmade following widening of the bridge in 1767). (Courtesy of the Master and Trustees of Eastbridge Hospital)

Henry's fears may have been realized, for there were local losses of corn and cheese in this year (probably stocks destined for Dover or Canterbury castles) 'through rapine by the Flemings'. When Henry reached London he enjoyed a modest triumph. The citizens turned out in their best attire and gave him an enthusiastic welcome, with every assurance that he need not fear for their loyalty. They escorted him to his palace at Westminster where, stricken in body, and exhausted and weighed down with worry, he took to his bed.

Far up in the north the dreadful conflict had continued. King William of Scotland failed to take Prudhoe and retired northward. Frightful brutalities were perpetrated upon peasants and townsfolk on the way. William dispatched two large forces with instructions to devastate the countryside, one under the command of Richard de Morville, brother of the murderer of Becket, while he himself settled down to invest Alnwick Castle on the Northumberland coast, where William de Vesci held out. Meanwhile a scratch force of knights and peasants loyal to Henry had been assembled and on the morning of Saturday 13 July (just as King Henry was rising from his fearsome round of penances hundreds of miles away at Canterbury), they emerged from a mist close to the castle and beheld the force of a hundred Scottish knights lying around in a meadow, their king among them. Action was immediately joined. The knights were almost all slain on the spot or in flight, though some who survived allowed themselves to be captured rather than desert their king. King William's horse was killed by a spear thrust. He himself was taken prisoner and hustled away from the scene.

The story of the sequel is told in French by a talented dramatist born out of due time, Jordan Fantosme, in the language of the participants, so much closer to contemporary trains of thought than Latin.[3] It was late on Thursday 18 July, as King Henry lay abed, that a shout was raised outside as a messenger demanded entry at the chamber door. 'Who are you?' demanded the chamberlain. He gave his name as Brian, sent by Rannulph de Glanville from the north. The chamberlain replied that the matter could wait until morning as his master was asleep. The voice without became more insistent. 'Let me enter, *chamerleng debonaire*!' The chamberlain answered, 'I daren't do it, the king is asleep.'

Henry started up at the sound of the voices. 'Open, Open!' he shouted, 'Who is it? Tell me!' 'Sire,' said the chamberlain, 'you shall know straight away. There is a messenger from the north. You know him well; he is one of Rannulph de Glanville's men, called Brian.'

'*Par ma fei*,' cried the king, 'that worries me. Bring him in.' In came Brian and saluted King Henry. 'Sir King,' he started, 'God who dwells in Trinity save you, first yourself and those about you.' Henry, all impatient and agitated, interrupted the courtesies. 'What news do you bring?' he demanded. 'Has the King of Scots got into Richmond? Is Newcastle on Tyne taken? Is Odelin de Umfraville [the loyalist castellan of Prudhoe] captured or driven away? Have all my barons given up their ground? Messenger,' he cried, '*par ta fei*, tell me the truth. Evilly have they served me and I'll be revenged!'

'Sire,' gasped the messenger, 'listen to me a little. Your barons up north are good people. *Do* listen to me on behalf of my lord. By me he sends greetings and friendship. You are wrong to worry,' and he at last managed to get out the words, 'The King of Scots is captured and all his barons too!' 'Are you telling the truth?' demanded King Henry incredulously. 'Yes indeed,' said the messenger, 'and you will know by morning. The Archbishop of York is sending two messengers. But I started first and I know the truth. For four days past I have hardly slept,' he went on, 'nor eaten nor had anything to drink, and I am very hungry.'

Said the king, 'Don't worry. If you have told me the truth you'll be well enough off. Is the King of Scots captured? Tell me truly.' 'Yes, Sire, in all faith, otherwise let me be crucified on a cross or hung on a gallows, or burnt in a great bonfire, if by noon tomorrow everything is not quite clear.' 'Then', said Henry, 'Thanks be to God and to Saint Thomas the martyr and to all the saints of God.'

The messenger Brian was then sent to lodgings to eat and drink his fill. The king went off at once to his knights' quarters, crying out the joyous news. Confirmation of the glad tidings came, as predicted, on the next day, sent by Archbishop Roger of York. Brian was allocated an income of £10 per annum as his reward.

Penance and remission, cause and effect: the connection was obvious. Both Henry and Thomas had triumphed. The saint had forgiven his enemy. Nothing could be more straightforward to the medieval mind. The revolt collapsed. Across the water on the Flemish coast the fleet assembled by Count Philip and Prince Henry was dispersed by a storm. All Henry's illness, probably mostly of psychological origin, vanished away. In a blazing burst of energy the now forty-year-old monarch (already very mature by medieval standards) took horse and rode the fifty miles northward to the enemy-occupied castle at Huntingdon, where he pressed local carpenters into service to make siege engines. Within a few days (by 21 July) he had cleared the fortress. Thence he sped sixty miles eastward to Framlingham, occupied by the rebel Earl of Norfolk, Hugh Bigot, who had no doubt by now heard of St Thomas's intervention into the fortunes of King Henry. The earl, whose relations with St Thomas during his lifetime had not been altogether happy, decided that the moment had come for complete submission. He came out to meet the king and on 25 July gave up not only Framlingham, but Bungay Castle in the same area as well. The Flemings in his service were allowed to embark and go home.

Though in pain from a kick on the thigh from a horse, Henry now moved quickly over to Nottingham, another journey of a hundred and twenty miles or more. He reached the town by 31 July. Here he received fealty from Hugh, Bishop of Durham, whose conduct in bringing forty knights and five hundred Flemish mercenaries into the kingdom had been, to say the least, dubious. From one castle after another across England, representatives came in with offers of surrender. To Nottingham was led Henry's new prisoner, King William of Scotland, who was not to disentangle himself from the results of his misfortune for very many years to come. As far as England was concerned the revolt was virtually over.

The Continent now demanded Henry's attention. The most immediate anxiety was Rouen, where King Louis was conducting a siege in defiance of a truce with Henry. By 8 August, only a month from his departure thence, the English king was back at Barfleur. He made for Rouen where Louis straight away withdrew back through the Vexin into France proper, while Henry's Welsh mercenaries plundered his baggage trains. A few more energetic forays and the king was master of his wide continental possessions as well.

Within a few days of his arrival at Westminster, Henry had confirmed by a charter what he had already granted verbally on Friday 12 July when he descended from his horse at Harbledown hospital outside Canterbury. Acting as witnesses to the document were people prominent in the Becket story, such as Gilbert Foliot, Bishop of London, Roger, Bishop of Worcester, and Richard of Ilchester the archdeacon, now Bishop-elect of Winchester, who in company with Earl William de Mandeville had been one of the party appointed to arrest Becket in 1170. By the charter (which was destroyed in the great air-raid on Canterbury on 1 June 1942), Henry confirmed the grant to the lepers of 20 marks each year from his revenues in Canterbury until he should find some other source. A mark is 13s 4d and 20 marks amount to £13 6s 8d. The sum can be found charged annually upon royal income in Kent, registered in the Pipe Rolls.[4] The lepers did not even have to wait until September and the beginning of the next full accounting year as would have been quite reasonable. Instead they were generously assigned 5 marks by King Henry for the very quarter in which the payment was initiated. Year after year the payment is entered either as 20 marks or £13 6s 8d paid *leprosis* or *infirmis de Herbaldun*.

In 1234 the citizens of Canterbury secured some measure of independence from the Crown by a charter of fee farm granted by Henry III, whereby they were allowed to compound directly with the Exchequer, instead of through the Sheriff of Kent as intermediary, for various royal rents with tolls and profits of justice, at the substantial sum of £60 per annum. The citizens were made responsible for paying the 20 marks due from the Crown to the hospital at Harbledown, and the £60 payable by them to the Exchequer was reduced by the same amount.

The oldest surviving account roll in the borough archives is dated 1272 and, covering a half year, mentions 10 marks paid to the almshouse. Payment went on all through the Middle Ages. It survived the Reformation. It survived the Civil War. By the eighteenth century there was some idea that it had been ordained by Henry VIII, of all improbable people! When the Municipal Corporations Reform Act came into force in 1835 the city treasurer decided that payment of ancient dues of this kind had lapsed, and for many years the sum went unpaid. Eventually, representations were made to the government on behalf of the almsfolk. The payments were restarted and arrears made good upon orders from Westminster. During the nineteenth century the nature of the payment was obscured even further when it was classed in corporation accounts as tithe.

The ancient day for payment is 10 October. This date itself calls for comment. In 1752 eleven days were dropped from the English calendar to bring it into line with the Gregorian scheme prevailing on the Continent. It was, however, provided that any payment or accounting day could be postponed to what would have been the due date for payment if the calendar had not been altered. Thus the government itself postponed its grand annual audit date of Lady Day (25 March) for eleven days, arriving at 5 April where it has stood ever since. The borough treasurer of Canterbury likewise postponed his settlement date in connection with the benefaction to Harbledown. Eleven days subtracted from 10 October takes one to 30 September, the old morrow of Michaelmas. Not only do the almsfolk receive a benefaction from Henry II but it comes at his ancient accounting period. There has been another adjustment. In 1971 British currency was decimalized. The odd half mark or 6s 8d, one-third of a pound sterling, could not be expressed exactly in decimal currency, and so the almsfolk now receive only £13.33 – or one-third of a new penny less than the sum laid down by King Henry II in 1174![5]

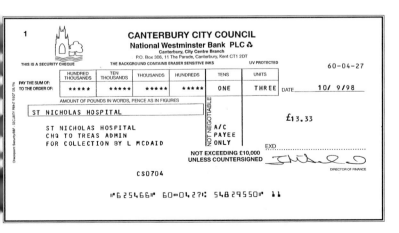

One of the annual payments which Canterbury City Council continues to make to St Nicholas Hospital in fulfilment of Henry II's endowment.

After the débâcle, father and son, old king and young king, made peace, and late in May of the next year both travelled to Canterbury on pilgrimage to the tomb of the now canonized St Thomas. With them (so it appears) went the young Queen Margaret for a stay of four days. The character of the young man is easily deduced from his actions. He was selfish, short-sighted and irresponsible, almost at times unbalanced. Like his brothers, whom King Henry senior tried to groom as viceroys in his various domains, he was a bitter disappointment (though Richard at least showed determination and military skill).

The younger Henry's revolt in 1174 is but one manifestation of his fecklessness. He remained quiet for some years, but in 1182 was again in arms against his father, who besieged him in Limoges where he managed to antagonize the townsfolk by plundering the shrine of their patron, St Martial. When he returned from a sortie they drove him away with insults. Undeterred, he then plundered another shrine, that of Rocamadour, whereupon he was struck down by fever, dying in a smith's house at Martel in ostentatious penitence, clothed in a hairshirt and lying on a bed of ashes. Yet somehow he had had, and still exercised, personal attraction. He destined his body for burial at Rouen but on the way it was seized by the citizens of Le Mans, to the anger of the Rouennais, who intervened successfully with Henry II for its transfer to their cathedral.

Some said that the quarrel with his father was fomented by the famous troubadour Bertrand de Born, a story given permanent currency in the pages of the *Inferno*. When Dante and Virgil have descended as far as the eighth circle, second only from the bottom, they encounter the terrible figure stalking around, holding in his hands his own head separated from his body. He explains his punishment:

> *sappi ch'i' son Bertram dal Bornio, quelli*
> *che diedi al re giovane i ma' conforti.*
> *Io feci il padre e 'l figlio in sé ribelli*

> Bertrand de Born am I, and I have given
> Such evil rede that sire from son is riven;
> Old king with young king through my fault has striven.[6]

The holy blisful martir

The whole of Christian Europe was unanimous in its view on the death of Thomas Becket: he had died as the great martyr to the cause of the Faith and Church. It was immediately assumed that not only had he made the supreme sacrifice for his priestly order, and (perhaps less clearly) for the layfolk as well, but that he had met his earthly end in circumstances of outstanding bravery and drama, at the swords of evil assassins. It was also assumed that he had met his death before the very high altar of Canterbury Cathedral itself, for reports soon circulated that the death took place '*coram altari*', meaning in fact only the side altar of St Benedict. However, as Latin possesses no definite article, 'an altar' soon became 'the altar'. The imagined scene, filled with vigorous action, was a gift to artists, and it is almost as if the talented designers of the age were waiting for a subject other than the Biblical scenes to which they were accustomed. The surging wave of emotion generated inspiration, and painters, sculptors, stained-glass designers, enamel workers and seal-engravers seized upon the new subject, producing vast numbers of images both then and right down to the end of the Middle Ages and beyond, changing fashions in arms and armour being reflected in their work.[1]

Archbishop Thomas was first buried in the eastern crypt at Canterbury, in a marble tomb which probably projected a few inches above the floor. It was some time before the threat of disinterment and the destruction of tomb and corpse abated, and so the monks strengthened the tomb. Many tales are told of this tomb, which is depicted no fewer than fifty times in the stained glass around the retrochoir of Canterbury, in illustrations of the miracle stories. Long-standing enemies of Becket fell silent and came to pray at the tomb, making heavy amends in terms of cash and humiliation. Nevertheless the tomb, which was now the objective of floods of pilgrims,

Part of a thirteenth-century 'miracle window' in Canterbury Cathedral. (Photograph: Dr Sebastian Strobl; the Dean and Chapter of Canterbury)

remained a humble and unpretentious monument in the eastern crypt of the cathedral, and must have been a disappointment to many coming from far away.

In some areas the cult of St Thomas became intense, as in the distant frozen north, where a great hero standing up to the powers of darkness was the theme of many a saga. Some Icelandic author, using a lost Latin *Life* of Becket, worked up the superb epic called the *Thómas Saga Erkibyskups*. In the warmer south, Thomas became an inspiration to French versifiers. Guernes de Pont Ste-Maxence added to the collection of *chansons de geste* with his *Vie de Saint Thomas*. Latin poets waxed rapturous, as in the joyous hymn to Canterbury, *Gaude Cantuaria urbs sanctificata*.

Clamour arose for recognition of the new hero of the Church, and Pope Alexander was besieged with appeals to canonize Thomas. The pressure upon him was enormous, although he had not a few unhappy memories of his difficult subordinate. The speed with which Thomas was made a saint was almost without parallel. The new martyr was declared a saint in a series of documents issued in March 1173, including the bull *Redolet Anglia* issued on 12 March and addressed to the clergy and people of England. Another bull was directed to the monks of Canterbury. It ordered that the new saint's 'birthday' (i.e. the day of his death and hence the start of his life in heaven) should be celebrated yearly henceforth. The body was to be decently conveyed to a shrine or altar, with proper processions and ceremony amid layfolk and clergy.

St Thomas appears to a leper. A scene from the 'miracle' windows. (The Dean and Chapter of Canterbury)

The great attraction of the new saint was his reputation for effecting miracles. The tomb soon became adorned with waxen images of cured limbs. An Icelander brought walrus teeth. A man condemned to hang at Perigord far away in France brought half of the very rope which had failed to extinguish his life when, at the last moment, he called on St Thomas. Two great volumes of miracles were set down by the Canterbury monks William and Benedict, who were by no means credulous receivers of every wondrous tale, though assessment of the particular therapy involved lies outside the scope of this book.[2]

Rich and poor alike came along the Canterbury road. In 1179 King Louis of France, in panic at the feared death of his son and heir Philip, who was sinking fast from exposure after having been lost in a forest, landed at Dover to pray at the tomb of his old acquaintance, promising annually the enormous amount of 100 *muids* of wine from the Poissy vineyards, at the same time giving a golden cup and the ring containing the stone called the *Régale*, an esteemed part of the French crown jewels. This ring had been coveted by Becket himself in his lifetime, so the story went, and now he secured it post mortem.

The most outstanding visitor, in terms of his future history, was Lotario di Segni, a young Italian studying at Paris. He arrived some time in the 1170s and seems to have sampled the local beer and experienced its effects. Years afterwards, as Pope Innocent III, he told English bishops who had just presented a muddled argument that they must have been indulging in their native beverage.

The quest for relics of St Thomas was fevered, and within a very short time many (including the doubtless spurious) were being hawked about. The tomb became a magnet for many monarchs. Henry II came and went. Richard I passed through Canterbury on his way to the crusade and conceived the idea of erecting a chapel in the Holy Land in honour of St Thomas. One of his knights from the area of Canterbury made an offering of property close to the cathedral gate by ceremoniously inducing his tenant to stand on the tomb as a visible sign of his gift. Richard was captured by the Germans on his way home and on his release in 1194 came with his mother, Queen Eleanor, to give thanks at the tomb in the cathedral crypt.

Tin-lead pilgrim badges. (Left) the head of St Thomas, recalling the life-size bust on the tomb which contained a portion of his skull. This seems to have been the most popular of all the many different designs. (Right) the return from exile. Both the badges shown here were found at Bull Wharf, London. (London Museum)

Towards the year 1200 there was a visitor to Canterbury from Scotland, described as Alan *dapifer*, i.e. the steward ('Stuart'). Overcome with devotion to the saint, he promised an annual gift of one whole mark (13*s* 4*d*) to the tomb. After riding away the good and thrifty Scot thought better of it, and when the monks received his remittance they discovered it was for half a mark only. However, at the great translation of St Thomas's body to its shrine in 1220, Alan's son Walter Stuart, who had come in company with Robert Brus, another name pregnant with future Scottish history, made up the grant to the whole mark.

Translation to a new shrine had long been mooted, but what with the crusade and the need to pay a colossal ransom for King Richard, together with the long-drawn-out crisis in John's reign which ended with the grant of Magna Carta and the king's submission to Pope Innocent, nothing was done. At length Archbishop and Cardinal

The pilgrim steps leading up to the Trinity Chapel. (Photograph: Dr Sebastian Strobl; the Dean and Chapter of Canterbury)

Stephen Langton brought about the erection of the new shrine in 1220. This was the most splendid thing of its kind in Christendom, a great casket covered with slabs of gold, some fifty square feet in surface area, standing high on arches. A mesh of gold wire allowed the offerings of the faithful in the shape of rings, brooches and personal trinkets to be attached to the shrine. From time to time they were cleared off and melted down by the unsentimental monks.

The translation from the old tomb to the new shrine on 7 July 1220 was celebrated with a splendour exceptional even in the pageant-loving Middle Ages. The young King Henry III, too small to act as coffin bearer, attended with the papal legate and the great magnates of the realm. No expense was spared and much of the 'great offerings' was used up in entertainment and the supply of free food and wine.

Accounts are available from 1198 and show substantial takings. As much as £405 was offered at the tomb in the crypt in that year. Offerings continued to be made at the old tomb after the shrine was set up. Throughout the thirteenth century there is no dramatic change in the takings, which were probably less than they might have been but for the barons' wars in the 1260s. But in the fourteenth century there clearly arrived the grand age of the pilgrimage, when offerings sometimes rose to £500 per annum. There was a profitable year in 1350 when frightened people, in terror of the Black Death, streamed to Canterbury and dropped £667 into the offertory box at the shrine, to which may be added large sums offered at the other cult-sites such as the Martyrdom, making £746 all told.[3]

Geoffrey Chaucer and his party probably came in about 1385, at a time when the Becket pilgrimage had assumed the character of a tourist excursion. The cult of St Thomas had its ups and downs even in Canterbury, where it assured some profits from the tourist trade. In 1327 the citizens were engaged in one of their periodic struggles with the monks and decided to loot the shrine, swearing that every man should wear on his thumb a ring from the tomb of Thomas Becket, as they contemptuously called him.[4] Citizens of Canterbury who decided to go on pilgrimage ignored the cult on their doorsteps and went off instead to places like Hailes where the Holy Blood was preserved.

Times and feelings were changing. Lollardy was growing and even heads of Oxford houses like John Wycliff of Canterbury College or Peter Payne, Principal of St Edmund Hall, were infected with heresy and doubts about the efficacy of intercession by the saints. For a long time, however, St Thomas remained the dominant saint of England and northern Europe. King Henry V came up the road from Dover to give thanks at the shrine after his victory at Agincourt in 1415. The pious King Henry VI made a trip to the shrine during one summer holiday, camping in the special tent called the 'hale', maintained for royal usage by the Canterbury city council at Harbledown, outside the walls.

Fervour for the cult of St Thomas diminished during the fifteenth century.[5] By 1428 a great code of practice for maintaining the shrine had grown up and in that year, when decline was setting in, the custodians decided to write down the Custumal which has come to light only in recent years. This tells of candles, square and round, in different colours of red and green. It tells also of one charming or grotesque feature, the 'Wheel of Dover', a great drum on which was wound a flexible candle between one mile and two in length, equal to the perimeter of that town, and trundled back and forth along the Dover road when the candle needed to be renewed. But it also tells of reduced takings in the offertory boxes, and reveals that allocations of cash, once ample to run cathedral departments such as the cellary or sacristy, were no longer adequate, owing to loss of faith in St Thomas on the part of layfolk.[6]

Every fifty years, 1270, 1320 and so on, there had been a special celebration known as the jubilee when indulgences were issued for

At the shrine of St Thomas, a drawing by Colin Dudley. This reconstruction of the shrine as it might have appeared in the fourteenth century omits the iron grille that surrounded it. The artist also points out that it is 'highly unlikely that poorer pilgrims would ever have been present when the shrine was being visited by nobility or wealthy'. The shrine is shown with its wooden canopy raised, and at the top edge of the picture can be seen part of Becket's hair-shirt. (Reproduced by kind permission of Colin Dudley)

Canterbury pilgrims, an early sixteenth-century miniature. (By permission of The British Library; Ms Royal 18D ii f.148)

reduction of time in purgatory. This brought great masses of people in 1370 when enormous crowds were unable to find either food or lodgings and slept hungrily in the streets. The better organized jubilee of 1420 was very well attended and was pronounced a great success in mutual congratulations between the city authorities and the monks.[7]

Throughout the fifteenth century enthusiasm waned and little is heard of the celebrations due in 1470, by which time the stirrings of the Renaissance (and the Wars of the Roses) were taking people's minds off the subject. In 1520 there were difficulties in securing papal approval and there is little to show that anything remarkable happened at Canterbury. Local records recount little more than a charge made against a man of beating up pilgrims 'in this year of grace'. Nevertheless King Henry VIII came with his guest Charles, very soon to become Emperor of Germany, his queen Catherine of Aragon and Cardinal Wolsey. They all formed up in procession and rode in great triumph through Canterbury to pay their respects at the shrine of St Thomas.

As in any popular tourist centre there was a brisk sale of souvenirs. Little 'Canterbury bells' tinkled at the bridles of pilgrims' horses returning home, and thousands of phials allegedly containing water impregnated with a drop of the saint's blood were sold. Whether anyone genuinely believed this must be doubtful, but certainly something resembling blood was on exhibition at the very end of the Middle Ages, stigmatized by Archbishop Cranmer as 'a feigned thing, and made of some red ochre'.[8]

In 1538 Henry VIII decided to confiscate the shrine and all its treasures. It was duly demolished (some of the monks actively helping) and eight men could scarcely stagger out of the cathedral with the looted bullion. The bones within were probably burnt, as there is sufficient evidence to show, though attempts have been made to discredit the story.[9]

There is a curious tale which has escaped attention though it has been in print since 1841.[10] A wandering Greek called Nicander Nucius attached himself to the German embassy to the English court in 1545. Despite the language barrier he picked up pieces of recent news on the way through Kent from Dover, such as the story

Eastbridge hospital (i.e. lodging place) for pilgrims was established on King's Bridge by 1180. Becket's nephew Ralph was probably its first Master. The undercroft, divided into cubicles, was the pilgrims' dormitory. (Reproduced by courtesy of the Master and Trustees of Eastbridge Hospital)

The late twelfth-century seal of the city of Canterbury depicts a royal castle on the obverse (top left) and the murder of Becket, flanked by censing angels, on the reverse (top right). Noticeably worn after more than three centuries of use (bottom left), the seal was altered in the reign of Henry VIII by literally cutting out the murder scene and substituting the city arms (bottom right). But Becket remains, for the city arms themselves incorporate his badge of three choughs. (Canterbury Cathedral Archives (Charta Antiqua *c.* 1154 and a loose seal). Photographs: David Pilcher)

of the Holy Maid of Kent from the decade before. He also learned of the destruction of the shrine 'ten years ago' (actually seven), and recounted that the bones of the saint had been burnt in the midst of Canterbury and then, he said, the ashes were forthwith put into a cannon and fired off into the air, thus finally dispersing the mortal remains of St Thomas. Could this story perhaps be true? Present in Canterbury at the time was Thomas Cromwell, the ex-soldier, and this is just what might be expected of his grim sense of humour. At all events no attempt was made in the reign of Queen Mary (1553–8) to re-establish the cult of St Thomas although his name was restored to the liturgy.[11] If any relics had been preserved, surely they would have come to light during the five years of her reign. At the dissolution of the monastery in 1540 the very vault where the sacrosanct body had lain in the first tomb for fifty years was downgraded into a coal store for the adjacent houses of the canons and so remained until the nineteenth century.

Through the years the fame of St Thomas was not forgotten. A Spanish ambassador made an offer for the glass in the great window above the Martyrdom showing appearances of the saint.[12] The same window was the special object of hatred from the Puritan fanatic Richard Culmer, when he smashed up the cathedral in 1643.[13] In 1660 Samuel Pepys, on his way back from the excitements at The Hague surrounding the restoration of Charles II, landed at Deal and rode to Canterbury, where he dined and looked at the tomb of Becket, as he asserts, though what he beheld is not clear.

The stubborn disinclination to accept that the bones of Thomas were destroyed seemed to be vindicated when in 1888 a skeleton was found in the eastern crypt of the cathedral, in a coffin adjacent to the site of the original tomb-shrine. There was much enthusiasm for assuming that the bones were Becket's. They were reinterred but brought out again in 1947 when a proper examination was made by two specialists.[14] Carbon-dating and other methods pointed to a twelfth-century date, but in a building where some five hundred burials are on record there could be no certainty of identification even within the limited period of a century. In 1920 Canon A.J. Mason brought out a short book on the problem entitled *What Became of the Bones of St Thomas?*, which provides a valuable assembly of theories, although strangely ignoring the anecdote about the disposal set on record by Nicander Nucius.[15]

Earlier this century strong Protestant opinion prevented Anglo-Catholic moves for revival of the cult. In about 1930 Father Tooth, a well-known ritualist, engaged designers to draw up plans for an overwhelming new (and untenanted) shrine which he offered to donate, and which would have dominated the whole cathedral choir. This scheme was happily prevented by the Fabian tactics of the then Chapter, and by the discovery on the promoter's death that no funds were available for his project.[16]

In the 1930s there was a simple annual ceremony on 29 December, held in the Martyrdom of the cathedral. This became more elaborate and was attended by the choir of the Roman Catholic St Thomas's Church, Canterbury. The cult in general has served as a rallying point for ecumenism, of which an important manifestation occurred in 1970 in joint Roman and Anglican celebrations of the eight hundredth anniversary of the murder.[17]

Ecumenism apart, there is a kind of secondary, popular cult of Becket displayed in enquiries made by visitors, continental and native, of all shades of information and belief. It certainly appears that Thomas Becket is the principal non-royal medieval personage occupying the imagination of the general public, with wide variations in grasp of the story of his calamities. Immediately upon entry into the cathedral many visitors ask to be shown the site of the murder, for a scene of blood-letting never fails to appeal. A second enquiry is regularly for the 'grave' itself, as news has failed to circulate of the destruction of the shrine. Devotion to the memory of the saint takes some very strange forms, in enquiries on the spot and in the substantial body of correspondence regularly handled at Canterbury.[18]

Intense interest in the events of that dark December afternoon over eight centuries ago persists, but this is matched by widespread ignorance about what really happened and why. For those who really want to know, however, a bridge over this 'information gap' already exists, in the remarkable set of records that has come down to us, and especially in the accounts given by the very able band of contemporary reporters.

Notes

Abbreviations used in Notes

Arch Cant:	*Archaeologia Cantiana*, Kent Archaeological Society, 1858–
Barlow:	Frank Barlow, *Thomas Becket* (1986; rev. edn, London, Orion Books Ltd, 1997)
Borenius:	Tancred Borenius, *St Thomas Becket in Art* (London, Methuen & Co. Ltd, 1932)
Butler:	John Butler, *The Quest for Becket's Bones. The mystery of the relics of St Thomas Becket of Canterbury* (New Haven and London, Yale University Press, 1995)
Collinson:	Patrick Collinson, Nigel Ramsay and Margaret Sparks, eds, *A History of Canterbury Cathedral* (Oxford, Oxford University Press, 1995)
Foreville:	Raymonde Foreville, *Thomas Becket. Actes du Colloque International de Sédières, 19–24 Août 1973* (Paris, Editions Beauchesne, 1975)
Knowles *Becket*:	David Knowles, *Thomas Becket* (London, Adam & Charles Black, 1970)
Knowles *Colleagues*:	David Knowles, *The Episcopal Colleagues of Archbishop Thomas Becket* (Cambridge, Cambridge University Press, 1951)
Knowles *Study*:	David Knowles, 'Archbishop Thomas Becket: A Character Study', *Proceedings of the British Academy*, XXXV (1949)
Mason:	A.J. Mason, *What Became of the Bones of St Thomas?* (Cambridge, Cambridge University Press, 1920)
Nilson:	Ben Nilson, *Cathedral Shrines of Medieval England* (Woodbridge, Boydell Press, 1998)
Rady:	J. Rady, T. Tatton-Brown, J.A. Bowen *et al.*, 'The Archbishop's Palace, Canterbury', *Journal of the British Archaeological Association*, CXLIV (1991), 1–60, Pls I–VIII
RS:	Rolls Series (*Rerum Britannicarum medii aevi scriptores*), (London, 1858–96)
Saltman:	A. Saltman, *Theobald, Archbishop of Canterbury* (London, Athlone Press, University of London Historical Studies, II, 1956)
Urry:	W.G. Urry, *Canterbury under the Angevin Kings* (London, Athlone Press, University of London Historical Series, XIX, 1967)
Woodman:	Francis Woodman, *The Architectural History of Canterbury Cathedral* (London, Routledge & Kegan Paul, 1981)
Woodruff:	C. Eveleigh Woodruff and William Danks, *Memorials of the Cathedral and Priory of Christ in Canterbury* (London, Chapman & Hall Ltd, 1912)

Notes

Dr Urry's manuscript contains very many footnotes referring to the various Lives of Becket, published in the seven volumes of *Materials for the History of Thomas Becket, Archbishop of Canterbury*, edited by J.C. Robertson and J.B. Sheppard, RS, 67 (1875–85), and elsewhere. It has been decided not to reproduce them here, on grounds of space and also because much of the same information is readily available in Knowles *Becket*, Knowles *Study* and the current standard biography of St Thomas, Barlow. A copy of Dr Urry's original text, including the notes, is available to students in the Cathedral Archives at Canterbury.

The footnotes that follow have been brought up to date as appropriate.

Prologue

1. In his manuscript Dr Urry writes that Osbert's name demands comment. 'In those days money was calculated in terms of the mark of 160 silver pence. Was this Osbert's figure for commission, 8*d* in the mark, and was it always on his lips? If he took one-twentieth in every deal, then he was the twelfth-century equivalent of Mister Five Per Cent!'
2. Dr Urry noted: 'I am much obliged to Professor I. Donaldson and Professor B. Matthews, Fellows of St Edmund Hall, Oxford, for discussion of the question.'
3. *Multiplicem* is discussed at length in Appendix VII of Knowles *Colleagues*, pp. 171–80. See also Barlow, pp. 153–6.
4. Knowles *Colleagues*, p. 180.

Chapter One

1. Knowles *Study*, p. 20.

Chapter Two

1. Dr Urry's manuscript contains a lot more information on the ancestry of the four knights than has been given here.

Chapter Three

1. Urry provides the background details referred to here. John son of Vivian is mentioned several times. The goldsmith brothers, William and Arnold, are mentioned on p. 155 and William the priest on p. 184.
2. Professor Barlow's plan is on p. x of Barlow. The quotation from Tim Tatton-Brown is on p. 4 of Rady, which records the excavations and building recording work carried out at the Old Palace in Canterbury between 1981 and 1986. Dr Urry's diagram is in Map 1(b) Large-scale, Sheet 4, in the Map Folder forming part of Urry. The same picture can be found in the plan of the monastic buildings at Canterbury on 29 December 1170 at p. 145 of Knowles *Becket*, which is based on the plan in Urry. The current thinking can be seen in the plan on p. 2 of Rady.
3. This so-called 'Waterworks Drawing' (MS.R.17.1, Trinity College, Cambridge) is reproduced in black and white in Woodman, p. 28, and in colour on the back cover of the dustwrapper. It was traced by Professor Robert Willis for his article 'The Architectural History of the Conventual Buildings of the Monastery of Christ Church in Canterbury, considered in relation to the Monastic Life and Rules, and drawn up from personal surveys and original documentary research', *Arch Cant* VII (1868), 1–206, between pp. 196 and 197, which tracing is reproduced in Collinson, pp. xxviii–xxix.
4. See Urry, pp. 182–3.
5. The name 'Thierlewda' can hardly relate to Throwley, near Faversham, as this was not a church at Becket's disposal. It was a possession of St Bertin (Saltman, p. 464). Harrow and 'Otherford' are the causes of grievances named in Becket's letter to the Pope early in December, but there is no reference to 'Thierlewda'.
6. The Beivin family is mentioned in Urry, A 23, B 86, 88, F 613, 658.
7. William FitzNigel (or FitzNeal) was involved in the fierce argument which erupted later in the twelfth century, when Archbishop Baldwin tried to establish a college of canons at Hackington, just outside Canterbury, to be funded at the expense of the monks of the cathedral priory. In January 1188 two monks were excommunicated by Baldwin, whom they had gone to greet at Wingham, a few miles to the east of the city. They returned to their monastery, pursued by William FitzNigel, to whom entry was refused. He broke in anyway, and occupied the outer offices of the precincts and in effect laid siege to the monks. The siege lasted for over a year. See Urry, pp. 165–6.
8. M.B. Hackett, *The Original Statutes of Cambridge University* (Cambridge, Cambridge University Press, 1970), pp. 46–7.
9. *The Letters of Arnulf of Lisieux*, ed. Frank Barlow, The Royal Historical Society, Camden Third Series LXI (1939), letter 57, pp. 102–3.
10. Saltman, letter 297, p. 523.
11. Knowles *Study*, p. 29, n. 85.
12. *Chronicles and Memorials of the Reign of Richard the First*, ed. William Stubbs, RS, 38, 2 vols (1864–5), vol. 2, *Epistolae Cantuarienses*, p. lx.

Chapter Four

1. Knowles *Study*, p. 21.
2. See Barlow, pp. 1–9, for a full discussion.
3. Isaiah 9:6.
4. Luke 22:53.
5. Knowles *Study*, p. 22.

Chapter Five

1. See Mason, pp. 53–4.
2. *Inventories of Christchurch Canterbury*, eds J. Wickham Legg and W.H. St John Hope (London, Archibald Constable & Co. Ltd, 1902), p. 133.

Chapter Six

1. 2 Samuel 1:17–27
2. See William Urry, 'Some Notes on the Two Resting Places of St Thomas Becket at Canterbury', Foreville, pp. 195–209.
3. *Chronique de la Guerre entre les Anglois et les Ecossois* in *Chronicles of the Reigns of Stephen, Henry II, and Richard I*, ed. Richard Howlett, RS, 82, 4 vols (1884–9), vol. 3.
4. Urry, p. 43, refers to this payment. A fuller account is given in William Urry, 'Two Notes on Guernes de Pont Sainte-Maxence: Vie de Saint Thomas', *Arch Cant*, LXVI (1953), 92–7, at pp. 96–7.
5. In November 1998 a letter was sent to Canterbury City Council's Director of Finance to check whether the payment was still being made. The reply was that 'indeed the payment you refer to is still made and made with some ceremony. On or about 4 December each year the Lord Mayor presents a cheque to the hospital at the feast of St Nicholas. The remittance is prepared in mid-September but without further research, which could take a considerable time, I am unable to say why this particular date. The description on our current payment records, albeit brief, reads, Tithe re 29 marks granted by Henry II out of his fee for farm rents in the City of Canterbury. As to the discrepancy over the number of marks, I am unable to say at this point which record is correct.'
6. Dante's *Inferno*, Canto XXVIII, 134–6.

Epilogue

1. See Borenius.
2. The matter is discussed in Ronald C. Finucane, *Miracles & Pilgrims. Popular Beliefs in Medieval England* (London, J.M. Dent & Sons Ltd, 1977), especially in Chapters 4 ('Faith-healing: Medicine and Miracle') and 5 ('Saintly Therapy in Action: Shrine-cures and Home-cures'), pp. 59–99.

   Further details of the miracles themselves can be found in E.A. Abbott, *St Thomas of Canterbury. His death and miracles*, 2 vols (London, Adam and Charles Black, 1898), and they are also discussed in Benedicta Ward, *Miracles and the Medieval Mind. Theory, record and event. 1000–1215* (London, 1982; rev. pb edn, Wildwood House Ltd, 1987), especially Chapter 5 ('The Miracles of St Thomas of Canterbury'), pp. 89–109.
3. Until very recently, the most accessible published details of offerings made in connection with the Becket cult in Canterbury was C. Eveleigh Woodruff, 'The Financial Aspect of the Cult of St Thomas of Canterbury as revealed by a study of monastic records', *Arch Cant*, XLIV (1932), 13–32. A much more detailed picture can now be found in Nilson, especially the Becket-related parts of Chapters 6 ('Shrine Accounts and Offerings') and 7 ('The Offerings Examined'), pp. 144–90; Table 2 ('St Thomas Becket: oblations to the four stations connected with the cult of St Thomas at Canterbury'), pp. 211–15; and Graphs 1 ('The offerings to the tomb of St Thomas at Canterbury to 1220, and to the shrine from 1220, from table 2') and 2 ('Income to the Corona, Canterbury, from table 2'), both on p. 234.

4. William Somner, *The Antiquities of Canterbury*, 2nd rev. and enlarged edn, ed. Nicholas Battely (London, 1703), p. 58.

5. Ben Nilson is more cautious: 'given the nature of the sources, it is impossible to declare that the cult of shrines was in serious decline much before 1500, and indeed seems to have been stable throughout the fifteenth century. . . . It is probable that what decline existed was not because shrines in general were no longer vital, but that the cathedrals that many of them were in no longer had a monopoly on religious attraction. Much of the devotion formerly directed towards saints' shrines in cathedrals was now given to those in smaller churches and to Marian shrines,' Nilson, p. 193.

6. BL Addl MSS 59616, fols 1–11, acquired by the British Library at the end of 1975 and described in D.H. Turner, 'The Customary of the Shrine of St Thomas Becket', *Canterbury Cathedral Chronicle*, 70 (1976), 16–23. Turner records that Dr Urry was one of those whose contributions enabled the British Library to acquire the MS.

7. A full account of the 1420 jubilee is to be found in Raymonde Foreville, *Le Jubilé de Saint Thomas Becket du XIIIe au XVe siècle (1220–1470)* (Paris, S.E.V.P.E.N., 1958), which also covers all the other pre-Reformation jubilees except that of 1520.

8. *Miscellaneous Writings & Letters of Thomas Cranmer* (Cambridge, The Parker Society, 1846), p. 378.

9. A useful collection of source material on the demolition of the shrine is to be found in Mason, especially Section III ('The destruction of the Shrine'), pp. 123–70, which to some extent follows H.S. Milman, 'The Vanished Memorials of St Thomas of Canterbury', *Archaeologia*, LIII (1892), 211–28. A more recent discussion is to be found in Butler, which also contains an account of five possible hypotheses as to what happened to Becket's remains after the destruction of his shrine. Professor Butler is careful not to say which he finds most convincing. Many will find it difficult to avoid the conclusion that wishful thinking is what motivates most of the so-called 'mystery', and that Dr Urry was right to conclude that the saint's bones were destroyed along with his shrine.

10. *The Second Book of the Travels of Nicander Nucius of Corcyra*, ed. and trans. J.A. Cramer, Camden Society, XVII (1841), pp. 74–5.

11. Woodruff, p. 302.

12. William Gostling, *A Walk in and about the City of Canterbury*, 4th edn (Canterbury, 1825), p. 342. Culmer seems to have heard a similar story: 'for which window (some affirm) many thousand pounds have been offered by outlandish Papists', Woodruff, p. 327. Gostling puts the amount at ten thousand pounds.

13. Woodruff, pp. 327–8, quoting Culmer's own description of the destruction of many works of art in the cathedral, and in which he mentions 'a minister being then at the top of the citie ladder near 60 steps high, with a whole pike in his hand rattling down proud Becket's glassy bones'.

14. F.J. Shirley, 'Scientists' Examination of Canterbury Bones. Becket theory disproved', *The Times*, 4 August 1951, p. 5. See also Butler, pp. 97–107.

15. See note 9 above.

16. See *Letters concerning the offer by the Rev Arthur Tooth to the Dean and Chapter of Canterbury Cathedral of an Altar Shrine in honour of St Thomas of Canterbury 1929–1931*, 2 vols, Canterbury Cathedral Archives: DCC/Tooth Correspondence.

17. The 1970 issue of the *Canterbury Cathedral Chronicle* (65) was largely devoted to Becket. The issue in the following year, 1971 (66), pp. 4–7, has a short account of what happened during 1970: Gerald Peacocke, 'The Becket Commemoration 1970. A Retrospect'.

   Since Dr Urry wrote this paragraph, a more fixed pattern of services has been established at the cathedral to commemorate St Thomas. On 29 December, the main feast, there is Evensong and Procession to the Martyrdom, a service attracting many people and normally attended by the Archbishop of Canterbury. When Evensong is over, all present process to the Martyrdom where there is another short service in which the archbishop reads a short portion of Becket's Christmas sermon from T.S. Eliot's *Murder in the Cathedral*. On 7 July, the feast of the Translation of St Thomas, there is Evensong and Procession to the Shrine, a 'normal' service in terms of numbers attending. The closing part of the service, involving the now empty site of the shrine, has varied in recent years. One year, the Dean and Chapter processed from the Quire to the shrine, said prayers and rather self-consciously censed the empty space. In July 1998 the whole congregation moved to the shrine area with the clergy, where a few simple prayers were said and an anthem sung. In 1999 the 1998 pattern was followed, but with the reintroduction of incense. On both feast days the Roman Catholic parish in Canterbury has an evening Mass at the high altar of the cathedral.

18. In his notes, Dr Urry quotes a correspondent who wrote to the cathedral library to say that 'I have become very interested in a man called Thomas à Becket who was shot or stabbed in Canterbury Cathedral'.

Further Reading

The starting point must be Frank Barlow, *Thomas Becket* (first published in 1986; revised edition, London, Orion Books Ltd, 1997), which is readily available in paperback. It has a short note on pp. 279–80 about where full bibliographies may be found. For 'the most readable and sympathetic short account' Professor Barlow recommends W.H. Hutton, *Thomas Becket* (first published in 1910; revised and enlarged edition, Cambridge, Cambridge University Press, 1926). Others might prefer Dom David Knowles, *Thomas Becket* (London, Adam & Charles Black, 1970), which was the biography to which Dr Urry referred in the text of his book. He also admired a slightly earlier popular work, Nesta Pain, *The King and Becket* (London, Eyre & Spottiswoode, 1964), which he felt got closer to Becket the man than any other book.

There is a perceptive account of Becket and his character in Beryl Smalley, *The Becket Conflict and the Schools* (Oxford, Basil Blackwell, 1973), especially Chapter 5 ('Thomas Becket'). Reference may also be made to the William Urry Memorial Lectures which have been given in Canterbury and Oxford and are published by the William Urry Memorial Trust with the Friends of Canterbury Cathedral (and available through the Canterbury Cathedral Archives), especially R.W. Southern, *The monks of Canterbury and the murder of Archbishop Becket* (1985), Frank Barlow, *Thomas Becket and his clerks* (1987) and Robert Franklin, *Thomas Becket and France* (1991).

There were several chroniclers of Becket, many of whom appear in the first four volumes of J.C. Robertson and J.B. Sheppard, eds, *Materials for the History of Thomas Becket, Archbishop of Canterbury* (London, Rolls Series 67, 1875–85). Vol. 1 is devoted to William of Canterbury, while vol. 2 contains Benedict of Peterborough, John of Salisbury, Alan of Tewkesbury and Edward Grim. William FitzStephen and Herbert of Bosham, together with miscellaneous material, appear in vol. 3. Vol. 4 has Anonymous I, Anonymous II (of Lambeth), the *Quadrilogus* and other material. Vols 5 to 7 contain the correspondence generated by the controversy. Anne Duggan, *Thomas Becket. A textual history of his letters* (Oxford, Clarendon Press, 1980) is a masterly study of the correspondence and related matters.

Guernes de Pont Ste-Maxence's Life has been translated by Janet Shirley as *Garnier's Becket* (London and Chichester, Phillimore & Co., 1975), now available as a paperback. Extracts from William FitzStephen's Life together with other contemporary sources were translated and edited by George Greenaway for *The Life of Thomas Becket. Chancellor and Archbishop* (London, Folio Society, 1961). The widest selection of source material on Becket in English, including extracts from the chroniclers and some items of correspondence and other matters, was printed in David C. Douglas and George W. Greenaway, eds, *English Historical Documents. Vol. II. 1042–1189*, 2nd edition (London, Eyre Methuen, 1981), pp. 749–828.

The Becket story has produced many novels about the clash between king and archbishop, and P.A. Brown, *The Development of the Legend of Thomas Becket* (Philadelphia, 1930) has never been bettered.

The subject of pilgrimage has been widely considered in recent times. Several relevant books are mentioned in the footnotes to the Epilogue. Jonathan Sumption's *Pilgrimage. An image of medieval religion* (London, Faber & Faber, 1975), is arguably the best book on the subject. For the later medieval period reference should be made to Eamon Duffy, *The Stripping of the Altars. Traditional religion in England, 1400–1580* (New Haven and London, Yale University Press, 1992), since reissued in paperback. It has a section on saints which includes a passage on pilgrimage.

Work continues to appear every year on Becket, and 1999 is no exception. For a paper delivered at the Battle Conference 1998 see Michael Staunton, 'Thomas Becket's Conversion', *Anglo-Norman Studies* XXI (1999), 193–211.

Index

Aa, river, 15
Adam, cellarer of St Albans, 57, 58
Adrian IV, Pope, 155
Agincourt, 175
Alan Stuart, 173; his son, Walter, 173
Alan, Abbot of Tewkesbury, chronicler, 157
Albert, Cardinal, 154, 155, 156
Alexander III, Pope, 7, 8–9, 10, 15, 16, 17, 19, 20, 21,
        23–4, 28, 29, 30, 42, 50, 51, 67, 70, 72, 83, 85,
        88, 95, 104, 105, 106–8, 109, 111, 150–5, 170
Alexander Llewelyn, 8, 12, 42–3, 61, 82, 85, 97, 120
Algar, 87, 115, 119, 153
Alnwick Castle, 163
Alphege, St, 82
Anonymous I, chronicler, 73, 90, 96, 98, 100, 102, 106,
        109, 116, 121, 137
Anonymous II, chronicler, 133
Ardres, 33
Argentan, 150
Arnold the goldsmith, 74, 142
Arnulph, Bishop of Lisieux, 71, 88
Arthur, King, 6
Ash, 45
Auvergne, 31
Auxerre, 3, 86
Avranches, 152, 156

Barfleur, 159, 166
Barfrestone Church, 92
Bartholomew the clerk, 57, 58
Bartholomew, Bishop of Exeter, 130, 155
Barton, Elizabeth, the Holy Maid of Kent, 180
Bayeux, 72; tapestry, 39, 92–3
Bec, Abbey of, 2, 88
Becquet, 1
Benedict of Peterborough, monk and chronicler, 96, 101,
        104, 107, 108, 110, 111, 113, 124, 171

Bernard, St, 21
Bertrand de Born, troubadour, 168
Black Death, 175
Bletchingley Castle, 86
Bologna, 3
Boston, 14, 15
Boughton, 87
Bramfield, 58
Breamore, 60
Bungay Castle, 165
Bur, 67
Bury St Edmunds, 158

Caen, 2, 25, 72, 75
Cahors, 5
Calixtus III, anti-pope, 154
Cambridge, 46, 87, 88
Canossa, 7
Canterbury, 5, 6, 10, 14, 15, 18, 22, 29, 36, 41, 42, 51,
        59, 60, 61, 62, 63, 74, 91, 94, 100, 101, 114,
        116, 125, 128, 135, 140, 142, 151–2, 154, 157,
        159–63, 163, 166–8, 171, 172, 175, 177, 178,
        180–1
    archbishop's palace, 15, 29, 63, 77–81, 94–9, 101,
        114–17, 120, 125, 128, 139, 141, 142
        mulberry tree in garden, 98, 114, 116
    Blean, hospital of, 159–60
    Burgate, 45, 86, 96
    Buttermarket, 45
    cathedral, 1, 31, 33, 39, 42, 43, 45, 74–5, 94, 96,
        101, 115, 116, 118, 119, 139, 140, 141, 143,
        144, 146, 154, 155, 157, 161–2
        altar of St Augustine, 148
        altar of St John the Baptist, 148
        altar of St Mary, 75, 127
        altar of St Mary in the crypt, 155
        cellarer's building, 78, 80, 120, 125

cellary, 176

chapel (and altar) of St Benedict, 74, 75, 123, 128, 134, 135, 169

chapel of St Blaise, 75, 124

chapter house, 46, 89, 122–3, 125, 152, 155

choir, 120, 123, 124, 128, 141, 144, 181

cloister, 75, 78, 80, 81, 120–6, 127, 138–42

crypt, 97, 123, 124, 127, 155, 157, 161, 162, 169, 180

dormitory, 122

high altar, 1, 46, 123, 142, 169

library, 18

nave, 120, 127–8, 138, 140–2, 160

north-west transept, the 'Martyrdom', 74, 75, 120, 123–39, 141–2, 160, 175, 180, 181

refectory, 121

sacristy, 176

shrine of St Thomas, 173–81

  Custumal, 176

  'Wheel of Dover', 176

speaking hole or tube in cloister, 81, 120

tomb of St Thomas in crypt, 148–9, 155, 157, 161, 162, 169–73, 175, 180

Trinity Chapel (retrochoir), 148, 169

washing-place, 121

works yard, 149

castle, 86, 163

Chantry Lane, 94

city walls, 18, 96

Dean and Chapter of, 39–40, 181

Dover Road, 94, 140, 176

Harbledown, 160, 175

  leper hospital, 159, 166–8

High Street, 160

King's bridge, 162

London Road, 160

Longport, 45

Mercery Lane, 45, 160

monks of, 7, 8, 16, 29, 63, 75, 113, 115, 119–24, 127–49, 150–2, 155, 160, 169, 170, 174, 175, 177, 178

Newingate, 45

New Street, 94

Northgate, 96

Palace Street, 116

Queningate, 96

St Augustine's Abbey, 94–6, 98, 114, 125, 140

St Dunstan's, 63, 160

St Laurence's Priory, 94

St Martin's Hill, 45, 46

St Peter's Grove, 81

St Thomas's Roman Catholic Church, 181

Staplegate ('Stablegate'), 80, 140

  Westgate, 63, 81, 160

Canute, King, 39

Charles II, 180

Charles, Emperor, 178

Chartres, 21, 25

Chaucer, Geoffrey, 175

Chaumont, 28

Cherbourg, 72

Chiddingstone, 61

Chinon, Tower of, 158

Clairmarais, Abbey of, 15

Clairvaux, Abbey of, 21

Clarembald, Abbot of St Augustine's, Canterbury, 25, 95–6

Clarendon, Constitutions of, 10, 17, 21, 23, 24, 36, 42; Council of, 10, 20

Compostella, 16

Constance of Castille, 4

Constance, wife of Count Raymond of Toulouse, 5

Cotentin, 72

Cranmer, Archbishop, 178

Cromwell, Thomas, 180

Culmer, Richard, 180

Dante, 168

David, Master, 70

David of Romney, 82

David, King of Scotland, 72

Deal, 180

Dol, castle of, 158

Domfront, 23

Dover, 33, 34, 35, 36, 38, 41–2, 50–1, 53, 86, 89, 90, 92, 158, 163, 171, 175, 178

Eadsin, Archbishop, 148

Eastry, 15

Edmund, St, 158

Edward I, 39

Edward Grim, 3, 63, 73, 81, 87–8, 89, 100, 110, 124, 125, 130–1, 133–5, 141

Eldemenstre (St Momelin), 15

Eleanor of Aquitaine, 3, 4, 53, 107, 157–8, 159, 172

Engelram de Bohun, 67

Engelram de Trie, 5

Ethelred, Archbishop, 148

Eton College, 71

Eudo, Count of Brittany, 67

Eustace, Prince, 3

Exchequer, the, 166

Faversham, 87

Fécamp, Abbey of, 71

Flanders, 14, 15, 35, 54, 162
Fordingbridge, 58, 60
Fordwich, 43
Framlingham, 165
Frascati (Tusculum), 30, 153
Frederick Barbarossa, Emperor, 17, 68
Fréteval, 25–6, 108–9

Garonne, river, 5
Geoffrey Grim, 87–8
Geoffrey de Mandeville, Earl of Essex, 68
Geoffrey Ridel, Archdeacon, 23, 53, 65, 83
George, a seafarer, 39
Gerald of Wales, 69, 97, 155
Gervase, monk of Canterbury and chronicler, 36, 41, 69,
        89, 135, 136, 140
Gervase of Cornhill, Sheriff of Kent, 36, 41–2, 63, 98
Gilbert Becket, 2, 72
Gilbert the citizen, 96, 98, 114
Gilbert Foliot, Bishop of London, 5, 10, 11, 15–16, 17,
        20, 21–3, 24, 28, 30, 34–6, 41–2, 48–52, 55,
        65–7, 83, 88, 104, 106–8, 153, 154, 159,
        161–2, 166
Gilbert de Glanville, 85
Giles, Bishop of Evreux, 70
Glastonbury Abbey, 147
Golgotha, 75
Grace de Tracy, 72
Gravelines, 15, 31
Gregorian calendar, 167
Gregory the Great, Pope, 22
Gregory VII (Hildebrand), Pope, 6–7
Guernes de Pont Ste-Maxence, 27, 41, 67, 71, 87, 89, 98,
        100, 101, 102, 103, 106, 110, 116, 117, 118,
        120, 121, 125, 129–30, 132, 135, 139, 140,
        142, 159, 160, 162, 170
Guisnes, 33
Gunter, one of Becket's clerks, 27, 33, 38, 61, 153

Hadrian's Wall, 159
Hague, The, 180
Hailes, 175
Harold, 67
Harrow, 56–61, 81, 83
Hastings, 72, 86
Haughley, castle of, 158
Henry I, 71
Henry II, 1, 3–4, 5, 7, 9–12, 13, 14, 16–17, 19–20, 21,
        23–4, 25–30, 31, 35, 42, 51, 52, 53, 54, 55, 57,
        62, 63, 65–70, 71, 72, 83, 95, 103–13, 115,
        128, 129, 139, 140, 142, 150–68, 172; his
        chamberlain, 164

Henry III, 166, 175
Henry V, 175
Henry VI, 175
Henry VIII, 167, 178; his queen, Catherine of Aragon,
        178
Henry IV, Emperor, 6–7
Henry of Auxerre, 86, 97, 120, 128
Henry of Blois, Bishop of Winchester, 1, 11, 14, 50, 55
Henry of Essex, Constable of England, 27
Henry, Prince, the young king, 1, 4, 8, 23–4, 25, 26, 27,
        28, 29, 41, 42, 52, 53, 54, 56, 57, 58, 59, 62,
        67, 69, 83, 86, 104, 105, 107–10, 152, 156–9,
        165, 168
Herbert of Bosham, 8, 13, 14, 15, 27, 37–8, 45, 46, 47,
        51, 54, 82, 83–4, 85, 87, 96, 97, 101, 137–8,
        141, 148
Holy Sepulchre, Church of, 75
Hubert Walter, Archbishop, 148
Hugh Bigot, Earl of Norfolk, 85, 158, 159, 165
Hugh, Earl of Chester, 158
Hugh, Bishop of Durham, 30, 165
Hugh de Gundeville, 69, 152
Hugh of Horsea, or Mauclerk, 5, 72–3, 115, 127–39
Hugh de Morville, 69, 71, 72, 91–6, 98–9, 101–20, 121,
        125–40, 154, 163; his father, Hugh, 72; his
        brother, Richard, 163
Humbert of Milan (later Pope Urban III), 8
Humphrey de Bohun, Constable of England, 158
Huntingdon, castle of, 165
Hythe, 27, 69, 90

Ipswich, 159
Ireland, 155, 156
Isabella, Countess Warenne, 9, 135

Jerusalem, 67, 75
Joan, Queen of Sicily, daughter of Henry II, 46
Jocelin of Arundel, 55–6, 57
Jocelin, Bishop of Salisbury, 23, 24, 28, 30, 34–6, 41–2,
        48–52, 55, 65–7, 83, 88, 104, 106–8, 153, 154
John, King, 173
John de Broc, 81
John of Canterbury, 61
John Cumin, 70, 153
John Grim, 87–8
John the Marshal, 10–11, 12
John of Oxford, Bishop of Norwich, 41, 43, 85
John *Planeta*, 85
John of Salisbury, 8, 27, 29–30, 61, 86, 88, 100, 109,
        112, 115, 116, 125, 135
John of Sudeley, 72
John, son of Vivian, 74

Jordan Fantosme, 164
Jubilees of St Thomas, 176–8

Knaresborough, 72
Knowles, Dom David, 20, 63, 96, 100, 124

Lambeth, 57
Lanfranc, Archbishop, 74, 159
Langton, Stephen, Cardinal and Archbishop, 173–4
Le Havre, 1–2
Leicester, 158
Le Mans, 168
Limoges, 168
Lincoln, 14–15, 71
Littlebourne, 45
London, 2, 22, 36, 54, 55, 61, 63, 81, 159, 162
    Cheapside, 1, 36
    Cornhill, 36
    Edgware Road, 57
    Holborn, 57
    London Bridge, 57
    Mercers' Hall, 1
Lotario di Segni (later Pope Innocent III), 171, 173
Louis VII, King of the French, 3, 4, 6, 15–17, 21, 25, 27,
    28, 30, 68, 85, 154, 157, 158, 166, 171; his son,
    Philip, 171
Lucius II, Pope, 67
Lympne, 90

Maidstone, 61, 63, 88
Manwood, Sir Roger, 40
Margaret, Princess, wife of the young king, 4, 25, 159, 168
Martel, 168
Mary, Queen, 180
Mason, Canon A.J., 180
Matilda Becket, 2, 4, 72
Matilda, Empress, 71
Matilda, a neurotic, 55
Matilda, Princess, 53
Matthew, Count of Boulogne, 33, 157, 158
Matthew Paris, 57, 58, 60
Medway, River, 63, 163
Merton Priory, 2, 7
Milo, Dean of Boulogne, 33
Monreale, 46
Montmartre, 23
Montmirail, 21
Mont St Michel, 156
Morville, 72
Mount Cenis, 7
Mount Pinçon, 72
Multiplicem, 20, 22

Nackington, 94
Newcastle on Tyne, 164
Newington, 54, 63
Nicander Nucius, 178, 180
Nigel de Sackville, 57, 83
Normandy, 24, 25, 27, 34, 51, 53, 65, 139, 140, 156,
    157, 158, 159
Northampton, 9, 11–14, 29, 36, 56, 83, 85, 87, 115, 158
Norwich Castle, 158, 159
Nottingham, 165

Odelin de Umfraville, 159, 164
Odo, Prior of Canterbury, 29, 45–6, 144, 145–6, 155,
    156
Orwell, river, 159
Osbern (Osbert), Becket's manservant, 7, 8, 13, 35–6, 87,
    115, 119, 141
Osbert 'Huitdeniers' or 'Eightpence', 2
Otford, 83
Oxford, 56, 87, 88, 97, 175

Papal legates, 21, 23, 154, 155, 156, 175
Paris, 2, 3, 4
Paschal III, anti-pope, 17
Payne, Peter, Principal of St Edmund Hall, Oxford, 175
Pegwell Bay, 39
Penshurst, chapelry of, 86
Pepys, Samuel, 180
Perigord, 171
Peter de Mortorio, 13
Pevensey, 31, 56
Philip of Alsasce, Count of Flanders, 33, 68, 157, 158,
    154, 165
Pipe Rolls, 162, 166
Poissy, 171
Pontigny, Abbey of, 17, 18, 19, 21, 60, 86
Prudhoe, castle of, 159, 163, 164

Quercy, 5

Ralph of Diss, 155
Ralph Morin, 86, 87, 113
Rannulph de Broc, 4, 12–13, 14, 17, 23, 27, 29, 36,
    41–2, 50–1, 56, 59, 63, 69, 81, 83, 90, 91, 98,
    109, 140, 154, 158, 162
Rannulph de Glanville, 164; his man, Brian, 164–5
Raymond, Count of Toulouse, 5
Reading, 88
Reginald, citizen of Canterbury, 90
Reginald, Earl of Cornwall, 53, 59, 60–1
Reginald FitzUrse, 25, 69, 71, 91–6, 98–9, 101–20, 121,
    125–40, 154; his father, Richard, 71

Reginald the goldsmith, 160
Reginald of Warenne, 36, 41–2, 59, 98
Rheims, 86
Richard I, 68, 168, 172, 173
Richard de Blosseville, Abbot of Valacé, 153
Richard le Bret, 69, 71, 73, 91–6, 98–9, 101–20, 121,
 125–40, 141, 154; his father, Simon, 71; his
 daughter, Maud, 71, 72
Richard the cellarer, 90, 120, 123
Richard the chaplain, 85
Richard, Prior of St Martin's, Dover, 52–4, 57, 58, 60,
 144, 145–6, 157
Richard du Hommet, 68, 69, 152
Richard of Ilchester, 23, 53, 65, 68, 159, 166
Richard de Lucy, 16, 23
Richborough, 41
Richmond, 164
Robert of Arden, Archdeacon of Lisieux, 153
Robert de Beaumont, Earl of Leicester, 1, 12, 67, 158; his
 son, Robert, 158–9; his son's wife, Petronilla,
 158–9
Robert de Brai, 14, 87
Robert de Broc, 4, 29, 73, 81–2, 83, 109, 114, 117,
 118–19, 125, 138–40, 141, 142, 154
Robert Brus (the Bruce), 173
Robert of Merton, 7, 125, 142
Robert, sacrist of Canterbury Cathedral, 27–8, 29, 36
Robert 'Shinbone', 8, 87, 114
Rocamadour, shrine of, 168
Rochester, 54, 63, 81, 86
 Castle, 158
Roger de Cave, 14
Roger of Pont l'Evêque, Archbishop of York, 2, 3, 24, 28,
 30, 34–6, 41–2, 48–52, 65–7, 69, 83, 104, 105,
 106–8, 153, 154, 164
Roger, Bishop of Worcester, 24, 55, 166
Rohesia, sister of St Thomas, 162
Rome, 3, 10, 16, 67, 72, 85, 120, 151, 152
Rother levels, 90
Rotrou, Archbishop of Rouen, 31, 70
Rouen, 2, 28, 31, 35, 72, 166, 168

Saga, 41, 90, 114, 121, 128–9, 132, 170
Saher de Quincy, 68, 69
St Alban's Abbey, 56–9
St Andrew's Priory, Northampton, 11, 13
St Bertin, Abbey of, 14, 15, 33
St Colombe, Abbey of, 21
St Denis, 23
St Drausius, shrine of, 8
St Martial, shrine of, 168
St Mary in Southwark, church of, 55

St Momelin, 16
St Omer, 14, 33
St Paul's, Dean of, 23
St Peter's Church, Dover, 35
St Philibert, 88
St Remi, 86
Salisbury, 10, 60
Saltwood, 94, 95, 98
 Castle, 27, 29, 69, 71, 81, 83, 86, 88, 90, 91, 135,
  140, 154
 Church, 88
Sampford Brett, 71
Sandwich, 15, 23, 38–42, 43, 46, 50, 59, 87, 89, 98
 Canterbury Gate, 41, 42
 House of St Thomas, 39
 Monken Quay, 39
 Strand Street, 39
Savigny, Abbey of, 156
Scailman, 14, 15
Sempringham, 15
Sens, 16, 17, 21, 23, 24, 28, 29, 31, 35, 36, 86
Simon de Beauchamp, 87
Simon de Crioil, 96, 114
Simon, Abbot of St Alban's, 58–9, 60
Simon, Archdeacon of Sens, 41–2, 87; one of his servants,
 139
Soissons, 8, 16
Solomon the mercer, 160
Southampton, 53, 159
Southwark, 55, 56, 61, 62
Stephen, King, 1, 3, 71
Stonar, 39
Stone Street, 94, 140
Stour, river, 39, 162
Streetend, 94
'Strongbow', Earl of Striguil, 156
Strood, 81
Stubbs, Bishop, 99

Thames, river, 15, 57, 61
Thanet, 39
Theobald, Count of Blois, 28, 158
Theobald, Archbishop of Canterbury, 2, 3, 5, 18, 24, 57,
 60
Theodwin, Cardinal, 154, 155, 156
Thierlewda, 83
Thomas Becket, background, 1–3; chancellor, 3–5;
 archbishop, 1, 5–9; quarrel with Henry II, 9–14;
 exile, 13–30; appearance, 4, 7, 46–9, 122; health,
 11–12, 18–19, 35, 47–8; return from exile,
 31–46; back in England, 48–64; plot against his
 life, 65–73; last days, 74–90; day of his murder,

91–9; meeting with knights, 100–26; murder, 127–39; burial, 144–9; aftermath, 150–68; cult, 169–81

Thomas of Maidstone, 89

Thomas de Turnbuhe, 55–6, 57

Tonbridge, 61

Tooth, Father, 180–1

Toulouse, 5, 7, 9

Tours, 25, 28

Tracy-Bocage, 72

Trie, 5

Turgis de Tracy, 72

Urs, 71

Vexin, 166

Vézelay, 8, 19–20, 21, 68

Wace, 72

Wales, 156

Walter, Abbot of Boxley, 144, 145–6, 162

Walter, the marshal of St Augustine's Abbey, 96, 114, 125

Walter, Bishop of Rochester, 54, 162

Walton on the Naze, 158

Watchet, 71

Westminster, 1, 5, 9, 11, 24, 57, 163, 166, 167

Wibert, Prior of Canterbury, 5, 16, 29, 46, 121, 123

Wildmore Fen, 14

William I, 67, 98; his daughter, Rainild, 67

William Beivin, 86

William, priest of Bishopsbourne, 74, 145

William, Subprior of Canterbury, 25, 29

William of Canterbury, monk and chronicler, 36, 41, 50, 52, 53, 58, 63, 65, 89, 100, 101, 110, 118, 125, 129, 130, 134, 135, 158, 171

William de Capes, 8, 14, 17

William, priest of Chiddingstone, 61–2, 85–6

William of Eynsford, 74

William FitzJohn, 69, 152

William FitzNigel, 8, 79, 86–7, 96, 97–9, 102, 112, 113–14; his son, Robert, 87

William FitzStephen, 13, 54, 61, 67, 69, 81, 82, 86, 95, 96, 97, 100, 102, 105, 108, 109, 111, 114, 115, 118, 119, 121, 124, 125, 128, 132, 135, 140, 141, 149

William the goldsmith, 74, 142

William the Lion, King of Scotland, 68, 157, 158, 159, 163–5

William, the Lord, 9, 135

William de Mandeville, Earl of Essex, 68, 69, 152, 166

William Mauvoisin, 67

William *medicus*, 18–19, 60–1, 97

William, son of Pagan, 114

William, assistant of Richard the cellarer, 98, 120, 123

William, Archbishop of Sens, 46, 85, 153, 154

William, Earl of Surrey, 9, 36

William de Tracy, 69, 71, 72, 91–6, 98–9, 101–20, 121, 125–40, 154

William de Vesci, 163

Williton, 71

Winchelsea, 89

Winchester, 29, 52, 53, 54, 58, 75, 104, 152

Windsor, 156

Wingham, 45

Wissant, 30, 33, 38, 69, 115, 152

Witham, River, 14

Wolsey, Cardinal, 178

Woodspring, Priory of, 71

Woodstock, 56, 57, 58

Wrotham, 61, 63

Wycliff, John, 175

Yonne, river, 21